The Sociology
of Psychotherapy

The Sociology
of Psychotherapy

Edited by

Paul M. Roman TULANE UNIVERSITY

and

Harrison M. Trice CORNELL UNIVERSITY

JASON ARONSON
New York

To Professor H. Warren Dunham

CONTENTS

PREFACE

THERE is little doubt that psychotherapy and its delivery systems are continually increasing in prominence in American life, both as the solution to the personal problems of individual Americans and as the solution to broader social system problems, particularly those based in urban community life. The roots of interest and commitment to psychotherapeutic attempts at problem solution are complex but constitute an apt, yet relatively neglected, subject for sociological analysis. To an extent, psychotherapy and its many modes of delivery may be viewed as a social problem, along with the other components of the ever-growing "problem industry" in American society.

This volume represents a range of sociological perspectives on psychotherapy, primarily analytical rather than critical in focus and intent. In Part I three basic issues are examined: the relationship of psychotherapeutic modalities to changing social values and ideology; the interfaces between processes of social disorganization and the sociopsychological processes involved in "working through" in the therapeutic relationship; and the development of lay-based therapeutic efforts in form of self-help groups, a development that has taken on many of the characteristics of a social movement.

The focus of Part II is on psychotherapists themselves: problems in socializing therapists for expanded role demands subsumed in the emerging speciality of community psychiatry; the prospects and problems of the role involvement of the sociologist on a full-time basis in a therapeutic delivery system; an examination of the personal and role problems reported by practicing psychiatrists working in different organizational settings; and a two-chapter exploration of the feasibility and consequences of populist assumptions that call for the involvement of the "indigenous nonprofessional" as a therapeutic agent in community-based treatment delivery systems.

The volume is a project of the Division of Psychiatric Sociology of the Society for the Study of Social Problems, conceived by the membership during the co-editors' chairmanship of the division. It is one of several volumes developed within the SSSP membership over the past two decades in which efforts have been made to summarize current knowledge on particular social problems. As an official project of SSSP, all royalties accrue to the organization for the furtherance of its work.

Our gratitude thus rests primarily with the contributors, not only for their scholarly efforts and for the patience and understanding that most of them have shown during the period required between first drafts and the printed page but also for their contribution to the work of SSSP.

We are particularly grateful to Dr. Hyman Rodman of the Merrill-Palmer Institute who, as chairman of the SSSP Editorial and Publications Committee, went far beyond the call of duty in helping us bring this project to fruition.

April 1973   PAUL M. ROMAN, *New Orleans, Louisiana*
HARRISON M. TRICE, *Ithaca, New York*

ACKNOWLEDGMENTS

AN earlier version of Chapter 1, "Ideologies and Utopias of Psychotherapy," has appeared in *The Sociology of the Future,* ed. Wendell Bell and James Mau (New York: Russell Sage Foundation, 1971). Permission was granted by the publisher for appearance in this volume.

Earlier versions of Chapter 3, "Psychotherapy without Psychotherapists," were presented at the Seventeenth Annual Meeting of the Society for the Study of Social Problems, August 1967, San Francisco, and at the Seventy-sixth Annual Convention of the American Psychological Association, September 1968, San Francisco. This investigation was not supported in any way by a grant or fellowship by any public or private agency.

The research for Chapter 4, "The Psychotherapist in Community Mental Health," was supported in part by a Public Health Service Grant, No. MH 10391.

The initial data for Chapter 6 were collected while the author held a research contract from the U.S. Army Research and Development Command: DA-MD-49-193-66-G 9209 and G 181. Collection of the remaining data and the writing of the final report were made possible through a grant to study problems of social change and social control in professions from the National Institutes of Health, HD 02776-02.

CONTRIBUTORS

Gary L. Albrecht
NORTHWESTERN UNIVERSITY

Pauline B. Bart
UNIVERSITY OF ILLINOIS COLLEGE OF MEDICINE

Rue Bucher
UNIVERSITY OF ILLINOIS COLLEGE OF MEDICINE

Arlene Kaplan Daniels
SCIENTIFIC ANALYSIS CORPORATION

Paul R. Dommermuth
STATE UNIVERSITY OF NEW YORK AT FREDONIA

Nathan Hurvitz
LOS ANGELES

Berton H. Kaplan
UNIVERSITY OF NORTH CAROLINA

George Ritzer
UNIVERSITY OF KANSAS

Charles W. Tucker
UNIVERSITY OF SOUTH CAROLINA

PART I

SOCIOLOGY
AND PSYCHOTHERAPY

INTRODUCTION

THAT psychotherapy does not operate in a social vacuum is an observation often made, both within psychiatry and within sociology. Many in these two disciplines would readily agree that they share numerous problems, considerations, as well as practices. Consensus declines considerably, however, when efforts aimed at explicitly spelling out the interface between sociology and psychiatry are made. What specifically does psychotherapy, in its many forms, share with sociology? Do dynamic, pervasive belief systems shape psychotherapy? If so, what new therapeutic forms emerge that reflect these social value shifts? How might specific sociological concepts about knowledge of the interface between social structure and disordered individual behavior be incorporated into psychotherapeutic efforts? What indigenous processes within societal belief systems produce psychotherapies that operate outside the institutionalized and professionalized systems of psychotherapy? The essays in Part I explore these interface questions, spelling out specific ways and forms in which sociological variables interact with psychotherapeutic efforts. The authors openly examine aspects of the interface, providing an opportunity for dialogue between psychiatrists and sociologists. Hopefully these authors will, in turn, stimulate a mutual examination of how these and other aspects of the interface between sociology and psychotherapy can be put into practice.

3

Professor Bart sets the stage in "Ideologies and Utopias of Psychotherapy" by examining how ideologies within American society act as dynamic forces shaping new forms of psychotherapy and altering old ones. Thus, ideologies challenging the established order have put under pressure current psychotherapeutic effort that adjusts the individual to society, discourages disloyalty, and uses drugs as a form of social control for the status quo. Civil rights and poverty concerns, as social movements with heavy ideological loadings, form the larger societal backdrop within which psychotherapy interacts and from which it cannot escape. Bart aptly terms the response of much of psychotherapy to these belief systems "psychotherapeutic quietism." Similarly psychiatric concern for community forces, especially those surrounding poverty and racism, have generated a massive upheaval in psychotherapy, producing an active awareness of the inevitable link between social systems and individual systems. Community psychiatry emerged from this aspect of the interface, espousing changes in institutional life before therapeutic efforts to alter personal behavior were attempted. Bart concludes that numerous psychiatrists have come to embrace the humanistic and democratic values lying in and behind the community psychiatry movement, thus focusing on institutional change, or, to use her phrase, "psychotherapeutic activism."

Probably more potent in its impact on psychotherapy and in its pervasiveness within American society is the current populist upsurge. Currently finding expression in such divergent sectors as politics, the youth culture, and pop art, populism has penetrated psychotherapy in a variety of ways. Bart, for example, describes in detail how Synanon has democratized its therapeutic process to the point that "patients" become "therapists" and academically trained therapists are either unnecessary or viewed as harmful. Such democratization provides a set of beliefs for encounter groups where humanistic psychology calls for interpersonal explorations among group members aimed at producing individual awareness, freedom, uniqueness, spontaneity, and capacity for living. At the same time the potent impact of technology and its belief system makes itself felt in behavior modification therapy—a strategy diametrically opposed to populism in its ideology. In many ways man is like other animals, and mechanical procedures can extinguish many of his dysfunctional anxieties and tensions without anyone—professional therapist or peer group member—rummaging about in his psyche. Additional mechanisms can reinforce desired behavior, further decreasing undesirable behaviors and feelings. Thus, well-trained psychologists can engineer desirable changes in emotionally disordered individuals in a rational calculated fashion, relying on observed learning principles originally established in animal studies.

In sum, Bart asks whether there can be *any* value-free psychotherapy and raises both esoteric and pragmatic research questions: How will current ideological reactions to present-day, deep-seated social changes reinforce particular therapeutic ideologies and strategies? What psychological and socioeconomic variables predict therapeutic results for one cluster of therapeutic ideologies and strategies, in contrast to results based in different approaches?

Professor Kaplan, in "Social Factors and Working Through," pursues the interface theme further by delineating specific dimensions of the "contact between the effect of the sociocultural setting and the experiencing individual." These dimensions come from Kaplan's detailed analysis of the reactions of a group of behavioral scientists to Dr. Alexander Leighton's work on the relationship between social disintegration and psychiatric disorder. From these raw materials, Kaplan extracts 13 "disintegrative interfaces"; for example, "instrumental disorganization," or the lack of social instruments whereby personal goals can be accomplished, represents the well-known concept of anomie as it impinges on individual behavior. Kaplan spells out the way in which each of these societal disintegrative interfaces have an impact on personal behavior. Thus "curing disturbances" in face-to-face interactions may result in an actor coping with persons who do not know how to communicate their needs. Again, intergroup conflicts produce classical role ambiguity and conflict, so that the individual is caught between incompatible demands.

But Professor Kaplan is concerned with substantially much more than an explication of these interfaces. He examines at length how knowledge of these disintegrative forces might be incorporated into traditional psychoanalytic therapy in which an enlargement of personal insight, hopefully, will lead to a change of behavior, or "working through." He first assumes that if the patient can learn from the therapist about processes involved in social disintegration that may impinge upon him, he (the patient) has a greater chance of using new insights to change his behavior. Kaplan next sets forth a frame of reference for thinking about the processes within a social system. If these could be taught to a patient in the working-through process, increasing his social system skills, he presumably would have more capacity to truly work through in the classical sense. Using a scheme developed by sociologists Parsons and Smelser for analyzing processes in a social system, Kaplan provides a scheme by which psychiatrists can teach patients how to locate their sources of social disintegration, and thus, provide them with a chance to correct these disruptive features. More important, however, these social insights should increase a patient's overall competence and his ability to move from personal insight into more healthy behavior. Clearly, Kaplan realizes that other schema might be used and other delineations of the interfaces put forward. His essay is not aimed at finality. It is, however, designed to consider how knowledge about socially disruptive forces can be operationalized within the therapist-patient relationship in a way that will increase the likelihood of therapeutic success.

Quite obviously Kaplan raises some interesting and important questions: Will therapists who have been trained to focus largely on intrapsychic phenomena incorporate social insight knowledge into their therapeutic efforts? To what extent can patients learn about social structure skills in conjunction with learning about personal insights? And, of course, the central question emerges: If they do learn about social structure skills, will this knowledge speed up the working-through process? In another view, Kaplan raises the exciting question: What characterizes those individuals, apparently a sizable majority, who live under substantially disintegrated social conditions but seem to cope enough to avoid psychiatric impairment of any magnitude?

In his article "Psychotherapy without Psychotherapists," Dr. Hurvitz concentrates on one of the major ideologies currently affecting psychotherapy, democratization of therapeutic efforts. Basically he examines the wide array of self-help groups "conducted by average members of the community who have had no training outside of their PSHPG (Peer Self-Help Psychotherapy Group) experience...." Thus he deals with such well-known self-help groups as Alcoholics Anonymous, TOPS (Take off Pounds Sensibly), Synanon and the less well-known Gamblers Anonymous, Narcotics Anonymous, and Recovery, Inc. Despite this diversity, a clear theme characterizes his analysis: the contrasts between conventional psychotherapy and the therapeutic efforts of nonprofessionals who suffer from a psychiatric impairment. Using participant observation, materials from clinical practice, and constructive typology, Hurvitz compares these two types of psychotherapy on five bases: structural and procedural differences; differences in reciprocity between therapist and client and between peers; differences in moral attitudes of the therapist and peers; differences between the social and psychological systems of therapists and peers; and differences in group therapy practices among therapists and peers. These comparisons lead Dr. Hurvitz to proposals for altering traditional psychotherapy: He suggests how conventional techniques might he substantially altered so that they incorporate many of the features of peer self-help groups. Within this broad theme, Hurvitz examines the problems of how to evaluate therapeutic effectiveness of the two basic types. Even though there is an absence of hard empirical data from evaluative research, he points out some of the cogent disadvantages that may come from peer self-help groups: for example, high drop-out rates and the unfavourable impact on self-concepts for those who try to affiliate but "can't make it." Despite these unintended consequences he demonstrates that peer self-help groups have grown naturally from historical social values relatively unique to American society. Although Alcoholics Anonymous is the best known self-help group,

Hurvitz uses his data and that of others to put all self-help groups into a historical and current perspective. He traces both the religious and secular sources of these groups, providing a thorough review of relevant literature. One point consistently recurs: Laymen often take therapy for their psychiatric problems into their own hands. And, as Professor Bart points out in her chapter, populism has already penetrated traditional psychotherapy, making it reasonable to hypothesize that peer self-help groups will proliferate even more in the near future. This is one of the chief questions Hurvitz indirectly raises: how can we more accurately catalog and describe the plethora of these groups? He also asks: What are the effects of dropping-out, both on individuals and on groups? What role do these groups play in the career pattern of mental patients? Do they, in effect, materially increase the overall treatment resources available? What kinds of persons readily affiliate and change their behavior, in contrast to those who respond to traditional psychotherapy? In yet another vein, what effect does their acceptance of the medical model have on general societal acceptance or rejection? What does membership do to the stigmatization process that surrounds mental illness? Last, returning to the major thrust of this section, Hurvitz raises a final basic question: How can the spontaneous processes present in peer self-help groups be articulated with the rational therapeutic strategies growing out of professionalized roles and occupations? Even more relevant, would it be a reasonable effort to make in the first place?

Chapter 1

Pauline B. Bart

IDEOLOGIES AND UTOPIAS OF PSYCHOTHERAPY

WHEN I moved from Berkeley to Chicago in 1970, I was struck by two differences: first, the omnipresence of shiny, new, enormous American cars, in contrast to the beat-up VW's that dominated the Berkeley scene; second, finding many people who were still in classical psychoanalysis, a treatment modality that, from my West Coast perspective, seemed quaint and old fashioned, like debates over whether or not sociology was a science. Changes in types of psychotherapy are not random but reflect societal changes. Likewise, regional and class variations in acceptance of such changes are also related to sociological factors.

Different psychotherapeutic orientations have different images of man, time focuses, concepts of society, assumptions of cause and effect, and orientations toward social change. These differences clearly reflect different values, hence the major conclusion of this chapter: Value-free psychotherapy is a myth.

American Psychiatry: From Moral Management to the Classless Clinic

Changes in the treatment of mental patients historically reflect changes in society. Before the great wave of immigration in the nineteenth century, mental hospitals had a therapeutic program called "humane care" or moral treatment. Cure was effected through interaction with the psychiatrist, and the atmosphere was what now might be termed a "therapeutic community." For example, the psychiatrist and the patient in that era ate their meals together.* (See Foucault, 1967, for a discussion of this type of treatment in Europe.)

This program was abandoned for the "warehousing" of inmates in asylums usually located far from urban areas. The only treatment given was somatic, and many patients merely received custodial care. This change in orientation and care occurred concomitantly with increased admissions of mentally ill immigrants to mental hospitals. The custodial ideology has now been abandoned—at least verbally—and the "humane" therapeutic community concept is once again in the ascendency. One wonders if the original change in policy did not result from the existence of a large number of patients different in ethnic background and social class from the psychiatrists—patients to whom the psychiatrists might have felt they could not comfortably "relate."

Folta and Schatzman (1968) suggest that the minimal care given mental patients in the past century reflected the ideology of Social Darwinism current at that time. The decline of that ideology and its replacement with the concepts of the New Deal and the Great Society—ideologies that insist that no groups be "written off"—are consistent with the changes in treatment of mental patients, particularly the current emphasis on treatment in the community. The growing importance in treatment programs of social workers and psychologists, many of whom were children of immigrants, accompanied the introduction of milieu therapy in hospitals. Their influence sensitized the population to problems of emotional disturbance and created a large clientele for psychotherapeutic services. Folta and Schatzman

* In my field observations in several mental hospitals I noticed a direct relationship between the eating arrangements and the social class differential between staff and patients. In the upper-class hospital staff and patients ate together; in the lower-middle-class hospital, while the same dining room was used, the staff ate at a raised platform at one end of the room; however, in the state hospital there were separate dining rooms.

predict the growth of an eclectic, pragmatic, public urban psychiatry, serving the varied urban populace, focusing on the client's present problem and its social determinants. In such a program even the well-documented social class differentiations found in clinics will disappear, since they are "uneconomical and ineffective."

Psychotherapeutic Pessimism: Freud

To understand the traditional quietist nature of psychiatry and its culture-bound character, one must examine some factors that influenced Freud's thought and his image of man and society. Freud has been admirably placed in a sociological and historical context by Rieff, Riesman, and Marcuse. Rieff (1959, pp. xiii, 4.5) sees Freud as a moralist: "the first out-patient of the hospital culture in which we live.... Once again, history has produced a type specially adapted to endure his own period: the trained egoist, the private man, who turns away from the arenas of public failure to reexamine himself and his own emotions." Freudian psychology supports this privatization, since it interprets "politics, religion, and culture in terms of the inner life of the individual and his immediate family experiences." This legitimation of the privatization of the self and the definition of radicalism as an expression of individual neurosis are ideological positions still affecting psychotherapy—an approach I call psychotherapeutic quietism.

Riesman (1954, p. 202) sees Freud as the bearer of the Protestant Ethic, who makes the "ascetic rationalist dichotomy between work and play." Freud's therapeutic techniques were shaped by his cultural and class outlook. Since Freud's patients and friends were upper-middle-class, he assumed that individualistic mobility motives were natural. His concept of work as the "inescapable and tragic necessity" and his position on "man's natural laziness and the futility of socialism" can be understood as products of a century dominated by scarcity, economics, and Malthusian fears (Riesman, 1954, pp. 176, 184).

Marcuse (1962, p. 224), on the other hand, considers

Freud's metaphysical theories radical but his psychotherapy conservative. Although Freud knew that the "sickness of the individual is ultimately caused and sustained by the sickness of his civilization," psychoanalytic therapy aims at curing the individual so that he can continue to function as part of a sick civilization "without surrendering to it altogether."

In *The Future of an Illusion* (1934), Freud has hope for increasing rationality among men, but his pessimism is shown in the conclusion of *Civilization and Its Discontents* (1961, p. 92).

> I can offer them [my fellow men] no consolation.... The fateful question for the human species seems to me to be whether and to what extent their cultural development will succeed in mastering the disturbance of their communal life by the human instinct of aggression and self-destruction.... Men have gained control over the forces of nature to such an extent that with their help they would have no difficulty in exterminating one another to the last man. They know this, and hence comes a large part of their current unrest, their unhappiness, and their mood of anxiety. And is it not to be expected that the other of the two "Heavenly Powers," eternal Eros, will make an effort to assert himself in the struggle with his equally immortal adversary (Thanatos). But who can foresee with what success and with what result?

Although Freud was pessimistic about social change, viewing civilization as "essentially antagonistic to happiness" and therapy as a "course in resignation," Marcuse considers the unconscious the "drive for integral gratification, which is absence of want and repression." Marcuse's (1962) reading of Freud is such that he can envision a society without "surplus repression" (p. 137), where there will no longer be the necessity for societal domination and individual alienation, a state "derived from the prevalent social organization of labor" (p. 128).

Freud's conception of human nature was Hobbesian; society is relatively unchangeable because of man's instincts. For example, Freud's traditional view of the woman's role grew out of his belief that her situation is rooted in her biology ("Anatomy is Destiny"); no change was possible. Freud's thought was generally deterministic, although the individual could increase the scope of his freedom through insight, freeing himself from actions determined by his unconscious.

Psychotherapeutic Quietism:
It's What's Inside That Counts

Certainly, if all problems and responses to problems spring from individuals' intrapsychic processes, then the society can be ignored except as a "superstructure." Social change, should it indeed be necessary at all, would have to be a function of individual change, which would occur because of the individual's awareness of the unconscious determinants of his behavior. If, however the radical "learns" that his desire to restructure society and overthrow its leaders is but a displacement of his desire to restructure his childhood family constellation and overthrow his father, the implication is that he should abandon his revolutionary activity, since it is but a symptom of his neurosis. Lest one think such an analysis is overdrawn, Anna Freud (1968) recently interpreted the protest movement among today's youth as not so much a result of real interest in solving social ills but a mask for concealing personal inadequacies. She considers introspective therapy and psychoanalysis to be exactly what the students need.

The psychiatric equivalent of original sin, "immaturity," can also be invoked to discredit radical political activity. For example, Lerner (1968, p. 96) states:

> In an organization such as the armed forces, the allegiance and loyalty of the psychiatrist to the organization must transcend consideration of the individual. If any organization—or, for that matter, society—is to endure, those persons who are in a position to affect the integrity and efficiency of the organization or of society must make a clear choice between the best interests of the individual and the best interests of society.
> . . . When the psychiatrist is concerned with evaluating an individual from the point of view of that person's loyalty

to his country and its way of life, the psychiatrist must make a decision so that his natural and customary concern for the individual is subordinated to his own personal obligation never under any circumstances to permit the best interests of his country and its way of life to be jeopardized. This calls for not merely honoring his oath and obligation, but utilizing psychiatric principles which foster maturity of the personality. The index of maturity of the personality is the capacity for conformity with the broad sanctions of society and loyalty to one's country and one's way of life. . . .

Rejection of the Father and/or the Mother figure closely parallels rejection of our country as an object of our concern and respect. We see symptoms of "disloyalty" or "rejection" in the person who develops patterns of behavior which are disturbing to his parents, his family, his community, or his culture. This hostility or disloyalty is a common *symptom complex* in psychiatric practice [emphasis added] . . . . Disloyalty of whatever nature is associated with

1. Emotional disturbance or psychiatric illness
2. Opportunistic attempts to achieve status, notoriety and power
3. The illusion that such activities will ameliorate personal, social, and economic status.

If concern with social problems or structural deficiencies in the society is merely a projection of one's inner dynamics, such dialogues as the following may take place. Goffman (1961, p. 377) reports a therapist dealt with:

a Negro patient's complaints about race relations in a partially segregated hospital by telling the patient that he must ask why he, among all the other Negroes present, chose this particular moment to express this feeling, and what this could mean about him as a person, apart from the state of race relations in the hospital at the time.

London (1964, pp. 9, 10) notes that this rhetoric of lack of concern with the external world may in fact be limited under certain circumstances. He reports an analyst's saying:

"When I am working in the privacy of the analytic session, I don't care if the world is coming down around my patient's ears on the outside." He does not stipulate, incidentally, whether his attitude would be the same if the financial world of the patient were collapsing, indicating that he would no longer be able to be paid, or if the patient were, on the outside "acting out" in a fashion that interfered with the analysis.

Also, London (1969, p. 41) observes that therapists can be irresponsible if they insist on totally denying responsibility for social change they may foster. They may become "insidious and potentially destructive" because the "potential of mental health experts for social engineering is quite large, though few of them are publicly concerned about it." This lack of concern with values and with society does not, of course, mean a value neutrality, because the failure to take a position is a position indicating values in itself.

Psychotherapists function today as priests did in the Middle Ages, and Seeley (1953) states that the mental health movement is vying for the vacuum caused by the passing of the church. Value-laden psychotherapy is possible because the imprecision of psychiatric theory, especially the ambiguity concerning "normality," permits the psychiatrist's moral preferences to be enunciated "in the disguise of scientific descriptions of fact" (Szasz, 1961, p. 105). Such ambiguity has resulted in the mental health movement being in effect the Protestant Ethic writ large (Davis, 1938, p. 580). At a Symposium on Preventive and Social Psychiatry sponsored by the Walter Reed Army Institute of Research (1957, p. 445), an army psychiatrist said supervisors in industry can promote the mental health of workers

by insisting that they perform adequately on the job. Any time a supervisor shows any preference or allows a worker to perform inadequately, he's doing both the group and the individual a great disfavor. (Note the alleged identity of interests between the two.)

The next psychiatrist "quite agreed" with him: "I think it is part of the mental hospital to establish this attitude inside the hospital as well."

The mental hospital as factory is a rather interesting model. Such an approach is not dated; the health book used by California elementary school children today, mouths the same platitudes under the guise of asking, "What is mental health?" (Byrd *et al.*, 1967, pp. 9–16). This book says a person with good mental health can handle disappointments as well as success, making "a good adjustment or adapting himself to the demands made upon him by his environment." The children are told that they have good mental health if they are truthful, loyal, cooperative, friendly and think positively instead of negatively.

Parsons (1951, p. 301) considered the process of psychotherapy

> the case in our society where those fundamental elements of the processes of social control have been most explicitly brought to light. For certain purposes it can serve as a prototype of the mechanisms of social control.

And Laing (1965, p. 12), the English existential psychiatrist, eloquently declares:

> Psychiatry could be, and some psychiatrists are on the side of transcendance, of genuine freedom, and of true human growth. But psychiatry can so easily be a technique of brainwashing, of including behavior that is adjusted, by (preferably) non-injurious torture. In the best places where straitjackets are abolished, doors unlocked, leucotomies largely foregone, these can be replaced by more subtle lobotomies and tranquilizers that place the bars of Bedlam and the locked doors *inside* the patient.

That psychotherapy is a form of social control and sanity "a trick of agreement" (Ginsberg, 1961, p. 13) has long been noted by poets and novelists. Though they may not be the unacknowledged legislators of the world, they do "see with the eyes of the angels" (Williams, 1956, p. 8). William Burrough's (1959) fictional psychiatrist, Dr. Benway, is the controller and advisor to the antiutopia Freeland Republic. He is a manipulator and coordinator of symbol systems and an expert in all phases of interrogation, brainwashing, and control. Kesey's (1962) depiction of a psychiatric ward reads like a dramatization of all the organizational analyses of mental hospitals. Though Big Nurse is the agent of social control, the patients are manipulated into cooperating in their own destruction. Big Nurse interprets any act of self-assertion as pathology, and the ward psychiatrist is generally unable to perform his therapeutic function (see Goffman, 1961; Caudill, 1958; Dunham and Weinberg, 1960; and Belknap, 1956, for sociological and anthropological analyses coming to similar conclusions).

Psychotherapy as social control bodes ill for an increase of human freedom and dignity in the future. In the Soviet Union individuals protesting political conditions have been confined in mental hospitals, since they were, of course, "sick." The cases of Ezra Pound, General Edwin Walker, and Governor Earl Long of Louisiana, however, show that this approach is not limited to other countries. In the latter two cases, the attempts to commit for psychiatric care individuals with deviant political stances failed. Long's case revealed no objective criteria enabling us to distinguish between paranoid schizophrenia (his diagnosis) and Long's "normal" behavior. General Walker, who led the opposition to integration at Ole Miss, considered his behavior appropriate for a patriotic American and a general of the U.S. Army. The government preferred to label him insane rather than admit that there are high-ranking members of the armed forces who think and act that way. Ezra Pound was labeled insane; thus, he could be shut up—in both senses—in St. Elizabeth's Hospital. And although the government was not placed in the awkward position of trying a major poet for treason, Pound could no longer publicly make pro-Fascist statements.

Attempts to discredit an opponent by labeling him sick rather than bad or incorrect have spread to the halls of Congress and to the Oakland police force. In response to reports linking cigarette smoking to lung cancer, the FTC sought to curb cigarette advertising. It was reported in *The New York Times* (1964, p. 12) that Representative Cooley of North Carolina, a tobacco-growing state, said, "I think someone in the FTC must be emotionally disturbed." More recently, the chief of the Oakland police stated on television that people who support the Black Panthers and the Peace and Freedom party were "sick."

Invoking psychiatric vocabularies to discredit behavior and attitudes with which one disagrees not only enables one to ignore the issues that are raised in the argument, but makes unnecessary a search for structural factors conducive to such behavior and attitudes. Each time there has been a multiple murder or an assassination, the individual has been defined as "some nut". And since the behavior of mentally ill individuals is believed by most people to be unpredictable, no safeguards or structural changes are presumed necessary. For example, according to the testimony of the clinical psychologist (San Francisco Chronicle, 1969) at the trial of Sirhan Sirhan, Robert Kennedy was assassinated because

> Sirhan's prime problem [became]...a conflict between instinctual demands for his father's death and the realization through his conscious that killing his father is not socially acceptable. The only real solution is to look for a compromise. He does. He finds a symbolic replica of his father in the form of Kennedy, kills him and also regains the relationship that stands between him and his most precious possession—his mother's love.

Sirhan's father was 55, yet Kennedy's image was always considered "boyish" rather than fatherly. Certainly, if the only way to prevent political assassination is to produce a world in which no one hated his father, then a solution would be impossible. Such wide invocation of psychiatric vocabularies for "explanation" has an "elective affinity" with psychotherapeutic quietism.

Psychotherapeutic Activism:
Yes, Virginia, There Is a Social Structure

Psychiatrists described as "psychotherapeutic activists" consider psychiatry a tool to build the good society. Federal and state financing has led to the burgeoning of community mental health clinics, and community psychiatry has become extremely popular. The 1967 research report of the American Psychiatric

Association was called *Poverty and Mental Health* (Greenblatt and Sharaf, 1967), and a recent compendium on psychoanalysis (Marmor, 1968) devotes one of its four sections to culture and society. Even in the clinical section, one chapter deals with social factors in the discussion of the treatment of low socioeconomic groups. These new foci in the field parallel social developments, lending support to the central hypothesis of the sociology of knowledge: Existential factors condition thought. Traditional psychotherapy, with its one-to-one relationship between the therapist and patient, reflected the "inner-directed man," whereas current trends—the discovery of the social structure and its impact on the individual and the growth of group therapy—are more appropriate to "other-directed" man.

Duhl (1963, p. 73) believes that the psychiatrist "must play a role in controlling the environment which man has created." He considers the ecological model more appropriate to our era than the linear causal model. Thus man is to be studied *in* society; disease is a socially defined condition. Duhl decries the post-World War II trend of psychiatrists committing themselves to "office therapeutics with little recognition of the possibility of working with environmental factors," and he notes that with the advent of research funds, programs, and training, as well as with increasing public awareness, a "major revolution has occurred" (Duhl, 1963, p. 65). Increasing interest has been shown in the biological and the sociopsychological aspects of mental illness, which has led to a focus on the processes of the family, the hospital, and the community as they relate to mental health and illness.

Where poverty has been discovered by the psychotherapists, the basic image of man has changed from passive client to active participant and planner in matters affecting his destiny. Duhl (1967) says that the time has passed when professionals define how services are given. When the poor in one community were polled concerning their needs, their priorities were markedly different from those of "the helping professions." One community member said that, while they might be viewed as a hard-core community with multiproblem people living in it, "We see you as being hard-core social workers. You're insulting with your belief that you have everything to give me. You forget that I not only know how to take, but I can give, too" (Geiger, 1967, p. 61).

The "activist" psychiatrists are aware of the intimate interaction between the social systems and personal system; they assume that in order to change the behavior of individuals, the institutions must be changed. For example, Peck *et al.* (1967) consider it their obligation as community psychiatrists to promote neighborhood service centers and become involved in voter registration, code enforcement in housing, and the organization of rent strikes.

In order to overcome "the customary professional constraints ordinarily required of those who work in the health field"—which have little meaning for the disadvantaged—techniques must be revamped. Storefront satellites, psychiatry not limited to a 50-minute hour, home visits, the use of indigenous workers to mediate between the professionals and the community—these are some of the techniques suggested (Rome, 1967).*

A focus on environmental change, particularly when working in poverty areas, is vital (Rome, 1967, p. 175) because:

> ...there is reason to believe...that much of the disproportion in the reported demographic and epidemiologic characteristics of mental illness is attributed to the direct and indirect effect of economics.... Economic factors exercise prepotent influence in the provocation of symptoms, the mode of expression of symptoms, as well as the selection of the appropriate remedial measures.

Although this concern with the economics of social problems is well grounded in empirical studies (e.g., Langner and Michael, 1963, found that money can cushion the effects of stress), psychiatrists formerly underestimated its importance. For example, I found that the psychiatric residents at the UCLA Neuropsychiatric Institute, when given a choice of eight major areas of external precipitating stress for their patients, chose "financial problem" least frequently; even "acute traumatic incident not

---

*See Reiff and Riessman (1965) and Chapters 7 and 8 in this volume for a discussion of the use of indigenous workers in the mental health field.

classified elsewhere" was checked more often (Bart, 1962). Now, however, some psychiatrists at that hospital are researching the effects of poverty on mental illness.

Race, as well as poverty, is now seen as a relevant variable. Contrast the following remarks with the statement quoted earlier in which the therapist gave an intrapsychic interpretation to a patient's complaints about segregation at St. Elizabeth's. According to Christmas (1966, p. 164), " . . . situational and environmental factors play a large part in the emotional problems of Negro patients and their families." Because of the complex interrelationship between the individual psychic process and sociocultural factors, therapy groups composed of many people having similar experiences, rather than individual treatment, are suggested. The goal is to enable the individual to function as a responsible actor rather than a powerless victim.

Coles considers these changes in psychiatric orientation and in models of patient–therapist interaction to be a reflection of world and national events and the changing social order (where problems of race and poverty are more salient). For example, he points out that Kenneth Clark set up a clinic in Harlem in the 1940s to work with delinquent and neurotic children, but the nature of his involvement has changed; now he is concerned with the effects of living in Harlem "not only as they are *reflected* in childhood pathology, but as they *generate* the social pathology" (Coles, 1967, p. 29, emphases added).*

Because the humanistic and democratic values of these activist psychiatrists are apparent, it is possible to infer their image of the future. They see, or would like to see, a world without racism and poverty, a world where the decision-making process is democratized so that individuals have some control over their own destiny. Their view is that only in such a society is it possible for those now in "the other America" not to contribute disproportionately to the ranks of the mentally ill; the social institutions themselves will have to be changed for these values to be

*We should not assume a one-to-one relationship between changes in psychiatric rhetoric and changes in psychotherapy practice. According to Spray (personal communication, 1968), psychiatrists working in community mental health clinics state that they use traditional psychotherapeutic techniques.

realized. These activists consider it their function as psychiatrists to act as midwives bringing about the birth of this good society.

Psychotherapeutic Populism: Psychotherapy as a Form of Recreation and Social Movement

Lift Your Burdens

If you cannot afford a Psychiatrist or a Psychologist, write box 2392 Santa Fe Springs, Cal. 90670, enclosing a self-addressed stamped envelope with three dollars for a reply: From MARIASHIN [Los Angeles Free Press, 1967].

Psychotherapeutic populism

The therapeutic process is becoming more democratic. Reiff (1959) pointed out that the standard relationship between the analyst and the analysand replicated the relationship between the Victorian father and his wife or daughter. In keeping with the "strain toward consistency" in society, as the family structure became more democratic, so also did the interaction between the therapist and his patient. In "encounter groups" democratic ideology defines the relationship between therapist and patient: as Stoller (personal communication, 1968) says, "It is important that the approach of one human being to another predominate over the roles of professional to client." Moreover, he considers "mutuality inherent in marathon group therapy" and facilitates this mutuality by having sessions in his home with his wife as a participant.

From this democratization of the psychotherapeutic process it is a simple step to considering the presence of a professional in the "helping professions" unnecessary, if not harmful—a position I term "psychotherapeutic populism."* The later position is taken by Yablonsky (1967, p. 370) when he attributes part of

---

* Another example of this diffusion of democracy can be found in the New Left's commitment to participatory democracy, again a reflection of the populist tradition in the United States.

the success of Synanon to the "patient's reversing roles with the therapist." He adds (1967, p. 368) that Synanon's position "that some of its 'patients' can become therapists seems to draw fire from many professional quarters."

The Diggers Creative Society, a hippie group, consider it their function to care for individuals on "bad trips." According to an informant, "The worst thing to do with a person like that is to take him to a doctor or a hospital" (a position consistent with that presented by Becker, 1967). Thus, in both, the case of Synanon and of The Diggers, the absence of academically trained therapists is not a makeshift arrangement caused by shortages of funds but part of a set of beliefs that such a system is better for the individual. In other areas, however, the ideologies of the two groups differ. The internal structure of Synanon is hierarchical and authoritarian; Chuck Dederich, the founder, is a charismatic leader. On the other hand, the hippies usually denigrate leadership. During the seminar one of the participants who was "coming down" from a trip refused to lead a group at a be-in in Griffith Park, saying "Nobody is a leader for anyone else. Everyone is his own leader. Everyone must help himself. I have my bag and they have theirs."

A more recent example of psychotherapeutic populism is the women's liberation "consciousness-raising" small group. During the first few meetings the women tell their life story; through group process their pasts are reconstructed so that what they considered private problems, stemming from their own inadequacy, are redefined as public issues, growing out of woman's situation in society. They learn that other women have undergone similar experiences because of "institutionalized sexism," and this knowledge is allegedly therapeutic. Furthermore, because of the ideology of sisterhood, subsequent emotional support is given (at least in theory) to the group members whenever they need it. I find it useful to conceptualize the women's movement, particularly the "small group," as an extended family, fulfilling many of the functions formerly met by one's kin—aid in life crises such as divorce, illness—and in large part avoiding the atrocities that can characterize relationships with one's biological extended family.

A final example of populism is reflected in the publication

The Radical Therapist, which was started by the Minot (North Dakota) Collective and moved to Cambridge in 1971. The paper includes articles critical of the medical model of mental illness and of current psychiatric practices, with a sharp emphasis on sexism in psychotherapy and a focus on alternative life and therapy styles. The collective considers change, rather than adjustment, to be the purpose of psychotherapy and is opposed to mental health professionals having a monopoly on helping people with emotional problems. In Chicago the Lincoln Park Guerilla Therapy Collective, composed mainly of clinical psychologists and social workers, attempts to put this philosophy into practice and break down the barrier between the patient and the "expert."

It is more difficult to say exactly what radical therapy *is* than what it is not: It is not psychoanalytic. It is not oriented to individual treatment but rather to group strategies. The therapist does not assume either an authoritarian or an expert role. Radical therapists follow Mills' (1961) dictum that many situations defined as personal problems are in fact caused by "crises in institutional arrangements." Such an assumption renders individual treatment irrelevant, since the problems transcend individuals' local environments and inner lives.

Radical therapists I have talked with differ in technique, but all operate under this assumption. One radical therapist said she has unlearned much of what she learned in graduate school in the process of becoming a radical therapist. By pointing out that some problems are caused socially, she can show patients that they are not ineffective human beings, and furthermore, that they do not have to adjust to traditional roles.

Another radical therapist, who works on drug abuse, has set up a therapeutic environment with an alternative set of institutions. She tries to obtain jobs for clients and give them responsibilities in these therapeutic communities.

Psychotherapy as recreation

Wife and I wish to start a bicycle club. (Psychotherapy included if wish) $1. a month membership. Lic. psychologist [Los Angeles Free Press, 1968].

Big Sur Mendocino High Sierras Weekend Mountain Encounter

With a naturalist and an encounter group leader $35 per person—$45 per couple—food and lodging included . . . . . Sponsored by the Institute for the Development of Human Potential [An officially recognized Student Organization, but not an integral part of The University of California, poster on bulletin boards at The University of California, Berkeley, 1969].

Psychotheraplay or "games" are now considered a form of recreation for the man who has everything. According to Szasz (1961), when people have a surplus of money, they expect to be happy, and they use their money to seek happiness. Therefore, the social function of therapy must be compared not only with religion but also with alcohol, tobacco, and recreation. Thus, Endore (1967, p. 9) refers to the Synanon games, which are similar to group therapy sessions, as "the human sport," the game "to make you grow up." The new, more flexible self-image that results occurs "by nothing more than a willingness to play an exciting game and have a good time while doing so." Endore and Frankie Lago, a long-time Synanon resident (former "dope fiend" and thief, who was the main speaker at the orientation held every Sunday for people considering joining the Synanon club and the "games") deny that the games are therapy. However, Yablonsky (1967, p. viii) in the preface to his book on Synanon calls the Synanons (as they were then termed) "a new kind of group therapy, an effective approach to racial integration, a different way of being religious, a new method of attack therapy, an exciting fresh approach to the cultural arts and philosophy."*

Lago considered the "games" "adult education." He continued, "dope fiends" are "afflicted with character disorders" and should be residents of Synanon, but the 1,000 nonresident players might be people who have had success in their lives and "now want to get plugged into something else." Yablonsky

---

* For one semester I participated in the "square" Synanons (those that include addicts and people who have never been addicts, or "squares") as part of a course I took from Yablonsky. It seemed like group therapy to me, except that all the supportive statements were omitted and the rule of confidentiality was not applied.

(1967, p. vi) said that the Synanon Clubs "are comprised of hundreds of people who never had serious emotional problems but seem to *enjoy the thrill* of personal discovery the Games seem to produce" (emphasis added).

Psychotherapy as a Social Movement

Synanon and The Diggers (and other hard-core hippies), as well as some of the encounter groups to be discussed below are social movements, complete with "true believers." Yablonsky (1967, p. v) states:

> A part of Synanon's character that has become more articulate is its significance as a social movement. The organization has steadily moved beyond the limited work of treating drug addiction and crime. The function of Synanon as a vehicle for constructive personal and social change has become clearer as the theory and method is increasingly utilized by people who were never addicts, criminals, or had any history of serious character disorders in their past.

Synanon has mushroomed since its inception in an armory in Santa Monica. There are Synanon houses on the East and West coasts (four in California), in Reno, in Detroit, and Chicago. Synanon Industries owns several gas stations. Residents' children now can go to a Synanon school. Synanon is not simply a "cure" for addicts but a full-blown social movement.

A striking example of therapy both as recreation and as a social movement can be found in the booklet describing Kairos, the mental health spa in San Diego, where self-actualizing encounter therapy takes place. Not only can individuals join the Kairos Club, they can give gift certificates of from $25 to $100 "for that person whom you know is open and really right for such an experience.... It provides the perfect Christmas gift from one or more friends or relatives." Can you imagine giving— or receiving —a gift for a psychoanalysis?*

* See the June 1968 issue of the *Journal of Health and Social Behavior* for articles on recreational drug use. Fred Davis' article, "Heads and Freaks," discussed the "Heads" use of drugs for self-improvement.

If, in fact, as at The Diggers and Synanon, professional therapists are not necessary but increasing self-knowledge should be a human goal, then the image of the future that these groups hold becomes clear. The non-speed-freak hippies would like to "turn on" the whole world in order to have a better society where "no one studies war no more." Although the "drugless trip" has achieved a certain status, it is still common to believe that the war in Vietnam could have been ended if only someone had turned on Lyndon Johnson.* Hippie communes exist in the West Coast cities, but a number of "free men" have moved to rural areas to set up psychedelic kibbutzim. They believe that if everyone were free to "do his thing" a better world would result. It seems to me that "doing your own thing" is a twentieth-century version of Adam Smith's "invisible hand."†

Synanon's adherents envisage the world as an enormous Synanon. Everyone plays the "games" and thus becomes mature. Unlike the hippies, Synanon is opposed to drugs—any drugs. People do not need chemicals of any sort to achieve a sense of well-being. Their image of man is more Hobbesian: A system of authority will continue to exist. Like the hippies, members of Synanon feel free to experiment with time. Recently the residents at Synanon changed their time arrangements so that they worked a stretch of 12-hour days, then participated in marathon group therapy, and finally had a period of free time (the cubic time schedule). Presumably, such experimentation would continue in the future since, although they believe in the work ethic, they do not limit themselves to conventional work arrangements.

The New Therapies

The most striking changes in psychotherapy have come from psychologists rather than psychiatrists. It is important to note

* The belief in drugs as a means of causing social change is a major difference between the hippies and the New Left.

† In his *Wealth of Nations*, Adam Smith developed the laws of the market where "the invisible hand" enabled each man by following his "private interests and passions" to arrive at what "is most agreeable to the interest of the whole society."

that Freud was opposed to limiting analysis to medical men.
And Reiff (1966, p. 28) considers the elimination of lay analysts
probably the most critical defeat suffered by psychoanalysis, one
for which the American analysts were largely responsible. The
view in the United States that only MD's are qualified to
receive training to become analysts seems to be patently ideological. It makes entry into the field extremely difficult for all
those who do not have the financial resources to pay for medical
school itself, as well as for the training analysis most psychiatrists consider necessary. As a result, psychiatrists either come
from upper- or upper-middle-class backgrounds or have been
successful in their desire for upward mobility. Their background
may be one reason for the image of man—private man—held
until recently by most psychiatrists. For people who are "making it" in society, societal factors are not perceived as being
very important.

On the other hand, psychologists have had many a running
battle with medical men for their right to treat clients. Their
lower status is reflected in lower fees. The radical changes in
psychotherapy have come from psychologists perhaps because
of their lesser commitment to classic Freudian models and the
psychiatric profession, but, more importantly, because of their
differing education. Psychologists have more likely been exposed
to other behavioral and social sciences. Thus, they would be
more aware of sociocultural variables. In addition, behavior-
modification therapy, one of the new trends, is a natural outgrowth of the learning theory they are taught.

Man the Self-Actualizer: Good-Bye Mr. Weber.

"Basic encounter" therapists work within an existential
Weltanschaung, which differs from traditional psychiatry in its
antideterministic stance and in its rejection of two assumptions
sometimes held in nonexistential psychiatry: Man should be
adjusted to society, and man may be reduced to a bundle of biological urges. Mendel (1964, pp. 26-27) states:

> It [existential psychiatry] conceives of the individual choos-
> ing and making his world rather than adjusting to it or suc-

cumbing to it. This view holds that the world is part of the existing human being, that he is part of it, and that he makes his world. The here and now is emphasized, since the patient needs experience rather than interpretation, for "learning and change occur only through activity."

Existential psychotherapy has for some time been popular in Europe but has been taken up only recently in this country. The most popular current offshoot is "encounter therapy" or "encounter groups."* Many encounter therapists, predominantly psychologists,† call themselves humanistic psychologists and, as such, have their own association and journal. (See Bugental, 1967, for a representative collection of their works.)

If Freud's thinking reflected nineteenth-century mechanistic physics, it is not surprising that with the discovery of the principle of indeterminacy in twentieth-century physics—a discovery that resulted in the perception that the objective was related to the subjective—psychology should once again focus on the more subjective aspects of the individual and a "humanistic psychology" should energe. (It is also interesting to note that a similar trend has taken place in sociology with the existence of a "humanistic underground," to use Bernard Rosenberg's term.) A new psychology was needed to reflect the increase of leisure time (at least for some segments of the population) and the decrease in the importance of the work ethic. Energy formerly required for mere survival could now be devoted to improving the quality of life through increased awareness both of oneself and of one's surroundings. Bugental (1967, pp. 345–346), a humanistic psychologist and advisor to the Esalen Institute, says that we are in the early stages of "another major evolution in man's perception

* Some therapists, such as Rogers (1967), differentiate between group therapy, which is for people who have problems, and encounter groups, which are for everyone. This distinction is, however, rarely made in practice, because "sick" people are thought to benefit by encounter groups, and I will use the terms interchangeably.

† I analyzed the Fall 1967 catalogues of Esalen and Kairos and found the following occupational characteristics of seminar and workshop leaders: 30 PhD psychologists, 12 PhD's in other fields, 9 MD's, and 42 others, ministers, artists and dancers.

of himself and thus the whole nature of human experience," due to the availability of this energy. He considers behavioristic psychology, with its view of man as "nothing but a complex of muscle twiches" and its disposal of concepts such as "soul," "will," "mind," "consciousness," and "self," inappropriate to present and future conditions although appropriate in the past.

This new psychological vocabulary, rather than emphasizing regularity, uniformity, and predictability, will highlight "the unique, the creative, the individual, and the artistic." More attention should be paid to man's internal subjective experiences, and it should be recognized that the supposed "law of causality" is:

> simply a useful heuristic aid....Some of man's behavior flows from *reason* and not from *cause*. The difference is revolutionary. Let this difference be accepted and developed, and the torch is lit which will burn away the whole of the mechanomorphic picture of man and illuminate the human enterprise to entirely new levels of realization [Bugental, 1967, p. 347].

Consequently, social institutions can be improved and better suited to man's evolving needs.

Perls, a founder of Gestalt therapy (which uses body movement and is similar ideologically to encounter therapy) and permanent resident psychologist at Esalen, agreed with Bugental that the traditional concepts of linear causation are no longer appropriate. In a fund-raising speech for the new Topanga Development Center, an Esalen–Kairos type of workshop located in a Los Angeles canyon, he stated that his approach was processual. In contrast to psychoanalytic thinking, he focused on "the now and the how" rather than on "the wild goose chase of the past" (brochure of the Topanga Human Development Center, 1967).

The goal of encounter therapy, in contrast to behavior-modification therapy, is not the elimination of discomforting symptoms. Indeed, one need not have any symptoms at all. It is the therapy for the man who has everything. As Wesley (1967) states, this therapy is for "anyone who has come to recognize a vague dissatisfaction in his life arising from the lack of expressive spontaneity, love and joy." Rogers says, "Encounter groups are for those who are functioning normally but want to improve their capacity for living within their own sets of relationships" (1967, p. 717).

The theory of human nature held by encounter therapists is that of Rousseau, and the assumption is made that the potential for growth present in each individual will develop through the permissive and accepting climate of an encounter group. As a result of this experience, people will be able to fulfill their potentialities.

Marathon group therapy, used at Esalen, Kairos, and by many encounter therapists (Stoller, 1968, p. 42) represents a challenge to conventional arrangements of time in that its basic characteristic is that of the continuous session ranging over one or more days. Regularly scheduled meetings of one or two hours duration, stretching out over many months or even years have been customary. The implications of the two basic approaches to people literally imply different views of men.

Traditional psychotherapists have criticized the marathons. In keeping with the nineteenth-century ideology out of which psychoanalysis developed, they believe that long periods of arduous work are necessary for any benefit to occur. They find it difficult to accept the claim that people may change as a result of participating in a 30-hour, two-day period of therapy.

Conventional attitudes toward sex are also contested in the new therapies. In contrast to the Freudian conceptualization of genitality, in which homosexual relationships are considered fixations, sexual activity not culminating in genital intercourse is considered polymorphous perverse, and promiscuity is considered immature, among some self-actualizing groups relatively free sex is considered part of the growth process. Thus Kairos offers a seminar entitled "Enjoying the Non-Permanent Relationship," the purpose of which seems to be to teach women to enjoy casual sex, since these nonpermanent interactions "constitute the majority of man–woman relationships." At Esalen, mixed nude bathing at the hot springs is part of the schedule; and although it is not required, it is expected.

The importance of relating to nature the anti-intellectualism, the emphasis on Eastern philosophy, techniques, and music, and the Rousseau image of man are found both among the hippies and the self-actualizers. They are like such American Romantics as Emerson (1837, p. 3), who said: "Why should we grope among the dry bones of the past or put the living generation into masquerade out of faded wardrobe? The sun shines today also." Neither group feels the past is relevant to present experience.

As a participant–observer at a "basic Encounter Group" that attempted to recreate the Esalen atmosphere, I noted the following differences between this group and conventional group therapy:

1. A nonverbal therapist, a dancer, was present whose function was to increase the group members' body awareness.

2. The meeting neither started nor ended on time. In conventional therapy, lateness is interpreted as resistance, an approach to time consistent with the requirements of an expanding industrial economy.

3. The relationship between the therapists and the group was relatively egalitarian.

4. Part of the encounter was devoted to nonverbal communication between dyads, which in two instances resulted in what can most parsimoniously be called "making out."

This group emphasized various sense modalities not previously highly valued in our society, geared as it was to production rather than consumption. The permissive attitude toward sex, the emphasis on body awareness, the democratization of the therapeutic process, all are associated with similar trends in other areas of our society and assume a future very different from the past.

The values of these therapists are freedom, spontaneity, intimacy and creativity. Their idea of the freedom man needs to grow is not simply Freud's goal of replacing id with ego but rather freedom to express feelings, to become close to people with less fear of interdependence and intimacy, freedom to express oneself through nonverbal as well as verbal means, through movement and art and nature. The structure of society, with its emphasis on role-appropriate behavior in interaction, is considered a barrier to full humanness.* Thus, individuals are encouraged not to become "victimized by the social rigging in which his life moves ... (which) chokes off the expansion of his life-self intimacy" (Kairos, 1967–1968).

An example of such an approach to changing institutions, and one that shows a Rogerian method of bringing about a society more suited for today's world, is the Educational Innovation Project of Carl Rogers and the staff of the Western Behavioral Sciences Institute working with the personnel and students of the Immaculate Heart Schools† (Rogers, 1967; Western Behavioral Sciences Institute, 1968). The purpose of Rogers' (1967, p. 717) "plan for self-directed change in an educational system" is to enable educational institutions to develop flexible and adaptive individuals who will be comfortable with rapid social change. "Basic encounter" groups with a maximum of freedom for personal expression, exploration of feelings, and communication are "one of the most effective means yet discovered for facilitation of constructive learning, growth and change—in individuals or in the organizations they compose..." (Rogers, 1967, p. 718). The whole system must participate for change to be effective. Otherwise the changed individual either becomes frustrated or returns to his previous method of interaction because of group pressure. Rogers believes that whole systems can be changed in a relatively short period of time.

Rogers, in a symposium with Skinner on control of human behavior, has set down his values and beliefs concerning the role

---

* This attempt to get through the presentation of self is also advocated by Synanon and the hippies. Synanon games propose to enable people to get away from the type of game playing that constitutes most of human interaction. The Diggers and other hippie groups believe that "tripping" enables a person to get to his "pure being" and away from his presented self.

† The sisters of the Immaculate Heart of Mary direct and teach in the college, secondary and primary schools involved in this experiment. Their innovations brought them into conflict with Cardinal MacIntyre of Los Angeles, a conflict that was finally mediated by the Vatican. One issue that disturbed more conservative Catholics was the encounter therapy, which they considered a means of breaking down traditional morality.

psychology should play. He suggests that the type of therapy he advocates will result in greater maturity, variability, flexibility, openness to experience, increased self-responsibility, and self-direction. He values

> man as a process of becoming, as a process of achieving worth and dignity through the development of his potentialities; the individual human being as a self-actualizing process, moving on to more challenging and enriching experiences, the process by which the individual creatively adapts to an ever-new and changing world; the process by which knowledge transcends itself... [Rogers and Skinner, 1956, p. 1063].

Thus, he attempts to learn if science can (p. 1063)

> aid in the discovery of new modes of richly rewarding living, more meaningful and satisfying modes of interpersonal relationships. Can science inform us on ways of releasing the creative capacity of individuals....In short, can science discover the methods by which man can most readily become a continually developing and self-transcending process, in his behavior, his thinking, his knowledge?

He believes that the therapy that he and followers practice express such values and produce a client who is "self-directing, less rigid, more open to the evidence of his senses, better organized and integrated, more similar to the ideal which he (the client) has chosen for himself" (Rogers and Skinner, 1956, p. 1063).

There are two limitations of this type of therapy. The development of each individual's full potentialities is possible only where there is an economic surplus. Maslow (1962) pointed out in his work on need hierarchies that self-actualization could occur only after other needs—safety, food and shelter—were met. Thus those portions of our society still poorly housed, fed, clothed and subject to the capricious behavior of police cannot afford the luxury of self-actualization (nor can most of the world). Stoller told me that when he applied the encounter techniques to welfare mothers and to drug addict prisoners, their structural situations made it impossible for the benefits they believed they obtained to be carried over into their daily life. Moreover, the goals of encounter therapy, which stress expressivity, would be most useful for individuals, who had traditional Protestant socialization emphasizing the virtues of stoicism and restraint. Other ethnic and class groups, white and nonwhite, whose significant others do not discourage expression of emotion and "acting out," would perhaps be better served by other modes of therapy.

Man, *"the Two-Legged White Rat or larger computer :"** Behavior-Modification Therapy*

Behavior-modification therapy is the antithesis of self-actualizing therapy. It is deterministic rather than indeterministic, is based on different theoretical groundwork, holds different views of human nature and of how society can and should be changed and thus has a different image of the future. It reflects the tendencies toward rationalization (in the Weberian, not Freudian, sense), dehumanization, and scientism in our society. Behavior-modification therapy, seems most adequately conceptualized as a continuation of the tradition of therapy as social control. The therapist controls the situation.

The image of man these therapists use is derived from the behavior of animals. Their position is unique, because it is derived from the branch of psychology known as learning theory (P. London, personal communication). These therapies are based on present observable behavior, rather than on unconscious factors or past events and they are designed to remove the symptoms causing the discomfort without "tampering with 'selves and souls' or even 'personalities'." (London, 1964, p. 37.) Many behavior-modification therapists believe that "the difficulties which bring people to therapy reflect learnings of fundamental behaviors which are at least as easily observed in lower animals as in people," and, thus, can be cured by mechanical procedures (London, 1964, p. 77). They try to change the system of reinforcements so that the symptom they want to "extinguish"

---

* Phrase taken from Bugental (1967, p. 345).

is no longer "reinforced" (rewarded). According to Kanfer and Phillips (1966), for this therapy to be effective, the patient must have a specific problem, such as a phobia, rather than the general problems of feelings of worthlessness, personal inadequacies, or chronic generalized anxiety. Mowrer (1963, p. 579) considers behavior therapy the "method of choice," because "the way to *feel better* is to *be better* in the ethical and interpersonal sense of the term." His position is different, however, from those behavior-modification therapists "who assume that all that is wrong with neurotics is that they have some unrealistics fears which need to be extinguished or counter-conditioned."

These therapists disagree with the Freudians who believe that insight will lead to changed behavior. They would more likely agree that changed behavior (which they would produce by manipulating reinforcements) would lead to insight. They are also opposed to the humanistic, nonscientific (according to their standards) approach of the encounter therapists, which they consider sentimental and muddleheaded. Thus, their papers have starkly mechanistic titles such as "The Therapist as a Social Reinforcement Machine" (Krasner, 1961, reported in London, 1964, p. 239) and "The Psychiatric Nurse as Behavioral Engineer" (Ayllon and Michael, 1959). Some techniques they use seem more akin to Dr. Benway (Burroughs' character) than to Dr. Kildare. Thus, in the Ayllon and Michael study, the nurse changed the behavior of a patient who insisted on being fed but who wanted to be neat. The nurse deliberately dribbled food on the patient when she fed her. The patient eventually fed herself, but she "unexpectedly" relapsed after a four-week improvement in self-feeding.

> No reasonable explanation is suggested by a study of her daily records; but, after she had been spoonfed several meals in a row, the rumor developed that someone had informed the patient that the food spilling was not accidental. In any event the failure to feed herself lasted only about 5 days [Ayllon and Michael, 1959, p. 331].

Ayllon and Michael believe patients' behavioral problems result from events "occurring in the patients' immediate or historical environment. They are not manifestations of mental disorder" (Ayllon and Michael, 1959, p. 323). (I do not understand their dichotomy.)

The logical extension of the model of man depicted in this section can be found in the work of Colby *et al.* (1966)—psychotherapy by computer. If the important part of therapy is not the relationship with the therapist, if a nurse can be "programmed" to modify behavior, why not make use of the new technology available and help solve the shortage of therapists? Colby (1966, p. 151) considers the therapist

> an information processor and decision maker with a set of decision rules which are closely linked to short-range and long-range goals. With time he builds up a cognitive model of the patient; carries on thought operations on the model, using first and second order inferences in a partially specialized language; and finally decides on a communication to offer to the patient in natural language ... guided by rough empiric rules telling him what is appropriate to say and not to say in certain contexts.

The person (as yet patients are not being used in the studies) types statements on a teletype, and the program types answers, substituting appropriate words in the responses for those found in the input sentences:

Person : My mother dislikes me.
Program : Why do you feel your mother dislikes you [Colby, 1966, pp. 148–149]?

The program should identify and keep statistical track of important topics for the formulation of future responses.

Efficiency is obviously a value of these researchers. The therapist is "much more efficient," since he can work with many more patients. Several psychologists with whom I have spoken think the programs are good; in the future they would give all the chronic patients, who at this time receive no therapy, the opportunity of conversing with a tape. But in view of Rioch's (Rioch *et al.*, 1963) success in training housewives in a brief period of time to be just as effective therapists as professionals with standard training, one wonders why so little attention is being focused on this alternative possibility? Choosing a computer program over a housewife–therapist certainly is a reflection of values.

The workers in this area admit that they do not know how effective computer therapy will be. The program cannot handle sarcasm, shouting, or changes in feeling and tone, and it still arouses some antagonism, which is assumed to be due to defects in the program rather than to the process itself. For example:

> *Person :* I hate you, you stupid machine.
> *Program :* What don't you like about me?
> *Person:* You have no feelings.
> *Program :* How do you mean [Colby, 1966, p. 150]?

It would be unfair to assume that the behavioral-modification therapists are monsters—men with no feeling who wish to produce a generation of robots, men who have turned their back on the humanistic tradition in Western civilization to become mad scientists in the laboratory. It is obvious, for example, that B. F. Skinner, on whose work much of the application of learning theory is based, is a man of good will, a man who would like to apply what he has found out about how pigeons learn, to create a world*

> in which there is food clothing and shelter for all, where everyone chooses his own work and works on the average only 4 hours a day where music and the arts flourish, where personal relationships develop under the most favorable circumstances, where education prepares every child for the social and intellectual life which lies before him, where—in short—people are truly happy, secure, productive, creative and forwardlooking [Rogers and Skinner, 1956, p. 1059].

In the above quote, Skinner is referring to the image of the

* Skinner appeared in September 1967 on a panel of five speakers at an Esalen-sponsored discussion in San Francisco, "The Scope of Human Potential."

future he presented in his utopian novel, *Walden Two* (1962). The book has been severely criticized for its *Brave New World* aspects and the lack of real freedom, but Skinner believes "All men control and are controlled. The question of government in the broadest possible sense is not how freedom is to be preserved, but what kinds of control are to be used and to what ends" [Rogers and Skinner, 1959, p. 1060].

Like the behavioral-modification therapists, and in contrast to the existential self-actualizing therapists, Skinner is deterministic. He does not believe that people behave in certain ways because of any innate goodness or evil but because they are reinforced for doing so [Rogers and Skinner, 1956, p. 1065]:

> The resulting behavior may have far-reaching consequences for the survival of the pattern to which it conforms. And whether we like it or not, survival is the ultimate criterion.

In his symposium with Carl Rogers (1956, p. 1065) he points out that there is no evidence "that a client ever becomes truly *self* directing."

> ...The therapeutic situation is only a small part of the world of the client. From the therapist's point of view it may appear to be possible to relinquish control. But control passes, not to a "self," but to forces in other parts of the client's world. This solution of the therapist's problem of power cannot be our solution, for we must consider all the forces acting upon the individual.

Therefore, in *Walden Two* Skinner (1962, pp. 296–297) designs a total environment, or, as some might say, a dictatorship, a total institution. Frazier, the designer in the novel, sees no conflict between dictatorship and freedom! People are trained, through positive reinforcements to "want to do precisely the things which are best for themselves and for the community. Their behavior is determined, yet they're free."

Frazier's (and Skinner's) goal is the control of human behavior, not for exploitation of others, nor for one's own benefit, nor for the benefit of some elite, but so that everyone may share in the advantages of the new technology of control:

"What remains to be done?" he said, his eyes flashing. "Well, what do you say to the design of personalities? Would that interest you? The control of temperament? Give me the specification, and I'll give you the man! What do you say to the control of motivation, building the interests which will make men most productive and most successful? Does that seem to you fantastic? Yet some of the techniques are available, and more can be worked out experimentally. Think of the possibilities! A society in which there is no failure, no boredom, no duplication of effort! [Skinner, 1962, p. 292]"

People marry young at Walden Two, but if the Manager of Marriages thinks there "is any great discrepancy in intellectual ability or temperament, they are advised against marrying. The marriage is at least postponed, and that usually means it's abandoned" (p. 135). A "series of adversities" is *designed* to develop the greatest possible self-control in children (p. 115). The approach is always pragmatic; every principle is experimentally tested. Thus, "History is honored at Walden Two only as entertainment" (p. 115). In sum (p. 14):

Political action was of no use in building a better world, and men of good will had better turn to other measures as soon as possible. Any group of people could secure economic self-sufficiency with the help of modern technology and the psychological problems of group living could be solved with available principles of "behavioral engineering."

A Radical Behavior-Modification Therapist

The common thread in behavior-modification therapy is the belief that behavior is related to the consequences of that behavior. Thus, the best kind of behavior therapy teaches the patient how to analyze the contingencies that control his or her behavior and how to control them so that he or she can better cope with life and not feel helpless and powerless. But behavior-modification therapists can also give male homosexuals shocks if they become aroused when they see a picture of a male nude. One particular therapist—a humanist and a political radical—would not use this method. If a gay person came for treatment, the person would first set up his or her own goals—whether to stop being homosexual or to make it a "less costly" lifestyle—rather than use standard criteria for "maturity" or have the therapist set up the goals, presumably heterosexuality. The behavior-modification therapist prefers not to use punishment or negative reinforcement for many reasons! As long as punishment is used the client has to be watched or monitored; furthermore, there are side effects. This therapist tries to help the client to find behavior that leads to pleasure and to avoid behavior that stops the pleasure.

Although not all behavior-modification therapists would agree with her, she considers this therapy a radical model because it focuses on external factors rather than on intrapsychic motivations. In this sense it is quite similar to the philosophical materialism on which Soviet psychotherapy was based. And of course, Pavlov, the Soviet psychologist, was a behaviorist, so these similarities are to be expected.

Better Living through Chemistry

Drug therapy is the province of medical men, since they are the only group allowed to prescribe medication. The use of such psychoactive drugs has increased greatly, especially for outpatients. In 1970, "202 million legal prescriptions for psychoactive drugs—stimulants, tranquillizers, antidepressants—were filled in respectable pharmacies for persons who saw their doctors first" (Lennard et al., 1971).

Lennard and his colleagues believe there is collusion, unwitting though it may be, between the pharmaceutical industry and physicians to promote increased drug use. The drug industry practices "mystification" in its communications to physicians, "relabeling an increasing number of human and personal problems as medical problems." Advertisements suggest that drugs be used when new students are anxious at college, children are afraid of the dark, and families cannot communicate with their children. The drugs mask the sources of such stress rather than enabling alterations in "human relatedness and social arrangements that determine the context and the substance of our existence" (Lennard *et al.*, 1971).

Such is certainly a possible interpretation of the giving of the stimulant Ritalin, to schoolchildren allegedly suffering from the ill-defined "minimal brain damage." Here, however, the school nurse or assistant to the principal administers the drug to the child. Amphetamines have a "paradoxical effect" on the child, actually slowing him down and calming him thereby making him easier for the teacher to manage. Such use of amphetamines presents the very real danger of introducing young children to the use of drugs to handle life problems, a practice that is condemned when the child is a few years older and obtains his psychoactive substances without the benefit of the physician. Perhaps it is the educational system rather than the nervous sytem that should be changed. In addition, newspaper accounts have recently told of Thorazine, a powerful tranquilizer, being administered to "trouble-makers" in schools for delinquent boys, in one case causing a boy's death.

In advertisements found in psychiatric journals, drugs are presented as the answer to the woman problem. For example, the makers of the tranquilizer Valium suggest it be used for the woman with a Master's in fine arts who, because of her three children, is not able to use her training. She manifests her unhappiness by having gynecological symptoms with no organic cause.

I will not deal at length with the use of drugs for in-patients in mental hospitals. While in many cases such drugs are an important adjunct to treatment, they can be used as a method of social control when the staff–patient ratio is so large that alternate methods are not possible. I vividly remember hearing a tape of a patient at Langley Porter pleading for a decrease in his dosage of thorazine, a request that was not granted. And those of us who have seen the film *Titticut Follies* cannot forget the staff meeting when a patient's request for less medication was considered part of his illness and "really" a request for more medication.

Soviet Psychotherapy:
A Test of the Sociology of Knowledge

It is the central tenet of the sociology of knowledge that existential factors condition social thought. According to Marx (1904, pp. 11–12), "It is not the consciousness of men that determines their existence, but on the contrary, their existence determines their consciousness." If, in fact, that is the case, not only should there be differences in psychotherapy through *time* but there should be cross-cultural differences as well. Szasz (1961, p. 54) noted that while Karl Marx was the "social thera-pist" for the impoverished masses brought together in the pro-cess of industrialization, "The basic value of the individual— as opposed to the interests of the masses or the nation—was emphazised, especially by the upper classes. The professions, medicine foremost among them, espoused the ethical value of individualism." Thus, forms of behavior that might be labeled "mental illness" in different national settings may be quite different. Comparing the United States with the Soviet Union, Szasz (1961, p. 296) says that differences

> arise from and reflect characteristic features of the social matrix of the therapeutic situation. They point to covert preferences of individualistic or collectivistic ethics and their attendant notions concerning the duties and privileges of citizens and state in regard to each other.

If we think of degree of socialism as one variable and of emphasis on the importance of sociological factors and of the community as another, we see that there is a positive relation-ship between the two, when examining the psychiatry in the United States, Great Britain and the Soviet Union. In the United States it was only when the federal and state govern-ments started funding community mental health centers and financing the training of social or community psychiatrists, in short, only when there was money in poverty, that community psychiatry and "psychotherapeutic activism" has burgeoned.*

In Great Britain since the National Health Act (1946) and with the added impetus of the Mental Health Act (1959), community mental health services have been greatly developed. According to Skottowe (1967, pp. 363–364):

> Aldrich has pointed out that British and American psychiatry had followed the same pattern up to 1939 but have diverged since the War. Whereas the main British developments have been in social psychiatry with particular reference to psychotic patients in hospitals, the main American developments have been in dynamic psychiatry with reference to ambulant neurotic patients. He tends to ascribe this...to the National Health Service. This has boosted mental hospital psychiatry... because it has brought mental hospital men out of their shells and has imposed on them the broader experiences to be found in outpatient departments, general hospitals, community work and domiciliary consultations.

Many observers (Field, 1960; Wortis, 1950; Zifferstein, 1966; Baburn, 1966) have noted the emphasis in Soviet psychiatry on environmental manipulation, or in plain words, on making the patient's real world more comfortable. In addition to different conceptualizations of the relationship between the individual and society in the United States and the USSR, perhaps the "it's what's inside that counts" ideology is so much a part of American psychotherapy because the therapist does

---

* The major funding of social psychiatric research and community mental health centers occurred in 1963 (for buildings) and 1965 (for staff) after President John F. Kennedy's message to Congress calling for such legislation. The National Institute of Mental Health (NIMH) was set up in 1946 in response to the great number of psychoneurotic exemptions, breakdowns and discharges during World War II; and in 1955 the Mental Health Study Act was passed, establishing the Joint Commission on Mental Illness and Health. Their policy recommendations emphasized the importance of the community, both in the etiology and the cure of mental illness (Felix, 1967). But it was not until the 1960s that psychiatric training included training in social psychiatry and that the psychiatrists became aware of the importance of sociological factors. Each year until 1968 financial support for NIMH has increased.

not have the resources available to manipulate the environment of his private patients. Thus, he must limit himself to focusing on the patient's internal world. This limitation is then transformed into the ideology that all that matters is internal.*

In the Soviet Union heavy emphasis is placed on the physiological basis of mental illness (Pavlovian theory), which is compatible with philosophical materialism and on environmental manipulation, which is compatible with the theory of individual dependence on society. Both Wortis (1950) and Field (1960) agree that Freudian or psychologistic explanations for mental illness are considered "undialectical" or "idealist" in the Soviet Union.

The problem of relating the psychology of man to his mode of existence in the Soviet Union becomes one of the main concerns of psychiatry. For this reason the most serious charges have been leveled against psychologists who seek to change people's minds without changing their activity and experience; and, conversely the greatest emphasis is placed on work therapy or on other forms of activity that serve to change people's minds (Wortis, 1950, p. 6).

Field (1960, p. 292) speaks of the somatic or physiological therapies (neurology and psychiatry are not two separate disciplines), psychological therapies, and the sociological therapies:

> The sociological therapies are based on the Soviet theoretical conception of the importance of the milieu for mental health and mental illness and the assumption that the care of the mentally ill is not only the responsibility of the psychiatrist, but also of others....Health, and particularly mental health, is much too important to be left exclusively to physicians. The idea is very strong that in many instances the patient may be treated more effectively through a change in his environment: transferring him to a different job, encouraging treatment at home or in the community in

* An American psychiatrist I know said that even the psychiatric social workers don't want to work with the patient's environment. They prefer to do dynamic therapy with their clients. On occasion *he* would attempt to get jobs for and introduce girls to his schizophrenic male patients. His colleagues derisively called him a social worker.

familiar surroundings and with people who care for the patient..., having the psychiatrist or a visiting nurse see the patient on his home ground if necessary.... I have already touched on the importance which attaches to work therapy; this type of treatment finds additional ideological reinforcement in dialectical materialism which holds that the consciousness of the individual is a reflection of the objective world, is formed by the process of social labor, and appears early during human activity.

In a more recent article Zifferstein (1966, p. 367) refers to "the Soviet Psychiatrists' Concept of Society as a Therapeutic Community." He contrasts the occupational therapy in the United States, where patients make sandals, stuffed animals and ceramics, with the work therapy in the Soviet Union, where patients make "real products" and are paid for their efforts. The therapy is directive and supportive. For example, a doctor thought that a patient with the capacity to be an engineer was unchallenged by the factory work he was doing and this contributed to his mental illness. The doctor, therefore, prescribed that the patient be enrolled in an engineering institute and paid his full salary during the entire period of his schooling. Not only is it "the doctors' role to rearrange his [the patient's] life so that he has a better schedule of work, sleep, recreation, etc." (Wortis, 1950, p. 84), each community clinic has an office of social assistance that "examines the working and living conditions of the patients and undertakes measures for improvement" (Field, 1960, p. 289). The emphasis on work in Soviet psychiatry as described by all the authors is in keeping with Marxian thought, because Marx emphasized the importance of meaningful work in man's fulfilling his species' nature. Needless to say, however, the use of patients labor in a society suffering from a labor shortage may have other than therapeutic motivations.

In sum, problems of human happiness in Soviet psychiatry are not basically considered to be psychiatric questions. Soviet psychiatry can best be understood if it is related to its three basic sources of influences: its social setting in a broad framework of public health services; its conformity with the general principle of dialectical materialism; and the teachings of Pavlov (Wortis,

1950). In the United States, where at least in the formal value system the individual is "master of his fate" and "captain of his soul," and where the psychiatrist, with the exception of those in the community health centers and the activist psychiatrists, does not have the power to manipulate the environment, the focus of therapy is on the individual and what he can do to change. In the Soviet Union, individual behavior is considered a result of social structural arrangements and psychiatrists have the power to manipulate the patients' environments. Thus, the focus is on physical treatment (consonant with philosophical materialism—the official ideology) and on changing the environment.

Soviet psychiatrists claim "that their type of society which has a clear-cut, well-defined goal and a collective orientation in its culture, leads to a lesser degree of mental illness than a capitalistic society with its antagonistic classes, its violent competitions, its irresponsible individualism, and its multiplicity of goals" (Field, 1960, p. 292). They, therefore, believe that social problems such as juvenile delinquency and alcoholism should have withered away and are chagrined at their continued existence. Nevertheless the Soviets do not consider psychotherapy the way to treat such problems. If the statistics presented by Field (1960) are valid, however, they have halved their rate of schizophrenia from 1940 to 1956, and we might expect that the rate would continue to decline, all other things being equal.

For the future, if an economic surplus becomes a fact of life of Soviet society, perhaps matters of individual happiness will become a matter of conern and, although they might even use self-actualization, Soviet psychiatrists would find behavior modification therapy more consistent with their Pavlovian tradition. The use of psychotherapy by computer would not be incompatible with the "rational" and "directive" psychotherapy used and with the high value on technology in the Soviet Union; if the relationship with the therapist is not considered the essence of the treatment, with proper programs available, the computer could well take over.

There is another more ominous possibility. The need for

social control, combined with distaste for traditional methods of terror, may increase the use of mental hospitals as repositories for political troublemakers. Already several intellectuals who have written in opposition to the regime have been defined as mentally ill and "sentenced" to mental hospitals.

Conclusion

London (1969) notes that mental health experts working privately can be irresponsible if they insist on totally denying responsibility for the social changes they foster. Their role can become "insidious and potentially destructive." Such a destructive role is brilliantly described by Keniston (1968) in a satirical image of the future, "How Community Mental Health Stamped Out the Riots (1968:78)." In his "projection," a psychiatric vocabulary is used to explain all forms of protest (much as Lerner did, 1968). Keniston projects the use of this vocabulary to justify incarcerating and "treating" rioters and potential rioters suffering from the "aggressive alienation syndrome."

Keniston further notes the relationship between psychological quietism and the developments he is "predicting." In this brave new world it is found that concern with "objectivist" issues such as housing, sanitation, legal rights and jobs lead to the patient's relapsing into violence; thus programs seeking to ameliorate these environmental factors are wrong, not only because they merely treat symptoms rather than the underlying personality of pathology, but because they "undermined the mental health of those exposed to these programs" (p. 23). Objectivism becomes "a prime symptom of individual and community dysfunction" (p. 23), for which therapy must be instituted swiftly and effectively. College students, intellectuals, and certain foreign countries become targets for the "total mental health" program because they show such "objectivist" pathology.

Perhaps Keniston hopes, by making us aware of the social control implications of a mental health rhetoric widely applied, that his image of the future will function as a self-denying rather than a self-fulfilling prophecy.

Other academics and therapists concerned with the social control aspects of therapy, and particularly of hospitalization, do not have an explicit image of the future. It is clear, however, that they would prefer a decrease in "total institutions" and an increase in the civil liberties of the patients or potential patients. Thus, they should approve trends toward day-treatment centers, night-treatment centers and out-patient care using drugs as a substitute for hospitalization (see Pasamanick *et al.*, 1967, for a study showing the superiority of such a program for schizophrenics over both hospitalization and nonhospitalization with placebos). Their rejection of the medical model may cause them to wince at terms such as "treatment" and items such as drugs. But because of the concern with "labeling" as a cause of deviance, any program diminishing hospitalization should meet with their approval, although ultimately the development of a society with an increased tolerance for nonconforming behavior seems to be preferred.

In general, the implications for the future seen by other writers sensitive to the problem focus on the nonmedical significance of psychiatric and psychological thought. Bensman and Vidich (1957, p. 57) believe that "the impact of psychoanalysis will ultimately be greater as a form of social awareness" and sensibility, than as a form of treatment for individual problems. Lindner (1957), like the therapists concerned with self-actualization, stresses the possibility of developing new potentialities and capacities, such as telepathy.

Rieff (1966) extends his 1959 thesis concerning the rise of psychological man, calling what is happening today and presumably tomorrow "The Triumph of the Therapeutic." Rieff's concern is: "How are we to be saved?" He (1966, p. 5) believes literature, sociology, and psychiatry converge, since their ultimate interest "turns on the question whether our culture can be so reconstructed that faith—some compelling symbolic self-integrating communal purpose—need no longer superintend the organization of personality." The decline of the work ethic is important: We are now learning "how not to pay the high personal costs of social organization," whereas "previously total social cooperation was necessary in order to survive hard reality in a world characterized by scarcity." The present trend toward "release" may be extended and permanent; "an infinity of created needs can now be satisfied" easily (1966, p. 239). Rieff is opposed to the new intellectuals because of their renunciation of the constraints of civilization and their worship of the self, disguised as the religion of art. They have an aversion to culture, and he considers their goal, the sense of well-being and impulse release, "the unreligion of the age" (1966, p. 10). This revolution is unlike others in that it is not being fought in the name of a new communal order, but rather for

> a permanent disestablishment of any deeply internalized moral demands.... For the culturally conservative image of the ascetic, enemy of his own needs, there has been substituted the image of the needy person, permanently engaged in the task of achieving a gorgeous variety of satisfactions [1966, pp. 239-241].

Rieff believes, further, that we need "compassionate communities" rather than the "trained egoists" of this therapeutic age. Given his commitment to a certain kind of culture and civilization, I do not believe he would consider the hippie communes such compassionate communities but rather a further example of self-indulgence and self-worship. He thinks (1966, p. 27) we must find the moral equivalent of the Protestant Ethic because "the rules of health indicate activity."

Rieff continues (p. 235) that although modern therapists may consider themselves social scientists and "the language of science is not revelatory," therapists today "must use a language of faith":

> A language of faith may be controlling or releasing, interdictory or counter-interdictory. It contributes vitally to what Mannheim called "collective definitions," not mere hypotheses or replaceable theories, but rather a "source of collective habits and actions."

Most therapists seem to be men of good will and humanitarian outlook, and they would envision a future in which psychotherapy would be available for all who need it. But social psychiatric studies have shown that the greatest need for this is among the lower socioeconomic status groups, precisely the groups that do not receive it. One problem is that psychotherapists do not know effective, sound methods of psychotherapy for the poor. But even if they could reach and "relate" to poor people with problems, "overwhelming socioeconomic stresses" make such help ineffective (Redlich, 1967, pp. 66–67).* Redlich suggests that techniques developed for these strata will probably involve group methods and nonverbal approaches. Tompkins (1967, p. 2) agrees that:

> The future of psychiatry will be determined in large measure by the extent we commit ourselves to joining with the rest of the health and welfare services in meeting these demands thrust upon us by socioeconomic and political forces in a changing world.

Although he believes that psychotherapy must continue as a part of medicine (for an opposing view, see Hollingshead and Redlich, 1958, p. 377), Tompkins notes the value of cooperation with other groups and thinks that the importance of private doctors making arrangements with private patients will diminish.

Greenblatt and Sharaf (1967) suggest several ways to train psychiatrists to treat lower-class patients:

1. Such patients should be accepted at teaching hospitals.†
2. Psychiatric residents could live as participant–observers in the homes of impoverished schizophrenic patients, because

---

* A psychotherapist who works with lower and working-class people, because psychotherapy is included in their union health plan, tells me: "If I were really doing my job, I'd teach my lower-class depressed patients to become revolutionaries."

† Training or university hospitals accept patients who they feel will be of use in teaching the psychiatric residents. Since some psychiatrists consider lower-class people unable to benefit from psychotherapy, and since some residents are being trained to do psychotherapy, such patients may not be admitted. Moreover, lower-class patients usually do not apply to university psychiatric hospitals. Some hospitals, such as the UCLA Neuropsychiatric Institute, require that patients come in voluntarily. Many lower-class patients are court-committed, and this practice excludes them. Thus, it was not surprising that in my research using five hospitals in the Los Angeles area, the UCLA Neuropsychiatric Institute patients ranked second in socioeconomic status; only the patients at an expensive nonsubsidized private hospital ranked higher.

"it may be that a tour of residence in the home...would teach the psychiatric trainee far more than many hours of office practice with the same patient" (p. 156).

3. Residents should be trained to be mobile, going where the need is, to the patient's home if necessary, and flexible, so they can delegate responsibility to other therapeutic team members.

Were these programs widely instituted, residents hopefully would be no longer trained to be what Paul Hoch termed "cream puff psychiatrists" (quoted by Greenblatt and Sharaf 1967, p. 151), men and women who are content to live out their professional lives dedicated to the welfare of a "thin layer of well heeled patients at the top of the economic heap." Even if such techniques are developed and effective in reducing psychic pain, "...as long as analytically-oriented individual therapy is regarded as *the* prestigious treatment, new modes will be implicitly declasse measures for declasse people" (p. 152).

Sociologists are among the agents of social change and have played roles in three major social psychiatric studies: the New Haven studies, the Stirling County studies in Nova Scotia, and the Midtown studies in Manhattan.

The New Haven team (Hollingshead and Redlich, 1958; Myers and Roberts, 1959) dealt explicitly with changes they advocated so that psychotherapy should not be the privilege of the rich and the shock box the medicine of the poor. As Hollingshead and Redlich (1958, p. 377) jokingly put it, "what America needs is a 'good five dollar psychotherapist'." Their projected program includes new treatment methods to develop effective and shorter methods of psychotherapy and professional training to train nonmedical "counsellors" or "psychotherapists" for the multitudes who cannot afford what people in Los Angeles call "couch canyon" (the few blocks in Beverly Hill where most analysts have their offices). In addition, they believe that public mental hospitals must change so that in the future "the present institution with its back wards of paupers and unwanted people should disappear when emphasis on the care of institutionalized mentally ill persons is shifted from commitment to treatment" (p. 379). Their third suggestion is for mental health education, so that people would be taught "the proper use of psychiatry" (p. 380). These men, a sociologist and a psychiatrist, have been agents of social change. Their findings, together with the availability of federal funds, stimulated the development and growth of some of the new techniques and approaches presented in this chapter.

The Stirling County studies (Leighton, 1960; Hughes *et al.*, 1961; and Leighton et al., 1963) have as their model of man *homo equilibriensus*, a man who must have stability to maintain his mental health. They found that, as a group French-Canadian women had the best mental health. Thus, their design for the future would include a consensus-making machine, with dissent not tolerated and adjustment rather than freedom the key.

The Midtown studies (Srole *et al.*, 1962; Langner and Michael, 1963) imply a massive attempt to reduce poverty, so that the normal stresses of living, such as death of parents and physical illness, would not weigh more heavily on the poor than on the rich. Their criteria of normality, however, include not only fulfillment of role responsibilities, but satisfaction in one's role as an individual in relation to family, social and civic life, the establishment and maintenance of a home, loving and giving, a mate and children, and so on, as well as the obligation to find and sustain a satisfying job. Not only are the former criteria based on middle-class ideals, but the latter seems increasingly difficult, given the increasing bureaucratization and rationalization of work.

If, on the basis of the New Haven and Midtown studies— because of their inclusion of poverty in the etiological scheme and because of the general growth of sensitivity to environmental factors such as race and poverty—psychotherapeutic *practice* as well as rhetoric changes on a significant scale, the following structurally deterministic model describes the sequence:

Changed Existential Factors→Changed Ideologies and Utopias→Changed Existential Factors

One indication of such a change in practice is the plan of the

University of California Medical Center's psychiatric teaching hospital, Langley Porter, to function as a community health center serving the neighborhood in which it is located and another is the several programs at Yale and Connecticut Health Center in New Haven based in the community.

In summary, as long as intrapsychic factors were considered the "real causes" of mental illness, psychiatry played an essentially conservative role in the society. One can consider the changes in psychotherapy a reflection of similar trends in other segments of society:

1. Apparent democratization of interpersonal relationships resulting not only in a democratization of the therapy sessions but in the advent of psychotherapeutic populism.

2. The presence of an economic surplus, so that many segments of our society are affluent and the work ethic is no longer a necessity.

3. The growing demand for psychotherapy, so that non-medical personnel, psychiatric social workers, and clinical psychologists are becoming psychotherapists in ever-increasing numbers.

4. The greater awareness of the problems resulting from poverty and racism.

The first three trends, combined with the growing popularization of a psychiatric vocabulary of motives, have resulted in the increasing number of therapy groups.

One can take the "vulgar Marxist" cynical point of view and attribute psychiatrists' growing concern with environmental factors to the money available for working with poverty. Nonetheless, psychiatric thinking *is* changing. The new therapies are based on diametrically opposite views of man and of the future: The concern with self-actualization seems appropriate only in an economy of abundance.

Perhaps an ideological analysis will do for psychotherapy what Freud hoped psychoanalysis would do for the individual; by making explicit the hidden assumptions and implications of different types of psychotherapy, where id was there ego shall be.

References

Ayllon, T., and Michael, J. (1959), The psychiatric nurse as a behavioral engineer. *J. Exp. Anal. Behav.*, 2:323–334.

Baburn, E. A. (1966), Legal rights of mental patients in the U.S.S.R. *Br. J. Soc. Psychiatr.*, 1:22–28.

Bart, P. (1962), Mobility and mental illness: A review of ideological analysis of the literature. Unpublished paper.

Becker, H. (1967), History, culture and subjective experience: An exploration of the social bases of drug-induced experiences. *J. Heath Soc. Behav.*, 8:163–176.

Belknap, I. (1956), *Human Problems of a State Mental Hospital.* New York: McGraw-Hill.

Bensman, J., and Vidich, A. J. (1957), The future of community life: A case study and reflections. In *Psychoanalysis and the Future*, 57–84. New York: National Psychological Association for Psychoanalysis.

Bugental, J. T. F. (1967), Epilogue and prologue. In *Challenges of Humanistic Psychology*, ed. J. Bugental, 345–348. New York: McGraw-Hill.

Burroughs, W. (1959), *Naked Lunch*, New York: Grove Press.

Byrd, O. E., *et al.* (1967), *Health* (6). Sacramento: California State Department of Education.

Caudill, W. A. (1958), *The Psychiatric Hospital as a Small Society.* Cambridge: Published for the Commonwealth Fund by Harvard University Press.

Christmas, J. J. (1966), Group therapy with the disadvantaged. In *Current Psychiatric Therapies*, ed. J. H. Masserman, 6:163–171. New York: Grune & Stratton.

Colby, K., *et al.* (1966), A computer method of psychotherapy: A preliminary communication. *J. Nerv. Ment. Dis.*, 142:148–152.

Coles, R. (1967), Discussion of Mr. Saul D. Alinsky's paper. In *Poverty and Mental Health*, ed. M. Greenblatt *et al.*, 29–31. Washington, D. C.: American Psychiatric Association (Psychiatric Research Report 21).

Davis, K. (1938), Mental hygiene and the class structure. *Psychiatry*, 1:55-65. Reprinted in *Mental Health and Mental Disorder*, ed. A. M. Rose, 573-598. New York: Norton, 1955.

Duhl, L. (1963), The changing face of mental health. In *The Urban Condition*, ed. L. Duhl, 59–75. New York: Basic Books.

———— (1967), What mental health services are needed for the poor? In *Poverty and Mental Health*, ed. M. Greenblatt *et al.*, 72–78. Washington, D. C.: American Psychiatric Association (Psychiatric Research Report 21).

Dunham, H. W., and Weinberg, S. K. (1960), *The Culture of the State Mental Hospital.* Detroit: Wayne State University Press.

Emerson, R. W. (1937), Nature. In *The Complete Essays and Other Writings*, ed. Brooks Atkinson, p.3. New York: Modern Library.

Endore, G. (1967), *The Human Sport.* Santa Monica: Synanon Foundation.

Felix, R. H. (1967), *Mental illness: Prospects and Progress.* New York: Columbia University Press.

Field, M. (1960), Approaches to mental illness in Soviet society. *Soc. Prob.*, 7:277-297.

Folta, J. R., and Schatzman, L. (1968), Trends in public urban psychiatry in the United States, *Soc. Prob.*, 16:60–72.

Foucault, M. (1967), *Madness and Civilization.* New York: New American Library

Freud, A. (1968), Annual Freud Lecture at the New York Psychoanalytic Institute Reported in *Newsweek*, April 4, 1968.

Freud, S. (1934), *The Future of an Illusion*, trans. W. D. Robson-Scott. London : Hogarth Press and the Institute of Psychoanalysis.

——— (1961), *Civilization and Its Discontents*, ed. J. Strachey. New York: Norton.

Geiger, H. J. (1967), Of the poor, by the poor, or for the poor: The mental health implications of social control of poverty programs. In *Poverty and Mental Health*, ed. M. Greenblatt *et al.*, 55–65. Washington, D. C.: American Psychiatric Association (Psychiatric Research Report 21).

Ginsberg, A. (1961), *Kaddish and Other Poems*. San Francisco: City Lights Books.

Goffmans, E. (1961), *Asylums*. Garden City, N. Y.: Doubleday (Anchor Books)

Greenblatt, M., and Sharaf, M. R. (1967), Poverty and Mental Health: Implication for training. In *Poverty and Mental Health*, ed. M. Greenblatt *et al.*, 151–159. Washington, D. C.: American Psychiatric Association (Pyschiatric Research Report 21).

Hollingshead, A. B. and Redlich, F. C. (1958), *Social Class and Mental Illness: A Study*. New York: Wiley.

Hughes, C. C., *et al.* (1961), *The People of Cove and Woodlot*. New York: Basic Books.

Hughes, S. H. (1961), *Consciousness and Society*. New York: Random House.

Kairos (1967–1968), *Kairos*. San Francisco: Esalen Institute.

Kanfer, F. H., and Phillips, J. S. (1966), Review of the area of behavior therapy. *Arch. Gen. Psychiatr.*, 15:114–127.

Keniston, K. (1968), How community mental health stamped out the riots (1968–78). *Trans-action*, 5:21–29.

Kesey, K. (1962), *One Flew over the Cuckoo's Nest*. New York: Viking.

Laing, R. D. (1965), *The Divided Self*. Middlesex, Eng.: Penguin.

Langner, T. S., and Michael, S. T. (1963), *Life Stress and Mental Health*. New York: Free Press.

Leighton, A. (1960), *My Name Is Legion*. New York: Basic Books.

Leighton, D. C., *et al.* (1963), *The Character of Danger*. New York: Basic Books.

Lerner, T. (1968), The psychiatrist's dilemma. *J. Am. Geriatr. Soc.*, 16:94–98.

Lindner, R. (1957), Psychoanalysis—2001 A. D. In *Psychoanalysis and the Future*, 143–144. New York: National Psychological Association for Psychoanalysis.

Lennard, H., *et al.* (1971), *Mystification and Drug Misuse*. San Francisco : Jossey-Bass.

London, P. (1964), *The Modes and Morals of Psychotherapy*. New York: Holt, Rinehart, and Winston.

——— (1969), Morals and mental health. In *Changing Perspectives in Mental Illness*, ed. R. Edgerton and S. Plog, 198–207. New York: Holt, Rinehart, and Winston.

Marcuse, H. (1962), *Eros and Civilization*. New York: Vintage Books.

Marmor, J. (1968), *Modern Psychoanalysis: New Directions and Perspectives*. New York: Basic Books.

Marx, K. (1904), *A Contribution to the Critique of Political Economy*. Chicago: C. H. Kerr.

Maslow, A. (1962), *Towards a Psychology of Being*. Princeton : Van Nostrand.

Mendel, W. M. (1964), Introduction to existential psychiatry. *Psychiatr. Dig.*, 25: 24–34.

Mills, C. W. (1961), *The Sociological Imagination*. New York: Oxford.

Mowrer, O. A. (1963), Payment or repayment? The problem of private practice. *Am. Psychol.*, 18:577–580.

Murphy, M. (1967), Esalen: Where it's at. *Psychol. Today*, 1:34–42.

Myers. J., and Roberts, B. (1959), *Family and Class Dynamics in Mental Illness*. New York: Wiley.

The New York Times (1964), January 20:12.

Parsons, T. (1951), *The Social System*. Glencoe, Ill.: Free Press.

Pasamanick, B., *et al.* (1967), *Schizophrenics in the Community.* New York: Appleton-Century-Crofts.

Peck, H. B., *et al.* (1967), Community action programs and the comprehensive mental health centre. In *Poverty and Mental Health,* ed. M. Greenblatt *et al.,* 103–121. Washington, D. C.: American Psychiatric Association (Psychiatric Research Report 21).

Redlich, F. C. (1967), Discussion of Dr. H. Jack Geiger's paper. In *Poverty and Mental Health,* ed. M. Greenblatt *et al.,* 66–67. Washington, D.C.: American Psychiatric Association (Psychiatric Research Report 21).

Reiff, R., and Riessman, F. (1965), The indigenous nonprofessional: A strategy of change in community action and community mental health programs. *Commun. Ment. Health J. Monog.,* 1:3–32.

Rieff, P. (1959), *Freud: The Mind of the Moralist.* New York: Viking.

—— (1966), *The Triumph of the Therapeutic.* New York: Harper & Row.

Riesman, D. (1954), Themes of work and play in Freud's thought. In *Selected Essays from Individualism Reconsidered,* ed. D. Riesman, 174–205. Garden City, N. Y.: Doubleday.

Rioch, M. J., *et al.* (1963), NIMH pilot study in training mental health counselors. *Am. J. Orthopsychiatr.,* 33:678–689.

Rogers, C. R. (1967), A plan for self-directed change in an educational system. *Educ. Leadership,* 24:717–731.

——, and Skinner, B. F. (1956), Some issues concerning the control of human behavior. *Science,* 124:1057–1066.

Rome, H. P. (1967), Poverty and mental health: A synopsis. In *Poverty and Mental Health,* ed. M. Greenblatt *et al.,* 172–175. Washington, D. C.: American Psychiatric Association (Psychiatric Research Report 21).

San Francisco Chronicle (1969), March 13:15.

Seeley, J. (1953), Social values, the mental health movement and mental health. *Ann. Am. Acad. Pol. Soc. Sci.,* 286:15–24.

Skinner, B. F. (1962), *Walden Two.* New York: Macmillan.

Skottowe, I. (1966), Trends and issues in British psychiatry. In *Current Psychiatric Therapies,* ed. J. H. Masserman, 6:360–366. New York: Grune & Straton.

Srole L., *et al.* (1962), *Mental Health in the Metropolis.* New York: McGraw-Hill.

Stoller, F. (1968), Marathon group therapy. In *Innovations in Group Psychotherapy,* ed. G. M. Gazda, 42–95. Springfield, Ill.: Charles C. Thomas.

Szasz, T. (1961), *The Myth of Mental Illness.* New York: Hoeber-Harper.

Tompkins, H. J. (1967), The future of psychiatry. In *Current Psychiatric Therapies,* ed. J. H. Masserman, 7:1–12. New York: Grune & Stratton.

Walter Reed Army Institute of Research and the National Research Council (1957), Summary and discussion of papers on social psychiatry in the community. In *Symposium on Preventive and Social Psychiatry,* 445–459. Washington, D. C.

Wesley, S. M. (1967), Experiential (experience) therapy: A way in, a way out. Privately printed brochure.

Western Behavioral Sciences Institute (1968), Educational innovation project. *Interim Report of the Western Behavioral Sciences Institute of La Jolla, California (April)* La Jolla.

Williams, W. C. (1956), Introduction. In *Howl and Other Poems.* A. Ginsberg, 7–8 San Francisco: City Lights Books.

Wortis, J. (1950), *Soviet Psychiatry.* Baltimore: Williams & Wilkins.

Yablonsky, L. (1967), *Synanon: The Tunnel Back.* Baltimore: Penguin.

Zifferstein, I. (1966), The Soviet psychiatrist's concept of society as a therapeutic community. In *Current Psychiatric Therapies,* ed. J. H. Masserman, 6:367–374. New York: Grune & Stratton.

Chapter 2

Berton H. Kaplan

SOCIAL FACTORS AND WORKING THROUGH *

T HE study of social processes associated with psychiatric disorder has a long and honorable tradition.† It is not our intention to survey this extensive literature; this chapter is solely concerned with the impact of psychiatric epidemiology on the further development of the social integration–disintegration hypothesis—in terms of two basic foci:

1. By focusing on the Stirling County †† experience [as expressed in the follow-up assessment seminar book (Kaplan, 1970) on this landmark study], how can we clarify the "powerful" social integration–disintegration hypothesis?
2. Next, by focusing on the study of the *individual*, how can we clarify sociological variables as they relate to mental illness?

* I am grateful to the editors Ellen Brauer Kaplan, and Robert N. Wilson for their comments; they cannot be blamed for any deficiencies. I am also very grateful to the Social Science Research Council for a fellowship to spend a year with the Cornell Program in Social Psychiatry, 1965-1966, during which time I worked on these ideas.

† See, for reviews and key examples, Pasamanick, *et al.* (1959), Plunkett and Gordon (1960), Clausen (1956), Leighton and Leighton (1967), Dunham (1965), Srole, *et al.* (1962), Hollingshead and Redlich (1958), Cassel and Leighton (1969), Lin and Standley (1962), Jaco (1960), Dohrenwend and Dohrenwend (1969), Leighton and Murphy (1961), Leighton (1959), Hughes, *et al.* (1960), D. C. Leighton *et al.* (1963), and Roman and Trice (1967).

†† See Leighton (1959), Hughes *et al.* (1960), and D. C. Leighton *et al.* (1963) for the three-volume series. See also A. H. Leighton *et al.* (1963).

My emphasis will be on the "working through" problem in individual psychotherapy, for, in my opinion, the study of working through is an overlooked focus for studying sociological variables as etiological or reintegrative.

Leighton's Definition of Integration–Disintegration

Alexander H. Leighton's classic, *My Name is Legion* (1959), integrated a voluminous literature on social integration–disintegration as it related to psychological integration–disintegration. Ten years later, during the Cornell Social Science Seminar (Kaplan 1971a), Leighton set forth his current conception of integration–disintegration:

"Some Notes on the Concept of Disintegration," by Alexander H. Leighton, M. D.: Any system by definition involves integration. Integration is part of the condition of being a system. When a system changes toward disintegration it is moving away from being a system. At absolute disintegration the system no longer exists, although its component parts may continue. A cell, a whole animal, a hive of bees, a community, an orchestra, a ship's crew, an army, are examples.

Systems perform functions. This is what is meant by dynamic. It follows therefore that as a system changes in the direction of non-existence, life is threatened, economic activity depreciates, music is badly produced, the ship is late, the army bungles, etc. Disintegration is not the sole possible cause of malfunction and one can see at times sufficient functioning in the face of some disintegration. This is because a system can often bring compensatory factors into play, or the disintegration may be localized within the system. In the long run, however, disintegration adversely affects function and at absolute disintegration all functioning has ceased.

The Stirling County and Yoruba projects attempted to check the hypothesis that socio-cultural disintegration causes psychiatric disorders. Cast in such general terms, however, this hypothesis can be misleading. It is important to indicate, therefore, that its point of reference is exclusively the small community. What it actually says is that the small community is a system such that the greater the disintegration, the greater the failure in community functions and the greater this malfunctioning, the more adverse the effect on the mental health of the members. The community is looked upon as a quasi-organism—an energy system with human components who exercise most aspects of their lives within the system. . . .

This brings forward the fact that it is the way the sociocultural environment impinges on the individual that is of crucial importance. We may call this contact between the net effect of the sociocultural environment and the experiencing individual the "interphase." The hypothesis may now be restated to say that disintegrated interphases produce psychiatric disorder. In disintegrated communities there are more disintegrated interphases than in well integrated communities.

By chance, of course, there will be some disintegrated interphases in all communities, even the best integrated. It may also be that the patterning of a community system is such that certain categories of persons' experience do not. We have some evidence that in Stirling County the village of Fairhaven is experienced as integrated by the men and relatively disintegrated by the women. The converse appears to be true of La Vallee. In many places it would seem that with advancing years, particularly between 60 and 70 a person is confronted with a progressively disintegrated interphase.

The concept of the disintegrated interphase is possibly an appropriate one with which to approach the problem of the environmental factors which affect mental health in large towns and cities. If we take the city as a community—a whole system—we can examine its patterns and structure to see if certain of the sub-systems regularly have a disintegrative effect during their portion of the interphase for any considerable number of people. Certain work situations, for example, might well fall in this category. We can then see if there are certain roles or categories of persons that regularly constitute totally disintegrative interphases because of the way they are linked to several disintegrated sub-systems. Thus the man who experiences a disintegrated work situation, a disintegrated housing situation and an impoverished religious, social and recreational life may be regarded as living in a disintegrated environment, even though the city as a whole nor even most of its sub-systems may not be properly so regarded.

The problem, then, becomes one of examining the sociocultural patterning and functioning of the city to see where large numbers of disintegrative interphases are being produced. These must be definable, of course, by objective criteria that are independent of the criteria used for estimating the presence or absence of psychiatric disorder.

What are these "disintegrative interphases?" The following review of the integration–disintegration hypothesis will help us to further examine this question.

The Concept of Integration-Disintegration Reexamined

After completion of the landmark Stirling and Midtown studies (Srole *et al.*, 1962; Langner and Michael, 1963), Alexander H. Leighton, then Director of the Cornell Program in Social Psychiatry, assembled 11 seminars called the Cornell Social Science Seminar, to reexamine how social processes are relevant to mental health, in particular, how to refine the integration–disintegration* process. The following disintegrative interphases, while not exhaustive, were extracted from the seminar discussions (Kaplan 1971b):

1. Instrumental disorganization
2. Normative interference
3. Environmental malfunctioning
4. Powerlessness
5. Cueing disturbances
6. Group conflicts
7. Level of integration
8. Need interference
9. Customary pattern interference

* The terms *disintegration* and *disorganization* are both used in this discussion.

10. Resource deprivation
11. Integration and number of interactions
12. Social discontinuities
13. Ineffective role-personality allocation

Instrumental Disorganization

Numerous shades of meaning attach to the concept of integration–disintegration. Isidor Chein,* (Human Relation Institute, New York University) pointed out that Merton's views on the concept of anomie could be labeled as "essential instrumental disorganization," that is, people have goals but no ways of satisfying them.

Normative Interference

Chein also referred to normative interference as a type of disintegration. What does an individual want in his particular context? What does he see himself doing? What gets in his way? What kinds of demands are being made upon him? What is he ready or unready to accept?

Chein pointed out (Seminar I, p. 14) that normative disintegration involves the following:

It seems to me that the disorganization issue always, once you focus on an individual, comes down to the use of his time. What gets in his way? What's pushing him around?

Furthermore, one can focus on the individual's view of social disintegration by studying commitments, barriers to goal attainment, and the degree to which the normative structure issues conflicting directions.

Normative interferences can also be studied in terms of *internalized* conflicts. As Chein stated (Seminar I, p. 35):

But it is prescriptions which get in my way. They not only get in my way, but when I internalize these, they're no longer coming from society; I find that these prescriptions

* Isidor Chein, Ph.D., All people cited participated in the Cornell Social Science Seminar.

get in the way of my fulfilling these internalized commitments. I am never just hungry. At the same time that I am
hungry or can anticipate hunger, I am also somebody who
needs recognition; I am also somebody who needs security;
I am also somebody who needs a sure position so I know
where I am; I'm also somebody who has to be helpful to
people, and I keep getting into trouble because I want to be
helpful.

Environmental Malfunctioning

It is also possible to focus on the *whole* system. In this case,
we assume that the *environment* that is not functioning properly
is potentially pathogenic. Chein observed (Seminar I, pp.
27–28):

*It is the question: does he move in an environment which is dis-
organized from a social point of view?* The focus of the question
is that people move in a social environment, and the working hypothesis is that when they get into trouble and this
"trouble" is something which helps to account for the etiology of their mental illness, and that seems to me to be the
focus.

Powerlessness

The question was raised whether or not a central factor in
the transaction between the individual and his environment
is the person's perception of his power or powerlessness. Nicholas
Freydberg (then with the Cornell Program in Social Psychiatry,
Cornell University) offered the following hypothesis (Seminar I,
p. 15):

I wonder if there is a kind of central factor in these aspects,
a person's perception of his own power or powerlessness, and
the degree to which this seems to be affected by someone
getting in his way, or some value system which he cannot
meet, such as goals of the society that are unattainable. His
mental health seems to be related to the extent that he is
rendered powerless by such events.

Cueing Disturbances

Integration–disintegration may be observed in face-to-face relationships; in fact, the "cueing system" is one way in which to study aspects of integration or disintegration. Chein referred to two dimensions of cueing disturbance: clarity of expectations, and communicative clarity (the Tower of Babel problem). He observed (Seminar I, pp. 15–17):

> The disintegration may manifest itself in his face-to-face relationships. *Take the cueing system.* Perhaps he cannot tell from the other individuals when to do things that will fit in with what they are doing in their face-to-face interactions, or perhaps he doesn't know whether he is in a situation *vis a vis* the other individual in which, to take a normative example, he is supposed to act in a symmetrical manner or in a complementary manner. What are the expectations of him?
>
> Face-to-face relationships do not necessarily take the form of any kind of formally distinguished group structures, but if he is dealing with people who do not know how to communicate their needs, he is in trouble wherever he confronts such individuals, it seems to me. This is a disintegrated dyad if he can't tell what it is that his patient is saying to him, whether it is expression, or behavior, or language, or what have you. If he gets the key to this, if the cueing system starts functioning, it does not matter whether he pursues a formal language or not, he knows what the other guy means. Take the classical example of disintegration, the Tower of Babel. Nobody knew what anybody else was saying, and they were all in trouble, but they were in trouble in terms of interpersonal relations.

Group Conflicts

One can look at the conflicting demands between groups; group members can be asked to do things that are not consistent. For example, we can find an individual who acts for the group caught between demands that are obviously inconsistent. In fact, his actions can get the group into trouble no matter how well integrated the group is internally. Chein observed (Seminar I, pp. 18–19):

> Take the police and the social workers. I can sympathize with Police Commissioner Murphy who once declared all these social workers were trying to make social workers out of the police. He finds that his group is being asked to do things which are not mutually consistent and if he agrees, the group is in trouble. It is a disorganized set-up, whatever its internal structure is, which may or may not be organized.

Level of Integration

It is very important to distinguish *levels* of integration–disintegration in terms of individuals, institutions and society. For example, a husband may meet his goals in a way that denies the wife her goals. You can also have situations in which something may be integrative for institutions but not for the individuals within it. What is integrative for society is not the same as asking what is integrative for the individual. It is important to distinguish levels of integration. Raymond Illsley (Professor of Sociology, Aberdeen University) and Lawrence Hinkle's (Human Ecology Division, Cornell Medical School) comments (Seminar II, pp. 26–27) are very relevant.

> *Raymond Illsley:* ...Let's take a problem that's likely to flare up fairly acutely in a society like Manhattan here where you've got a large number of people coming into the society, the immigrants—shall we say the professional groups—coming into the society and seeking a job. For them, one of their goals is success in their careers. This may be shared between the husband and the wife. It may be necessary, too, from the point of view of an institution, the work institution, that people should move around in this way, to get the right kind of person in the right kind of place at the right kind of time. He comes into Manhattan, and he may get a great deal of satisfaction out of the work he does.
>
> He brings, however, his dependents into this situation where they themselves may find, particularly if this is a recurrent process, moving around from one group to another,

from one area to another. You then have disintegration of the family relationships, and for the relationships of these people to people in society at large. You may have here two institutions, the family and work, which are each in a way attempting to integrate themselves, but which are mutually contradictory.

I can see where it becomes important to distinguish between what is integration for an institution, or for a system, and what is integrative for the individual.

Hinkle: I go along with this very much. I think what you are saying is that you may have a large community and a large social system which is perhaps integrating and growing, and in the process of integrating, it may be disintegrating to certain sub-systems belonging to certain people within it. This may or may not be disintegrating to certain aspects of the individuals' lives. But I think what you study depends on the view-point when you ask the question. I would not necessarily assume that the phenomena of integration or disintegration in a society, or in a sub-section, is the same thing as asking a question about disintegration of interpersonal relations.

Personal Need Interference

Katharine Fales (Department of Psychiatry, Cornell Medical School) asked: How are individual needs satisfied in the community or group? From this point of view the problem is one of *needs* whether people are living in communities and subgroups that satisfy personality needs, for example, affiliative needs. As Thomas Langner (Department of Sociology, New York University) pointed out : What would a community be like if it were in line with the individual's needs?

Customary Pattern Interference

William Foote Whyte (Industrial and Labor Relations, Cornell University) noted that changes in *customary* patterns of interaction can be another type of disintegration. Whyte observed (Seminar I, pp. 34-35):

I want to suggest that by the time he reaches maturity, the individual has developed a certain customary pattern of interaction, and substantial changes in this pattern could lead to mental health problems, problems which could be avoided if he were able to re-establish this pattern. We should not be surprised to find an individual who has led a quite isolated life being relatively symptom-free, but we should expect when an individual involved in very active social relationships has something happen so that he is cut off from these interactions, to have this isolation bring on some kind of mental health problems. I think it is not just a matter of how much interaction, but how it changes over time. You have to think of rewards or penalties that would occur. In brief, one way of looking at this problem is through examination of the interaction problem with particular emphasis on changes through time.

Resource Deprivation

It is clear that some people live in disorganized communities but are able to do reasonably well. Resource availability or resource deprivation might help account for differential adaptations. Whyte's observations are very relevant (Seminar I, pp. 28–29):

It seems to me to test this we need to do something like this. There has been a lot of work in this Program to characterize a disorganized community, and then a lot of work on response of individuals, the symptoms that arise and so on. What is apparently lacking is some kind of charting of the way of individual finds his way through this community. It may be that when you get this gross picture of a disorganized community, you can predict that there's a higher hazard, that the likelihood of succumbing to mental illnesses is higher, as in a plant where the chances are that somebody working on a dangerous job is more likely to be injured than somebody sitting at a desk. Somehow there's a differential response to this community situation. It seems to me research has to find some method for charting the way individuals find themselves through this community so that some individuals in an overall disorganized community, if you characterize it so, still find some kind of stable pattern of social adjustment in it, whereas others are completely lost. Apparently you are at the point where you can roughly predict, in this kind of community, that the chances of the inhabitant breaking down are greater than in this other kind of community. But can you follow the individuals who do and do not break down and see how they handle it?

Integration and Numbers

The relative involvement in group memberships is an often used dimension of integration–disintegration. Yet an isolate may be doing well until pushed into personal relationships.

Laurel Hodgden (College of Human Ecology, Cornell University), observed (Seminar II, pp.1-2):

I think one could even hypothesize a situation where an individual who had been an isolate, and who for some reason had been forced or pushed into organizational patterns, might react as strongly as the person who was in a reverse situation. For example an isolate, or a slightly schizoid individual, who was drafted into the service could have a very violent reaction to this transfer into an organization.

Social Discontinuities

The broad range of phenomena known as social and cultural discontinuities can constitute another type of disintegration. For example, Isidor Chein pointed out that some gang members may be incapable of functioning elsewhere. When the gang disbands they in effect turn to narcotics to cope with the social discontinuity.

Poor Role-Personality Allocation

There may be a discrepancy between role demands and personality types. Chein referred to poor career channeling within an organization as a possible example of this problem. The channels for advancement in an organization can determine the proper or improper use of an individual's capacities. Chein noted (Seminar II, pp. 19–20):

> We can take the channels that social organizations offer for advancement, as, for example, the group workers. This is a field in which the basic training of the people is for one level of work. They are highly sensitive to functioning in small groups. They can fit into it, they can facilitate the operation by encouraging the youngsters to develop and all sorts of things. It is a relatively new profession so vertical mobility is very rapid.
> You get somebody say, who graduates from the New York School of Social Work, and in a few years he's the assistant head of a large agency. He has moved now into a new level of responsibility for which he is totally unequipped. Everything that he has ever learned about group work may suddenly vanish, and then he becomes a tyrant, unreasonable, petty, all kinds of things which he would never be if he were functioning as a group worker.

It is important to point out that the concept of integration–disintegration has been a useful hypothesis in studying diseases other than mental illness, such as hypertension (Henry and Cassel, 1969), and strokes (Neser *et al.*, in press) as examples.* However defined it appears to be a reasonable generalization that social disintegration is associated with a wide range of psychologically or physically deleterious consequences.

The problem of levels of integration (self, dyads, roles, groups, intergroup, community, cultural and societal levels), however, requires clarification and systematic statement.† For example, a need exists to specify levels, units and processes of integration–disintegration in global sociocultural variables (e.g., urbanization, acculturation), social institutions (e.g., socialization groups, family, work, religion), sociopsychological constructs (e.g., sentiment, needs, etc.) psychological constructs (e.g., satisfaction, achievement), and behavioral constructs

---

* See also Mechanic (1968) and Wilson (1970).

† A. H. Leighton has suggested we sort out a dictionary of definitions of integration much like that done by Kluckhohn and Kroeber. I think we need to check out the status of our tree of hypotheses on the social environment and mental disorder, as in *My Name is Legion* (Leighton, 1959).

(e.g., anxiety, fear). Linking these levels are the questions: How are the global processes, such as anomie or urbanization related to key institutional experiences in the home or school? How are industrialization and job experience (global and institutional) mediated by one's status in the community, family cohesion, needs, and expectations, that is, by concepts that link the individual to the institution and significant others in his environment? How then is the person satisfied (on a psychological level) by his roles and needs? Finally, behaviorally, are the person's actions adaptive or maladaptive?

In keeping with the spirit of "successive" approximations,* the following fresh definition of integration–disintegration by Isidor Chein is helpful (Seminar II, pp. 73–74):

A social group or social context, or social what-have-you is integrated to the degree in which, a) the individuals involved are facilitated in carrying on with the major activities to which they are committed and the activities which are expected of them, and find their personal commitments congruent with what is expected of them; and b) the dialectics of change are such that the transformations in commitments and/or expectations which are consequent upon such carryings on or upon the maturation of the individuals involved will not disrupt the balance described in (a). What I tried to put into this is the notion that people are involved in activities. They're involved in activities because they want to be involved in activities, because these are things that are expected of them, and there's a potential source of disintegration in defects and impatients. Secondly, I put into this the fact that doing things requires support; we can't operate if there's a possibility of disruption emanating from the failure to provide a space dimension of facilitation. And I put into it the notion that things don't remain

---

* Abraham Kaplan's observation that every "taxonomy is a provisional and implicit theory (or family of theories). As knowledge of a particular subject-matter grows, our conception of that subject-matter changes; as our concepts become more fitting, we learn more and more. Like all existential dilemmas in science of which this is an instance, the paradox is resolved by a process of approximation: the better our concepts, the better the theory we can formulate with them, and in turn the better the concepts available for the next, improved theory. "V. F. Lenzen has spoken explicitly of 'successive definitions.'" It is only true of such successions that the scientist can hope ultimately to achieve success (Kaplan, 1964, pp. 53–54).

the same. Consequently, the changes that occur, if these are changes which lead into it progressively, from the point of view of facilitation and harmony within the ranks, then the expectation is for a well-integrated situation. If from this point of view the situation progressively deteriorates, because successive outcomes lead into situations that are no longer compatible with the harmony of either the supports and the activities, the two sources of the activity, this is a bad situation, and from a temporary point of view, this is not a well integrated situation.

Individual View: The Problem of Working Through

The problem of "working through" in classical psychoanalysis offers an excellent "case example" of the interface disruptions between the social system and personality. More specifically, and in an historical sense, I am talking about the problem posed by the relationship of Durkheim's work to that of Freud: the internalization of norms (Parsons, 1964). How do social "rules" contribute to the development or "cure" of mental disorders?

The further study of the working through process should contribute to our understanding of how social processes are implicated in the etiology of mental disorders and how social processes contribute to mental health. It is important to approach the problem of social processes and mental health from both a system and an individual point of view, from a population or epidemiological focus, and from a clinical focus.

It is almost a cliche of the analytic process that the expansions of insight do not necessarily lead to changes in behavior or working through. These are the cases of "sour" analyses the years on the couch with little behavioral change. Why is this so?

This question is well established by several eminent psychiatric observers. For example, Allen Wheelis (1950, p. 135) in a very interesting paper entitled "the Place of Action in Personality Change" observed that:

All psychotherapists who attempt seriously to intervene in the neurotic ways of life of their fellow human beings are faced recurrently with a disturbing question: Why do some patients not get well? Why do they not modify such unpleasant aspects of their environment as they can and accept the rest? Why do they not seek and obtain the real gratifications of achievement and enjoyment as they can and accept rest? Why do they not seek and obtain the real gratifications of achievement and enjoyment for which they have the requisite endowment? Why—despite insight and working through—do they cling still to neurotic mechanisms and live in a twilight world of anger, frustration and distorted partial gratifications. Therapists are faced also with a question of an opposite nature: why do other patients get well? This question is not nearly so disturbing to the questioner, but often equally difficult to answer.

More recently, Wolberg observed (1954, p. 757):

A basic assumption in insight approaches is one made originally by Freud which was to the effect that, once the individual becomes aware of his unconscious motivations, he can then alter his behavior and get well. That this fortunate consequence does not always follow (a circumstance also recognized by Freud) is the disillusioning experience of many young therapists who have predicated their futures on the premise that analysis of resistances will inevitably bring forth insight and cure like a sunbeam breaking through a cloud.

One of the basic problems posed in working through involves this question: Does the analytic treatment model lack a sufficient sociological analog to permit insight to then be transmitted into social system skills, which would then help energize behavior and behavioral changes? In effect, does psychiatric theory lack an adequate theory of adult socialization (and the nature of social exchange) that ties psychic and social processes into their natural interlace?

What is meant by *working through*? Greenson's "preliminary definition" is as follows (1965, p. 282):

We do not regard the analytic work as working through before the patient has insight, only after. It is the goal of working through to make insight effective, i.e. to make significant and lasting changes in the patient. By making insight the pivotal issue, we can distinguish between those resistances which prevent insight and those resistances which prevent insight from leading to change. The analytic work on the first set of resistances is the analytic work proper: it has no special designation. The analysis of those resistances which keep insight from leading to change is the work of working through. This may consist essentially of repetition and elaboration of the same procedures as performed in ordinary analytic work. In certain cases special problems may develop which may prevent insight from becoming effective and which may require special interventions.

Greenson summarizes as follows:

Working through is the analysis of those resistances and other factors which prevent insight from leading to significant and lasting changes in the patient.

This focus on resistance may be excessive, incomplete, and in need of the sociological correlates. Are there not social contexts that *promote* working through? Are there not normative correlates to successful psychotherapy?

One way to examine this question is from the point of view of the problem of competence motivation, a concept developed by Robert W. White (1960, 1965).*

It is important to indicate what White means by competence motivation. White (1965, p. 203) points out that:

this feeling of efficacy is one of our most fundamental and biologically important affects, the basis of our persisting attempts to achieve whatever mastery we can over the environment, the thing that lies behind our unceasing attempts to enlarge the sphere of our competence. It is the root of the sense of competence that is so central to self-

* Although this paper was conceived before Lennard and Bernstein's (1969) book, I also am concerned with clinical sociology and with similar questions about interaction processes. Sharing a common concern with social contexts as a part of therapeutic intervention (not as solely individually focused), I differ in my specific focus on the working through issue as an entry into the relationship between the individual's pathology and his social environment.

esteem. Chronic ineffectiveness of the kind I have hypothe-
sised will have far reaching consequences for development.
Attention will be less sharply focalized, intention will be
less clearly felt, action will be less vigorous, effects on the
environment will be smaller and less frequent, there will be
fewer experiences of efficacy, and a smaller base will be laid
for a sense of competence and self respect. The world will be
experienced as operating largely in ways that cannot be
influenced. Having built up little power to control his surroundings, the person is bound to feel more or less under
their control.

I find White's "competence" thought provoking, with the
following reservations:

1. Given the efficacy motive, what *specific* kinds of interpersonal skills are involved?
2. How can we better classify the social system skill areas
that are relevant to an increased sense of competence?
3. How can the concept of competence motive be integrated into a social action schema, especially since White gives
so much emphasis to competence considerations of observing
and thinking about the consequences of social action?
4. From a clinical viewpoint, what strategy norms are
involved? What normative skills should a therapist attempt to
teach as appropriate? How much of sociology, social anthropo-
logy and social psychology should be an integral part of a psychiatrist's therapeutic skills? (For example, a patient with "power"
relationship problems may profit from the contemporary knowledge of social psychologists who study power dependency
processes.)

I am fully aware that there are therapeutic strategies that
involve treatment of the "system," e.g., the pioneering work
on family therapy of Ackerman (1958) and Cleveland (1957)
and Stanton and Schwartz (1954).* But family therapy is a
different focus from the one presented here. I am concerned

* I am indebted to Robert N. Wilson for pointing out that the patient's insight
into system strains may only lead to more satisfactory living *if* the system itself can
be changed. In practice, this will no doubt vary. It would depend on the kind of
problem involved.

with the working through process in *individuals* as a point of inquiry into learning more about disruptive social experiences as etiological and the patient's increased competence in the nature of social system processes as an important ingredient in "successful" therapy.

Working Through and Social System Skills

One of the tenets of psychoanalysis is to make the unconscious conscious, thereby strengthening ego functioning. "Where id was there ego shall be." Following this analogy, I am concerned with making the significant aspects of one's social situation more conscious. Where social ignorance was mastery there shall be, thereby potentially raising the level of competence in ego functioning and hence facilitating the working through situation.

In order to do this, it is necessary to have some way of systematically looking at events in a social system as a process. The scheme below, developed by Parsons and Smelser (1956), includes six fundamental variables as determinants of behavioral outcomes: conductivity, strains, generalized beliefs, precipitating events, mobilization processes and social controls.*

Structural Conductiveness

Structural conductiveness involves seven "skill" dimensions. First, this concept refers to the extent to which any structure encourages a particular type of reaction. Do the structural arrangements directly encourage a particular response, for example, hostility? Do these arrangements prohibit or limit other types of reaction? In the first case, to what degree are you invited to choose a particular response? In the second case, to what degree does the existing structure drive you into hostile outbursts, or helplessness?

---

* There are other important sociological frameworks useful in working out better analog with psychiatry, see, for example, Thibaut and Kelly (1959) and Blau (1964) on the social-exchange literature.

Second, conductiveness involves the possibility of reconstituting the existing structure. In other words, how can situational facilities be redefined (e.g., correct information)? Can one attack responsible agents? Can the existing troublesome norms be negotiated? Can the existing troublesome values be redefined?

Third, under the possibility of strain, conductiveness refers to the possibility of minimal to maximal stress. Thus, it is possible to live in a system that is loaded with malintegrations of various sorts, or vice versa. Certainly some social positions, for example, are far more "stressful" than others. Some social attributes can make life impossible!

Fourth, conductiveness involves the possibility of withdrawal from danger. Panic or other kinds of reactions for example, are not as likely if escape routes are well conceptualized and open.

Fifth, conductiveness implies the adequacy of the existing communication channels as very important to adaptive success or failure. For example, with minimal communications over a possible threat or strain, confusion and individual terror may arise more easily. Effective communications channels can also minimize "stress."

Sixth, are the major social rewards freely disposable or are they locked up around a very limited range of acceptable behavior? The nature and balance of the rewards and social costs is crucial to adaptive success or failure. For example, are the rewards allocated solely for the overachievers?

Seventh, conductiveness refers to identifying the possible means to reconstitute, that is, correct, the strains in the existing structure. This raises the question of alternate opportunities and of the individual's ability to "repair" his situation.

Strains

Strains refer to the malintegration of system parts. Specifically, Smelser defines *strain* "as an impairment of the relations among, and consequently inadequate functioning of the components of action" (1959, p. 47). First, strain involves situational *facilities*—an ambiguity as to adequate means for a given goal. Second, strain has to do with *mobilization of motivation*, involving relationship between responsible performance in roles and accrual of rewards. The third type refers to *normative strains*, implying competing demands of different roles for the expenditure of time and energy. Finally, a fourth kind concerns *value strains* —the legitimacy of the values in question. In summary, "value strain imposes the issue of commitment; normative strain concerns the integration of human interaction; strain in mobilization concerns a balance between motivated activity and its reward; strain on facilities concerns the adequacy of knowledge and skills" (Smelser, 1959, pp. 64–65). The sources of *system*-induced strain should be well known to the patient, if working through is to be more successful.

Generalized Beliefs Used To Assess and Explain Situations

These definitions provide the cultural as well as the individual definitions of the situation. Smelser (1959, p. 83) suggests five major types of *generalized beliefs*: *Hysterical* beliefs transform an ambiguous situation into an absolutely potent generalized threat; *wish fulfillment* beliefs reduce ambiguity by positing an absolutely efficacious generalized wish (e.g., salvation ethic); *hostility* beliefs remove some agent or object perceived as a generalized threat or obstacle; *normative*-oriented beliefs envision the reconstitution of a threatened normative structure; and *value*-oriented beliefs foresee the reconstitution of the threatened value system.

If a therapist is interested in how the patient assesses his life situations, a knowledge of his personal and group belief structure would be useful in enlarging the psychiatrist's understanding of the relationship between the patient's reactions, his response sets, and his social situation.

Precipitating Factors

What transforms anxiety into fear? Precipitating factors confirm the generalized suspicions and uneasiness of anxious

people. What are the specific *concrete* and *actual threatening* events
that precipitate certain kinds of reactions? Thus, the precipitating factor involves the event, the confirmation of a culturally
conditioned anxiety, and the interpretation of it as a source
of anxiety.

Mobilization Process

People under strain mobilize either to reconstitute their
situation or to react to the social order or themselves in some
way. Once the first four determinants have been established, the
next step is the mobilization of action. At this point there is an
onset of such emotional reactions as anger, anxiety, panic,
hostility, or agitation.

Some of the important problems in mobilization are:

1. Who exercises what kinds of leadership in the formulation
of beliefs and the encouragement of certain action?
2. Is the reaction process, a slow and searching coping process? Does it accelerate fast? Or does panic, for example, set in
before any evaluation or attempts to cope?
3. How successful are specific coping tactics that have been
used in the past? What are the directions of coping after various
successes and failures?

Problems of Social Control

Controls are those counterdeterminants that prevent, inter-
rupt, deflect, or inhibit the accumulation of the foregoing five
dimensions. It is convenient to divide social controls into two
broad types: (a) those social controls that minimize strain;
(b) those social controls that are mobilized only after an
episode has begun to materialize. These determine how fast,
how far, and in what direction the episode will develop.

In this scheme, there are four types of social controls:

1. *Facilities* involves the development of informational skills
and knowledge. For example, information can be used to diminish anxiety: At the point of strain, corrective information can

be given; at the point of precipitating factors, information can indicate that the precipitating factors are harmless.

2. *Organization of mobilization* is concerned with the structure of roles that enable an individual to resist a condition that builds up towards, for example, panic or anxiety. For example, the individual's relationship to the role structure of his group may be more clearly defined, which could be anxiety-reducing.

3. *Norms* are an important source of control; they can provide directives as to how to contend with threats, and how to direct behavior toward some more desirable kind of activity.

4. Finally, *values* are an important source of control. Faith, for example, can serve as a protective function in threatening situations. Value commitment can be an important kind of control. A well-trained psychiatrist, particularly in the working through situation, should have a reasonable knowledge of the nature of value systems as social controls. The more the therapist can teach the individual about these social processes, the more *competent* the individual will become.

What is the point of these six dimensions?

1. They help map the individual's sources of social integration–disintegration.

2. They represent possible areas of increased social consciousness of one's setting and the opportunity to correct the "noxious" elements in the social situation.

3. Learning how to assess one's life situation and its sources of social disintegration/personal disintegration should lead to increased competence in White's terms.

4. Working through involves the ability to translate insight into action, which requires an increased understanding of *social* as well as ego processes.

The problem of "working through" and the process of social integration–disintegration are related problems in the following ways:

1. The translation of insight into behavioral changes reveals

how "bad habits" are unlearned, "unrewarding habits internalized."

2. This should necessarily free us to reexamine how social
reintegration takes place and how social and personal integration are feedback processes.

3. The social attributes that need to be extinguished reveal,
from the individual's point of view, those aspects of his *personal*
community that operate as disintegrative interphases, which
should permit us to clarify the social attributes that promote
integration or disintegration. At this point the concern with
social integration–disintegration converges with the problems
of working through.

4. At a clinical level, how can sociological skills be better
incorporated into the training of psychiatrists and other
clinicians? Maybe "successful" therapy is in part the successful teaching of socially integrative behavior patterns (Smith,
1963).

Conclusion

Why a selective review of the concept of integration–disintegration as it is related to mental illness; and why then the
assessment of the concept of working through? There are at
least four congruences between these seemingly disparate
questions:

1. The 13 types of disruptive interphases between the individual and his social environment—whether discontinuities,
conflicts, role-need allocation, etc.—are assumed to be points
at which participants are put at risk to emotional discomfort or
disorder. Working through involves these related questions:
How does an individual come to understand the social sources of
his emotional difficulty? How does an individual come to know
social system processes, increasing his social competences and
coping with his environment, rather than being "punished" by
his ignorance or lack of competence skills.

2. There is a need to flesh out and refine the developing tree of hypotheses on social variables and mental disorder. Thirteen types of social-risk (Kaplan, 1971a) variables have been outlined as well as a list of six types of social risk or social skill variables from another frame of reference (Smelser, 1959). Surely, there are complementing concepts between the two schemes: conductiveness is a useful addition to Leighton's scheme; the list of disruptive interphases refines Smelser's notions of strain.

3. There is a need to build up our knowledge on social processes and mental illness from at least four feedback types of approaches: epidemiological, clinical, experimental, and literary. (I have dealt with the first two only.)

4. By combining an examination of effective social systems (integration–disintegration) with an analysis of more effective psychotherapy ("working through"), it may be possible to learn more about how to strengthen the social system and make it less "noxious," as well as how to do more successful psychotherapy and help teach the individual (sick or well) to cope in healthier ways.

References

Ackerman, N. (1958), *The Psychodynamics of Family Life*. New York: Basic Books.

Blau,Peter M. (1964), *Exchange and Power in Social Life*. New York: Wiley.

Cassel, J.,,and Leighton, A. (1969) *Epidemiology and Mental Health*. Washington. D. C.: Department of Health Education, and Welfare.

Clausen, J. (1956), *Sociology and Mental Health*. New York: Russell Sage Foundation.

Cleveland, E. J., and Longaker, W. D. (1957), Neurotic patterns in the family. In *Explorations in Social Psychiatry*, ed. A. H. Leighton *et al.*, 167–200. New York: Basic Books.

Dohrenwend, B. P., and Dohrenwend, B. S. (1969), *Social Status and Psychological Disorder*. New York: Wiley.

Dunham, H. W. (1965), *Community and Schizophrenia*. Detroit: Wayne State University Press.

Greenson, R. (1965), The problem of working through. In *Drives, Affects, and Behavior*, ed. M. Schur. New York: International Universities Press.

Henry, P. and Cassel C. (1969), Psychosocial factors in dessential hypertension. *Am. J. Epidemiol,* **90**:171–200.

Hollingshead, A. B., and Redlich, F. C. (1958), *Social Class and Mental Illness.* New York: John Wiley.

Hughes, C. C., *et al.* (1960), *The People of Cove and Woodlot.* New York: Basic Books.

Jaco, E. G. (1960), *The Social Epidemiology of Mental Disorders.* New York: Russell Sage Foundation.

Kaplan, A. (1964), *The Conduct of Inquiry.* San Francisco: Chandler.

Kaplan, B. H. (*ed.*), in collaboration with Leighton, A. H. Murphy, J. M., and Freydberg, N. (1971a), *Psychiatric Disorder and the Urban Environment.* New York: Behavioral Publications.

Kaplan, B. H. (1971b), Seminar assessment of the integration–disintegration framework. In *Psychiatric Disorder and the Urban Environment,* ed. B. H. Kaplan. New York: Behavioral Publications.

Langner, T. S., and Michael, S. T. (1963), *Life Stress and Mental Health.* New York: The Free Press.

Leighton, A. H. (1959), *My Name Is Legion.* New York: Basic Books.

————, and Murphy, J. M. (1961), Culture as causative of Mental disorders. *Milbank Mem. Fund Q.,* **39**:341–383.

————*et al.* (1963), *Psychiatric Disorder among the Yoruba.* Ithaca:Cornell University Press.

Leighton, D. C., and Leighton, A. H. (1967), Mental health and social factors. In *Comprehensive Textbook of Psychiatry,* ed. A. M. Freedman and H. I. Kaplan, 1520–1533. Baltimore: Williams & Wilkins.

————*et al.* (1963), *The Character of Danger.* New York: Basic Books.

Lennard, L., and Bernstein, A. (1969), *Patterns in Human Interaction:An Introduction to Clinical Sociology.* San Francisco: Jossey–Bass, Inc.

Lin, Tsung-yi, and Standley, C. C. (1962), *The Scope of Epidemiology in Psychiatry.* Geneva: World Health Organization.

Mechanic, D. (1968), *Medical Sociology.* New York: Free Press.

Neser, W., *et al.* (in press) (1972), Social Disorganization and Strokes.

Parsons, T. (1964), *Social Structure and Personality.* New York: Free Press.

————, and Smelser, J. (1956), *Economy and Society.* Glencoe Ill.: Free Press.

Pasamanick, B. (ed.) (1959), *Epidemiology of Mental Disorder.* Washington, D. C. American Association for the Advancement of Science.

Plunkett, R. J., and Gordon, J. E. (1960), *Epidemiology of Mental Illness.* New York: Basic Books.

Roman, P. M., and Trice, H. (1967), *Schizophrenia and the Poor.* Ithaca: New York State School of Industrial and Labor Relations (ILR Paperback ‡3).

Smelser, N. J. (1959), *Social Change in the Industrial Revolution.* Chicago: University of Chicago Press.

Smith, H. L. (1963), *Adaptation: Clinical and Social.* Chapel Hill: Institute for Research in Social Science.

Srole, L., *et al.* (1962), *Mental Health in the Metropolis.* New York: McGraw–Hill.

Stanton, A. H., Schwartz, M. (1954), *The Mental Hospital.* New York: Basic Books.

Thibaut, J. and H. Kelley. (1959), *The Social Psychology of Small Groups.* New York.

Wheelis, A. (1950), The place of action in personality change. *Psychiatry,* **23**:135–148.

White, R. W. (1960), *Competence and the Psychosexual Stages of Development. Nebraska Symposium on Motivation.* Lincoln: University of Nebraska Press.

————(1965), The experience of efficacy in schizophrenia. *Psychiatry,* **28**:199–211.

Wilson, R. N. (1970), *Sociology and Health.* New York: Random House.

Wolberg, L. R. (1954), *The Technique of Psychotherapy.* New York: Grune & Stratton.

Chapter 3

Nathan Hurvitz

PEER SELF-HELP PSYCHOTHERAPY GROUPS: PSYCHOTHERAPY WITHOUT PSYCHOTHERAPISTS

SELF-HELP programs and activities of various kinds are continually being organized. While many of these disappear, others grow; and the self-help movement as a whole is gaining strength and being given increasing attention by social and behavioral scientists and by psychotherapists. This growth is due to (a) the increasing number of people who require assistance with social, psychological, and emotional problems, (b) the failure of traditional psychiatric, psychological, social work, and psychotherapeutic efforts to aid significant numbers of people with these problems, and (c) the need for alternative methods to help those people who require assistance.

Many different kinds of problems or deviant behaviors such as alcoholism, drug addiction, gambling, criminality, obesity, "neurosis," etc., are defined as psychological, and many psychotherapeutic theories and practices are utilized by psychotherapists to eliminate or change such problems or deviant behavior. However, despite many years of experience with various psychotherapeutic theories and practices, many psychiatrists, psychologists, and social and behavior scientists question the effectiveness of conventional psychotherapy. They recognize that there is no objective evidence that shows that a particular theory and practice of psychotherapy is more helpful than any other (since all report about two-thirds "success") or than an individual's life experiences (Eysenck, 1960; Fox, 1957; Frank, 1961; Hill and Blane, 1967; Schorer *et al.*, 1968). Certainly, we have the testimonials of those who say they have been helped by psychotherapy. But we must evaluate these testimonials in the same way, and with the same skepticism, that conventional psychotherapists and their supporters evaluate the testimonials of clients and patrons of dianetics, faith healers of various kinds, fortune tellers, etc.

Types of Self-Help Programs

The enthusiasm for self-help programs and the desire to call so many different kinds of activities self-help comes from two sources: Self-help concepts and practices fit the professed American democratic ideal and the democratic ideals of the helping professions. These concepts also match the demands for community control of institutions designed to assist minority group members, the demands of welfare recipients to control the agencies and services that exist because of their need, and the economic need for many low-paid aides to deal with the large numbers of patients and with deviants who refuse to participate in or have not responded to traditional programs. Self-help is thus one of the current shibboleths of the helping professions and a euphemism for a particular type of cooptation (Billington *et al.*, 1969), as well as an authentic movement to assist many people who have not been helped previously to overcome problems or deviant behavior (Sobey, 1970). At least seven different types of self-help organizations and programs are reported in the psychiatric, psychological, social work and sociological literature. They are as follows:

1. Participation of middle- and upper-class citizens in voluntary groups, primarily nonprofit, health-oriented associations, to secure better care for themselves, their kin, and the community as a whole; to arouse public interest; and to raise money for programs and research. Examples are the National Association for Mental Health, American Schizophrenia Association,

Planned Parenthood Federation, American Heart Association. Studies of such voluntary associations have focused on the demographic characteristics of the members (Wright and Hyman, 1958) and types of voluntary associations (Gordon and Babchuk, 1959). Other studies have reviewed the relationship between volunteers and professionals and between the national organization and its local chapters (Sills, 1957). Such groups have always played an important and respectable part in American life.

2. Participation of people from various sectors of the community in groups organized about a condition or characteristic that marks the members as different or deviant in order to alter their condition or characteristic or live more comfortably with it (Sagarin, 1969). This type includes such organizations as Parents without Partners (Egelson and Egelson, 1961), Little People of America (Weinberg, 1968), and others. Although the condition or characteristic that identifies the members of these groups may cause psychological and emotional problems that require psychotherapeutic intervention, these groups have a social, rather than a psychotherapeutic, function. The members of these groups have organized on their own behalf directly and only incidentally serve or assist other members of the community.

3. Participation of members of the recipient community (e.g., "poor people") as non-professional "helpers" in traditional social welfare programs and activities (Grosser et al., 1969; Kramer, 1969; Millman and Chilman, no date; Reiff and Riessman, 1965; Riessman, 1965).

4. Participation of students, housewives, patients, and others as quasi-professional staff members, as non-professional volunteers, or paid aides in community, hospital, clinic, or agency programs and projects (Carter et al., 1962; Ellsworth, 1967; Guerney, 1969; Holzberg et al., 1966; Katz et al., 1967; Poser 1966; Rioch, 1966; Rioch et al., 1963; Sobey, 1969; Torrey, 1969; Verinis, 1970). These quasi – and non-professionals are not involved in welfare programs and activities and are not members of the group or community in which they render their assistance.

Members of the recipient community and students, house-wives, and other quasi-professionals and "indigenous nonprofessionals" are trained to perform traditional roles in traditional settings. Those concerned with the utilization of non-professionals have established procedures for finding, screening, selecting, training, assigning, supervising, evaluating, and terminating them. As the non-professional is conducted through these procedures, he is recreated in the image of the established —and establishment—professional. He uses their theories, concepts and practices and identifies with their institutions, values, and goals. As helpful as these non-professionals may be the established professionals use them in programs in which the professionals are in charge and maintain authority. And as benign and as well-intentioned as this authority may be, it displays the continuing effort of professionals to resist the effort of people to take over the management of their own affairs.

5. Participation of primarily well-educated, middle-and upper-class members who are looking for new experiences rather than for help with a distressing psychological problem in "leaderless encounter groups" in "growth settings." These programs are presented by psychotherapists variously identified as members of a "humanist," "existentialist," or "third-force" movement and by opportunist promoters looking for an exploitable gimmick. These programs, which stress authenticity, openness, identity, self-actualization, transcendental experience, sensory awakening, consciousness expansion, meditation and similar experiences, are presented by psychotherapists of various professional backgrounds who imply that, although their programs will not help the participants overcome specific problems, they will enhance each participant in some way psychologically and take him "beyond therapy."

The tantalizing programs, in which one can participate with or without clothes, can be examined in the lavish brochures of such places as the Aureon Institute, Elysium Institute, Esalen Institute, Kairos, Topanga Center for Human Development, and others. There are serious questions whether the participant in encounter groups can utilize the attitudes and methods he learns and assumes in the idyllic growth setting.

Away from the irritating detail of everyday life with his family
and at work, and in the company of kindred souls who are
seeking joy through play therapy for adults, he learns to shed
his fears, to be open and to express his feelings. In the real
world he finds that despite his efforts to be open and express his
feelings, he is constrained by the demands of his fellow members
of the individualistic, competitive and exploitative society to
behave in ways that he wants to change.

6. Peer self-help psychotherapy programs involving the
participation of professionals in some continuing responsible
role in half-way houses (Connecticut Association for Mental
Health, 1968; Fleischl and Waxenberg, 1964; Grob, 1963;
Rausch and Rausch, 1968), psychiatric rehabilitation programs
(Wilder, 1963), therapeutic social clubs such as Daytop Village
(Bassin, 1968; Shelley and Bassin, 1965), or Integrity Groups
(Drakeford, 1967; Mowrer, 1966, 1969). Where peers have
joined in self-help activities under professional supervision, or
have formed voluntary associations, the principles that guide
them are no different from those of any voluntary association
of peers (Katz, 1970). Instead of being directly involved, professionals may "program" such groups (Berzon and Solomon,
1966); and they may foster their humanist concerns for the
group members by instructing them via tape recordings (Berzon
and Reisel, 1970).

7. Participation of people from various sectors of the community in peer self–help psychotherapy groups (PSHPG's).
These groups are formed by people who have problems or
display behavior currently defined as deviant and assumed to
have a psychological origin or component. These groups enable
their members to overcome their problems by developing their
own psychotherapeutic activities without utilizing professional
psychotherapists in any capacity.PSHPG's, which may or may
not be affiliated with an national organization or movement,
are under the complete control and direction of their members,
who define their goals and determine their methods for achiev-
ing them. Such groups include Alcoholics Anonymous (AA),
Synanon, Recovery, Inc. (The Association of Nervous and
Former Mental Patients). PSHPG's differ from the preceding six

types of self-help programs in that only PSHPG's serve a specifically psychotherapeutic purpose for their members without utilizing professional psychotherapists. It is PSHPG's that we are concerned with in this chapter.

Peer Self-Help Psychotherapy Groups: Pros and Cons

The PSHPG movement was initiated with the organization of AA in 1934 and Recovery, Inc., in 1937; since then many other self-help groups, programs, and fellowships have been modeled on the concepts and practices they originated and developed. Mowrer, who was the first to draw professional attention to PSHPG, reports (1964) that in 1961–1962 a directory of PSHPG's entitled *Their Brothers' Keepers* compiled by Dr. Maurice Jackson, listed 265 different groups, some of which are undoubtedly defunct. A recent listing of self-help groups published in "Constructive Action," the newsletter of the American Conference of Therapeutic Selfhelp/Selfhealth/ Social Clubs (ACT), reports 126 groups and fellowships including AA and Recovery, Inc., which itself has 750 clubs in the United States with over 12,000 members (Burghard, 1970). AA reports 9,047 community groups in the United States with a membership of 156,817 and 12,274 groups including those in Canada, in prisons, hospitals, etc., for a total registered membership in the United States and Canada of 234,077 in 1969 (Alcoholics Anonymous World Services, 1970).

The only research and most impressionistic reports about PSHPG's have been published about AA (Anonymous, 1949; Bales, 1944; Blum and Blum, 1967; Co-Founder, 1957; Eckhardt, 1967; Fox, 1957; Gellman, 1964; Maxwell, 1962; Ripley and Jackson, 1959; Smith, 1941; Stewart, 1955; Tiebout, 1944; Trice, 1958, 1959; Trice and Roman, 1970a, 1970b). Impressionistic reports and anecdotal accounts have also been published about Synanon (Casriel, 1963; Cherkas, 1965; Collier, 1967; Endore, 1968; Holzinger, 1965; Mueller, 1964;

Volkman and Cressey, 1963; Yablonsky, 1965), TOPS (Take
Off Pounds Sensibly) (Wagonfeld and Wolowitz, 1968), Adults
Anonymous (Eglash, 1958), Gamblers Anonymous (Scodel,
1964), Narcotics Anonymous (Patrick, 1965), Recovery, Inc.
(Dean, 1969; Lee 1966, 1971; Low, 1945, 1959; Wechsler,
1960), Samaritans (a British group) (Bagley, 1968), the Seventh
Step Foundation (Fagin, 1968), Forum Anonymous (Cook and
Geis, 1957). Grosz (1972) prepared a preliminary report of
a survey undertaken by Recovery, Inc. There has been one
attempt to interpret PSHPG's as a social movement (Toch,
1965) and two reviews of several PSHPG's (Drakeford, 1969;
Sagarin, 1969). There are several histories and statements about
the guiding principles of various movements by their founders
(Alcoholics Anonymous World Services, 1965; Co-Founder,
1957; Egelson and Egelson, 1961; Low, 1950; Sands, 1964)
and a great many feature articles in newspapers and magazines.

The evidence that PSHPG's help their members is primarily anecdotal and based upon the testimonials of PSHPG's
members and their families—the same kind of evidence that
was rejected about conventional psychotherapy. The absence
of definitive research findings means there is neither objective
evidence for, or a challenge to the credibility of, the anecdotal,
impressionistic, and testimonial evidence about the value and
effectiveness of PSHPG's.

In addition to the testimonials of PSHPG members and
their families are those offered by knowledgeable professionals.
Most of these are for AA, Synanon, and Recovery Inc. Marty
Mann (1970) of the National Council on Alcoholism states that
AA is a proven success in bringing hundreds of thousands of
alcoholics to recovery; she also states that AA "has often been,
simply, a miracle" (1958, p. 163). Fox (1957, p. 167), a psy-
choanalyst who has had a great deal of experience treating
alcoholics, states, "Probably the single most effective method
of treatment [of alcoholism] is that of Alcoholics Anonymous."
Blum and Blum (1967, p. 164) report that "Unquestionably,
AA can be recommended" for the treatment of alcoholism;
they also suggest (1967, p. 158) that Synanon, during the first
10 years of its existence, has helped a greater proportion of

drug addicts who have participated in its program than any other type of treatment for addicts:

> Since 1958, the date of incorporation of Synanon as a non-profit foundation, it has treated nearly 500 addicts and persons with severe social and psychological problems. The majority have been addicted to narcotics, dangerous drugs, and alcohol. Of 860 who have come to Synanon, 55 per cent have stayed and kept free of addiction, even though the door is open at all times.

Dean (1969), a psychiatrist and early supporter of Recovery, Inc., states that patients who received psychiatric care from him and who also participated in Recovery, Inc., showed better progress than those patients who did not participate.

Not all informed professionals are so enthusiastic. Among those who deny the value of PSHPG's, specifically AA, are conventional pschotherapists with a psychoanalytic orientation. Nearly 25 years ago Simmel (1948, p. 21) commented:

> The unconscious conflict of the wish to destroy the mother on whom he depends, and the need to hate when he wants to love, are of the deepest significance to the addict's fight for and against his drinking....Identification with his mother within the ego is substituted by drinking as a physical introjective prototype of incorporation. By drinking her, as it were, he becomes one with her and thus approximates a return to her womb.

According to Simmel, "the therapeutic principles employed in AA's psychotherapeutic endeavor correspond basically to psychoanalytic findings" (1948, p. 31). However, these are not spelled out.

Some conventional pscyhotherapists accept Simmel's model of the maternogenesis of alcoholism; however, they do not acknowledge that AA employs psychoanalytic findings in its therapeutic principles. Thus Koegler and Brill (1967, p. 173) accept Simmel's interpretation of the "dynamics" of alcoholism and ascribe the therapeutic value of AA to "the maternal role which AA performs in the life of its members." Hayman (1966) agrees that alcoholism has its origin in a disturbed mother–child relationship and suggests that the alcoholic conducts a continuing effort to achieve reunion with his mother through alcohol and the bottle. Hayman reports a study of psychiatrists' attitudes toward alcoholism in which he states (1956, p. 490):

> Although psychiatrists estimate the results obtained by A.A. in rather modest ways, they overwhelmingly approve and refer patients to them, thus indicating their belief that A.A. is superior to their own methods and techniques.

Chafetz and Demone (1962) also agree that the alcoholic substitutes alcohol for the mother lost during the earliest stage of psychosexual development. Membership in AA then becomes "a gratifying maternal reunion symbol like that formerly played by alcohol" (p. 161). Chafetz and Demone conclude (p. 163):

> In our opinion, A.A. is really not interested in alcoholics in general, but only as they relate to A.A. itself. By action and by rules, A.A. expresses more interest in strengthening and perpetuating Alcoholics Anonymous than in helping alcoholics.

Koegler and Brill (1967, p. 168) also "question whether successful graduates can ever break with Synanon" and ascribe what effectiveness it may have to the charisma of its founder, Charles Dederich.

PSHPG's do have limitations. Most people with a problem that defines a particular group never attend a PSHPG meeting, despite the considerable publicity some of these groups receive. Many of these people do not believe they need help; they do not identify themselves as being like the PSHPG members and state that the group is "not for me" for reasons they cannot or will not explain. Some may believe that they do not have the simple social and verbal skills required for group participation. Others may not have the self-regard or support from others that is required for comfort in the group, for a feeling that others will accept them, and for a belief in one's ability to participate. Others do not investigate the group because they know or have been told of real or alleged instances of dissatisfaction or harm caused by a particular group principle or practice. They may fear that some members may misuse the information learned about them or attempt to use their participation in the group for their personal gain.

Many people attend one or more meetings and drop out before the group and its members become important and helpful to them. These people do not feel accepted by the members because of their self-concept or because they believe that real or assumed differences in social status, educational level, income, race, ethnic background, religious identification, etc., affect the way others behave toward them. Some may drop out because of problems in the group: poor organization or management by the indigenous leadership, differences between the local group and the national organization, or destructive conflicts between members for leadership or between cliques for group control. Others drop out because they reject some group principle or practice, for instance, the religious or inspirational quality. Finally, some may drop out because they do not want to share their intimate shame and guilt experiences publicly or because they do not want to share these experiences with a particular audience. Unfortunately, there is no way to determine the number or proportion of drop-outs or where to find them and learn why they left the group.

PSHPG's appear to have characteristic problems and dangers. Members of the fellowship become extremely important to the new member. In order to demonstrate his appreciation and his regard for his peers and to repay them for the assistance and care they give him, he may attempt to assume all the responsibilities that must be fulfilled in the group. Some members pass through a period of such intense involvement that they appear to work for the group every available moment. Because former friends have been estranged by the individual's problem behavior, the group becomes the sole source of friends, and other group members, their activities and their common problem become his only interest. Some involve their spouses and other family members in group programs and activities. Others may develop conflicts with their family.

PSHPG members have problems, some very serious. Because of their problems they are more tolerant of others who have problems. Therefore, some very disturbed people are attracted to PSHPG's. These people may have attempted to join and participate in other groups composed of "normal" people in the community but were rejected by them. When they are accepted by PSHPG's they may create difficulties for the group members and may disrupt the group. The PSHPG policy of accepting anyone who wants to participate makes it more difficult for the group to achieve its purpose. It is one of the major causes of the shortlived existence of PSHPG's, which are open to former patients of mental hospitals. It is also the basis for the decision of some PSHPG's to exclude or expel members who are unable to conform with basic expectations. Groups such as Recovery, Inc., Neurotics Anonymous, and those that work with drug addicts and former criminals are particularly vulnerable.

Any group in which men and women meet may become the setting for sexual involvements. Intimate friendships between a married man and married woman may develop more quickly and intensely in PSHPG's because both have a significant common problem and use and respond to the ploy, "My wife (husband) does not understand me." In addition some PSHPG's appear to attract a particular type of hustler who understands the self-feelings and loneliness of women members and preys upon them.

Many PSHPG members become very informed about their common problem by reading the popular press and the psychiatric and psychological literature; many hours are spent discussing their problem. Some members come to believe that they are better informed and more capable than the professionals concerned with their problem. Because of the negative experience many PSHPG members have had with professional psychotherapists, the group becomes a place in which these negative attitudes are expressed and reinforced.

Those who drop out of PSHPG's because of their own real or assumed limitations, because of group problems, or for reasons they themselves do not understand or cannot verbalize may devalue themselves and develop a stronger, negative self-concept. This may be especially true for those who joined the group believing it was the last possible source of help. Failure of PSHPG experiences may then lead to self-blame, to a depressive response, and to greater feelings of inadequacy. These feelings, in turn, may precipitate the kind of situation that characteristically leads to the problem behavior that caused the individual to come to the PSHPG in the first place.

The PSHPG movement has gained a kind of negative ultimate achievement with the establishment of franchised PSHPG's and therapists are invited to "be the first to own the X franchise in your community." Some people are critical of the direction recently taken by Synanon (Collier, 1967) and question whether other PSHPG's will follow.

PSHPG'S are involved with their own members and with their acceptance in the community; they do not generally participate in community affairs as a pressure group. Although PSHPG members are particularly competent to speak out on certain issues, AA does not take community action against alcoholism; Neurotics Anonymous and Recovery, Inc., do not help inform the community about the conditions that prevail in many mental hospitals; Seventh Step Foundation does not fight for penal reform. PSHPG's and their members have the responsibility to help create communities and a society in which PSHPG relationships are established in the society as a whole. Each PSHPG is part of a movement that has demonstrated how well it can help people with problems and change deviant behavior. The movement has yet to learn that it must assume the additional responsibility to help change the community and society as the Fortune Society for ex-convicts is doing.

Thus, whatever effectiveness PSHPG's do have is of critical importance. This importance lies in the circumstance that conventional one-to-one psychotherapy is conducted by highly trained professionals who have completed a lengthy and expensive training program. These professionals command a very high hourly rate for their services, which continue over long periods of time and which are performed in expensive settings. PSHPG's on the other hand, are conducted by average members of the community who have had no training outside of their PSHPG experience; members do not charge for their services, which continue over indeterminate periods of time in all kinds of available settings.

The effectiveness of PSHPG's must also be related to the severity of the problems treated in psychotherapy. On this basis the PSHPG accomplishment may be even greater than the results of conventional psychotherapy. This is so because psychoanalysis is "limited to the more healthy neurotics" (Rangel, 1968), and conventional therapists tend to establish criteria for treatment by which they exclude those who have the most serious problems or deviant behavior. These criteria have been expressed as the "Yavis" syndrome: youthful, attractive, verbal, intelligent and successful (Schofield, 1964). The syndrome may be modified to "Yafvis"—the *f* for female (Koegler and Brill, 1967). In contrast, PSHPG's are open to anyone who has the type of problem that defines the group. Thus, if a PSHPG achieves even the two-thirds success rate common to all psychotherapeutic endeavors, its accomplishment is greater than that of conventional therapy.

The fact that PSHPG's help their members to the extent that they do suggests that there is some element, quality, or characteristic in PSHPG's that makes them more helpful than conventional psychotherapy for some people who have psychological problems. It is therefore important to attempt to discover what it is about PSHPG's that makes them effective and how to utilize this information to modify present psychotherapy to make it more effective than it is. To do so requires an examination of the religious and secular sources of PSHPG's.

The Religious Sources of PSHPG's

The religious sources of PSHPG's are discussed by Drakeford (1969) and Mowrer (1969). Mowrer states that when people sin, that is, break the rules of their community that they have incorporated as their conscience, they feel guilt. These guilt feelings estrange them from their community and arouse other unpleasant feelings that dispose them to learn behavior defined as inappropriate or deviant and to manifest "symptoms." The individual can overcome his alienation from the community, his unpleasant feelings, his inappropriate or deviant behavior, and his distressing or disabling symptoms by confessing his sins to his "significant others" in the community and where appropriate, by making restitution to them. He is thereby reunited with the community and exemplifies the original meaning of religion, which comes from the Latin *ligare*. Re-ligion literally means a reconnection that can be achieved by confession and restitution. Through reconnection with his community one learns appropriate behavior and is encouraged to live it.

Mowrer draws upon John T. McNeill's *A History of the Cure of Souls* (1961) to discuss oral community confession of personal sins as a way of expiating guilt for these sins in Hinduism, Buddhism, Confucianism, and Islam (and also in contemporary primitive peoples). Early Christianity, under the influence of Judaism and Greek and Roman thought, was characterized by small groups that practiced open confession of sins. This is expressed in James 5:16, "Confess your sins one to another and pray for one another that ye may be healed." Mowrer reports that public confession ended after 325. By the twelfth century confession was no longer a congregational or group activity but was made in secret to a priest.

The Protestant Reformation led to the development of a large number of sects. One sect, initially a small movement within the Church of England, became the Methodist Church under the leadership of John Wesley. As Methodism developed, it consisted of societies made up of smaller units referred to by various names. Wesley himself liked the old English word "band," which later came to be known as "class meetings."

Piette (1936) noted that the weekly meetings of the Methodists were marked by self-revelation—to which only the initiated were admitted after solemnly promising absolute sincerity. However the meetings were called nests of debauchery and hotbeds of immorality and became the object of the most virulent attacks launched against Methodism. Piette rejects these charges, reporting that Wesley took great care to avoid their abuse by separating men and women and married people from

young unmarried people. Another significant aspect of the
Methodist "class meeting," according to Drakeford, was the
use of lay preachers.

Frank Buchman, a Lutheran minister, further developed the
group confession early in the twentieth century. Buchman
resigned from a boys' home that he founded because of differences with its trustees. While on a trip he had a dramatic conversion experience, which led him to send an apology to the
trustees. He shared his apology with the son of his host who was
impressed and was converted. According to Drakeford (1969,
p. 8), "This experience may have set the pattern for much of
Buchman's later theorizings and techniques of action."

Buchman subsequently developed a new movement initially
known as the Oxford Group and then as Moral Rearmament.
The Oxford Group worked with college students and emphasized the "Changed Life," one based upon several central assumptions: men are sinners; men can be changed; confession is a pre-
requisite to change; and those who have changed must change
others (Clark, 1951, p. 168). Members of the Oxford Group
aspired to four absolutes: absolute honesty, absolute purity,
absolute unselfishness, and absolute love; and these became the
standards for evaluating an individual's progress. The way to
achieve these absolutes was by the practice of confession, called
"sharing," which was characterized by the group members'
standing before an audience to tell about their failures. The
confession or "sharing for witness" included the member's discussion of his own personal struggles with life, the sins he may
have committed in the past, and the way he triumphed over
them. In this way, the individual who was being proselytized
could see the example of change and therefore accept membership in the Oxford Group.

Two men, both alcoholics, who had participated in the
Oxford Group met in Akron, Ohio, in 1935. Bill W. had come
in contact with the Oxford Group at the Calvary Episcopal
Church in New York, which conducted a mission for alcoholics.
Dr. Bob, a surgeon, had also been associated with the Oxford
Group. Their meeting, at which the Oxford Group principles
were applied, was mutually beneficial. They unknowingly
repeated the practices of the Washingtonians, an earlier anti-

drunkenness movement that started in 1840 and apparently was active to the end of the century. The Washingtonians, who acknowledged that they were habitual drinkers, gathered to hear each other's story of drunkenness; some were able to persuade others to quit drinking and become missionaries on behalf of their cause (McCarthy, 1958).

The success of their encounter led Bill W. and Dr. Bob to seek out others; and as they succeeded with them, their group grew. At the end of 1937 the Akron group had 40 members, and in the spring of 1939 when the name Alcoholics Anonymous was chosen, the 100 members in the Akron–Cleveland group were divided into two groups. AA's growth was slow until it received publicity in the local *Cleveland Plain Dealer* and national *Liberty* in 1939 and in the *Saturday Evening Post* in 1941. Following this publicity the organization grew rapidly. The first International Conference, which 7,000 delegates attended, was held in Cleveland 15 years after the establishment of the movement. The organization has continued to grow and became the model for other "Anonymous" groups such as Gamblers, Neurotics, Overeaters, Addicts, among others, as well as Alanon for nonalcoholic members of families of alcoholics and Alateens for teenage children of alcoholics. All of these subscribe to the Twelve Steps (Alcoholics Anonymous World Services, 1965).

The founders of AA, who were introduced to public confession in a religious setting, secularized confession; and they formed a fellowship based upon the concept and practice of public confession with one's peers as a way of overcoming behavior that estranged them from their fellows.

However, although the mutual and open confession of sin in small groups was one way the churches helped their members achieve moral discipline and maintain their ties with the community, it was not the only way. The churches also saved their members' souls by exhortation to live right, by warnings against damnation, by advising prayer, good deeds, repentance, restitution, and Bible study.

The efficacy of any method of saving one's soul, gaining remission of sins, expiating guilt feelings, or overcoming distressing or disabling "symptoms" must be conducted in accord with the psychological belief systems of the society. For in any period, as

Mencius proposed, the mind works according to the theory by which it is supposed to work. The "client" and "therapist" must both subscribe to the psychological belief system, and the client must also believe that the therapist has the power to bring about the results he seeks (Frank, 1963). In a society that proclaims confession of sin, exorcism of a dybbuk, adjuring the departure of evil spirits, "insight" into one's unconscious motivations, a ritual sacrifice, supplication of a god, performing a prescribed task, or the magic of native healers to be psychotherapeutically effective (Wintrob and Wittkower, 1968), some members of the society will indeed be helped by confession, exorcism, adjuration, insight, sacrifices, supplication, performance of the task, or native magic. The founders of AA accepted the well-established belief of their time that open confession of guilt-causing behavior helps individuals overcome problems, and that alcoholism is a symptom associated with guilt feelings. The founders formed a small group outside any established church; yet they believed in "a power greater than ourselves," and "Made a decision to turn our will and our lives over to the care of God *as we understood Him.*"

The Secular Sources of PSHPG's

The failure of traditional psychodynamic psychotherapy to help a large number of people with problems or deviant behavior stimulated two different approaches: The biological approach led to the development of the psychoactive drugs, and, although they are the greatest boon yet to psychotics and many neurotics, they will not be discussed here. The sociological–educational approach, called here the secular, led to the development of psychotherapeutic theories and practices that directly and indirectly fostered the PSHPG movement. These secular sources include the following different but related processes and philosophies:

1. The acknowledged limitations of psychodynamic psychotherapy based upon the one-to-one relationship of the

"medical model." Chafetz and Demone (1962) suggest that because conventional psychotherapists "failed the alcoholic, AA came into being" (1962, p. 161). This failure encouraged experimentation with other psychotherapeutic methods, particularly those based upon learning theory.

2. The psychologization of human behavior—or the psychologistic conception of human nature (Davis, 1949, p. 374)—that fostered the expectation that any method of helping people with problems or deviant behavior would be a psychological one.

3. The professed American ideal of democracy and the philosophies of pragmatism and instrumentalism that encouraged self-help and mutual aid and the formation of voluntary associations.

Fifteen years ago Albee (1959) recognized the problems inherent in trying to help people with psychological problems through individual psychotherapy. He indicated that the mental health of the American people is becoming such a great problem that all the professionally trained psychotherapists cannot offer the required assistance. More recently Albee (1968) again and Arnhoff (1968) pointed out that the need, supply, and demand for manpower in psychology was out of balance. Although the lack of manpower did not cause a revolution in the conceptualization of the theory and practice of psychotherapy, it did raise questions about traditional concepts and models of one-to-one psychotherapy and create a permissive environment for the participation and utilization of nonprofessionals.

The effectiveness of nonprofessionals in self-help programs has been reported by many investigators; it raised still another challenge to traditional psychotherapy and the "medical model" upon which it is based. There was increasing awareness that psychotherapy is a learning experience and that "mental illness is a myth" (Szasz, 1961a, 1961b). To an increasing extent psychotherapists did not search for the "underlying causes" of "symptoms" to cause psychological change. These psychotherapists regarded the "symptom," the maladaptive, deviant, or problem behavior as learned in interaction through differential association with significant others, often during a time of emotional distress and not as the "acting out" of putative unconscious instinctual strivings the individual cannot control. Psychotherapy is thus a process in which the therapist helps the client to learn more effective behavior. And if new behavior can be learned in interaction with psychologists, social workers, psychiatric technicians, housewives, students and others, as well as with psychiatrists, then one does not need medical training to function as a psychotherapist.

Despite their inadequacy, psychodynamic theories, concepts and practices were accepted by many outside the professions in which they were developed and led to the psychologization of human behavior and problems. Davis (1949) points out that the American open-class society and the prevailing Protestant ethic strongly affected the acceptance of psychological concepts of human behavior by the "mental hygiene" movement.

The failure of liberal social solutions to the human problems of a capitalist society and the fear of proposing and working for revolutionary solutions also led to the acceptance and support for psychological solutions drawn primarily from psychodynamic theories. Theologians and religious functionaries who are bound to the social order in mutual support found that the mythology and mysticism of psychodynamic theories, concepts, and interpretations were ultimately compatible with their own religious beliefs and attitudes. Poets, novelists, dramatists, and other creative persons utilized the same mythology and metaphors derived from psychodynamic theory. Political scientists, economists, sociologists, and anthropologists, who could not otherwise explain the social phenomena they study without challenging society, indicated their progressivism by abandoning instinct theories for the concept of a dynamic unconscious (Berger, 1965; Hook, 1960; LaPiere, 1959; Larrabee, 1960; Nelson, 1957; Parsons, 1951; Rieff, 1961; Ruitenbeek, 1962; Seeley, 1967; Stein et al., 1960; Sutherland, 1959; Wilbur and Muensterberger, 1951).

Finally, psychotherapists who utilize psychodynamic principles and practices have reinforcing experiences, since all psychotherapeutic activities "work" about two-thirds of the times they are used; and they are also reinforced by testimonials. They are united with philanthropists, educators, social workers, and friends and supporters of psychotherapy (Kadushin, 1966) in a mental health establishment or power structure (Andriola, 1956; Blanck, 1970; Graziano, 1969; Johnson, 1956; Sargant, 1964; Thigpen and Cleckley, 1964) that has promulgated the belief that mental illness is a disease that is curable by psychotherapy and that social problems are diseases of many people curable by lots of psychotherapy (Group for the Advancement of Psychiatry, 1966).

Although psychodynamic theories and concepts became the accepted world view, the failure of psychodynamic practice to aid masses of people emphasized the need for new and different psychotherapeutic methods and practices. The response to this need was associated with American "humanitarianism," which Williams (1960) considers to be a major value-orientation in America. Despite the considerable evidence that can be amassed to indicate antihumanitarian elements in American life, Williams proposes that American society is marked by "disinterested concern and helpfulness, including personal kindliness, aid and comfort, spontaneous aid in mass disasters as well as the more impersonal patterns of organized philanthropy (1960, p. 426). In its larger sense it is related to the professed American ideal of an equalitarian democracy—although it is obvious that not all who profess the ideal participate in efforts to achieve it. This ideal is identified with the Judeo–Christian religion and the pioneer and immigrant past; with a belief in the value of life, liberty, and the pursuit of happiness; with the conviction that the state exists for the individual; with the assurance that personal rights are more important than property rights; and with the belief that equality of opportunity must not perish from the earth.

The concept and practice of democracy was brought into psychiatric hospitals and introduced into the mental health field by social group workers (Maier, 1965; National Association of Social Workers, 1960; Trecker, 1956), who, despite their psychodynamic training, tend to have a social-action orientation and are partial to interaction rather than introspection. These social workers organized groups and encouraged the members to achieve group goals through discussion and social action. They also established councils in which members decided upon group goals and methods in settlement houses, community centers, and summer camps. They brought their concepts and experience with participant self-government into institutions that had never experienced such activity before. They led traditional therapy groups and special activity groups and experimented with role playing with their particular understanding of group dynamics. They also formed residents' councils and ward self-governments for they professed that participation in the democratic process is itself a psychotherapeutic experience. The activity of these social workers was a part of and an encouragement to the development of milieu therapy (Bierer, 1951; Bion, 1961; Cumming and Cumming, 1961; Jones, 1953), which also gave the hospital patient greater responsibility for therapeutic programs and activities.

The American philosophies of pragmatism and instrumentalism were developed by William James (1925). According to the pragmatists the meaning and truth of an idea depends upon its practical consequences and a problem is real if its solution affects our behavior and lives. The utilitarian approach of pragmatism was further developed by John Dewey (1925) with his philosophy of instrumentalism. Dewey proposed that the significance of an idea is realized only when it is applied to a socially useful purpose. Thus, for Dewey philosophy or ideas were instruments to change the world through action, to apply knowledge gained in the laboratories and academies to understanding and changing man in interaction through "learning by doing" in a changing society.

The professed democratic ideal and the philosophies of pragmatism and instrumentalism fostered the development of voluntary associations in the United States. Americans were known to be a nation of joiners prior to the twentieth century, and Alexis de Tocqueville noted, "Americans of all ages, all conditions, and all dispositions constantly form associations" (de Tocqueville, 1835). While America exalted the individual it also fostered his participation in and cooperation with his community.

Among the voluntary associations developed were those related to "mental health." Significantly the major national organization in this field was founded by a former patient, Clifford Beers (1948). Now many lay people are members of the National Association for Mental Health; they participate in local affiliate groups, raise money for national and community projects, and perform various services. Their participation in mental health programs and organizations that are headed by professionals fosters their dependence upon the professionals and upon their concepts and practices in the mental health enterprise. At the same time, however, their participation also enables them to learn the professionals' limitations.

The development of psychotherapeutic theories and practices such as the group concepts and methods of Moreno (1960) and the nondirective psychotherapy of Rogers (1951) offered psychotherapists alternative models by which to practice. Moreno originated his psychodrama theories and practices in Austria in the early 1920s and brought them to America somewhat later. His ideas and his work with groups were rejected by the regnant psychotherapists who practiced according to the psychoanalytic model. It was not until World War II, because of the need to help large numbers of patients in the military setting, that group therapy was widely accepted; and those who had experience with it in the military utilized it in their subsequent civilian psychotherapeutic activities. Group therapy is now accepted as a useful psychotherapeutic modality, and many different theories and techniques of group therapy have developed.

Rogers introduced another challenge to psychodynamic therapy with his emphasis upon the interpersonal relationship between the therapist and client as the effective psychotherapeutic agent. He rejected the value of information about the developmental process, unconscious motivations, and insight and interpretation as the way to help the client recognize the inappropriate sources of his present behavior. Instead he proposed that a relationship based upon the therapist's "openness," "genuineness," and "unconditional positive regard" is the necessary and sufficient condition for psychological change. However, unconditional positive regard for another is not a skill or property of a professionally trained person. Stupid lovers can demonstrate it; many men acknowledge that their wives' unconditional positive regard made a mentsch out of them; and it can be demonstrated by group members for each other.

The concepts and practices of psychodynamic psychotherapy were the domain of medically trained psychotherapists. Many, if not most, psychiatrists resisted the attempts of nonmedically trained psychotherapists to practice, although they cooperate with social workers in various supervisory and financial arrangements. Considerable intra- and inter-professional strife characterizes the psychotherapy community on this issue. Some psychiatrists deny the competence of any nonmedical therapist; others propose that the nonmedical therapist practice under medical supervision; still others accept the nonmedical therapist as a colleague. The nonmedical therapist, in most instances, asserts his competence to practice independently and calls for medical assistance if it is needed.

A related issue is the considerable length of time it takes to become a psychodynamic therapist, a *bona fide* member of one of the societies, and to become eligible for referrals. In addition to the tightly controlled educational programs, an often lengthy personal psychotherapy experience is also a requirement. Neither Moreno nor Rogers were concerned whether the therapists who utilized their theories and practices had a medical or nonmedical education. In comparison with the training programs required for psychodynamic therapists, their training programs were very brief. And because their straightforward psychology and techniques could be utilized in various settings, particularly in schools, their systems and methods spread rapidly.

Each of these secular sources fostered the development of self-help activities in general and peer self-help psychotherapy groups in particular. Clients, as members of the psychologized society, learned that "mental illness" is a "disease," but they also learned that unlike other diseases, some mental disease can be cured by people who are not doctors. They learned that people like themselves can help themselves and others on hospital wards, in half-way houses, and in the open community as social service assistants and aides, as community organizers, street workers and in other jobs—most of which required them simply to be a good friend to someone else. This was right and proper, for helping yourself is the American way; and working together with others during a crisis is also the American way. And if people with problems can help others, who among those who can help another is more suited to the job than someone who has experienced and overcome the problem from which the other still suffers?

Many had had group experiences. Some had participated in voluntary organizations and they shared their know-how with others as peers and not as volunteers directed from above. Some had been members of residents' councils. Some had been members of therapy groups. Some had participated in self-help programs in the hospital. Some recognized the worth of the group process. Many experienced the value of sharing their pathogenic secrets in public. And many recognized the value of openness, genuineness, and unconditional positive regard for those who have problems, are troubled, have lost hope, and are desperate. Some experienced support and concern from others, and they felt an obligation or desire to offer their support and concern to others in return. There were PSHPG's being organized in which they could get and give help to peers who experienced what they did in a community that welcomed them, a community in which help did not come from the outside but from the members themselves.

The Method of Investigation

My method of investigation included participant observation (Becker and Geer, 1957; McCall, 1969; Trow, 1957), discussions with members of self-help groups and with colleagues who are knowledgeable about such fellowships, and review of the literature. Self-help groups whose meetings I have observed—all in the Los Angeles area—are AA, Alanon,

Gamblers Anonymous, TOPS, Recovery, Inc., Neurotics Anonymous, Seventh Step Foundation, Weight-Watchers, and a local group, Psychiatric Club of America; and I have attended Saturday night Open House programs at Synanon.

The comparison of conventional psychotherapy and PSHPG's is based upon sociological "constructed" or "ideal" types. The ideal type has four distinguishing characteristics: The term "ideal" does not imply a value judgment regarding perfection or merit; it is a logically constructed organic unity of abstract elements that does not exist in reality; it is not an average that can be computed, but an extreme that must be imagined; and it is constructed to formulate concepts, to measure social reality, and understand social relationships by comparison with other ideal types (McKinney, 1966; Weber, 1947).

The constructed type of conventional psychotherapy has been developed from about 20 years of study and practice; and the constructed type of PSHPG has been developed after observation of about a dozen different groups over a four year period. The constructed type of conventional psychotherapy is the neopsychoanalytic interpretation and insight approach to which is added the interpersonal attitude of the nondirective school as I assume these approaches exist outside of the hospital setting. Some may object to this ideal type and claim I am adding apples and oranges. However, I want to elicit the uniqueness of PSHPG's in contrast to conventional psychotherapy, and the neoanalytic and nondirective schools represent the prevailing conceptual systems that claim the greatest number of trained psychotherapists. In addition, there are many different neopsychoanalytic schools, and each has its own emphasis and metaphor that have been developed and modified from classical psychoanalysis. Both schools are guided by humanitarian values and develop strong positively affective relationships between therapist and client. Both acknowledge that psychotherapy is in large part a learning experience but do not use learning theory and practices in their concepts or methods.

The constructed type of PSHPG is the self-help fellowship or social movement such as AA, Recovery, Inc., or Synanon, which offers an opportunity for maximum interaction between members and for mobility within their fellowship or movement. PSHPG "theories," procedures, and activities also differ in the many different groups; and there are significant differences between the "Anonymous" groups and other fellowships. All the "Anonymous" groups, however, subscribe to the Twelve Steps and display the AA "prayer." Because of the preponderance of Anonymous groups and their basic similarity, it should not be assumed that the present comparison of PSHPG's and conventional therapy is based upon an ideal type derived solely from AA. Distinct elements of Recovery, Inc., and Synanon are contained in the ideal type.

Peer groups have different organizational forms that determine different kinds of interaction between members. Some groups may meet once a week in each other's homes; AA members may meet each other several times weekly at their meeting hall, or a member may attend several different group meetings each week; and Synanon members participate in a voluntary community that houses all but its "graduates" and controls all important aspects of its members' lives. Neither do the PSHPG's have the same philosophy or attitude about "religious," "inspirational," and "spiritual" expressions and activities or about ridiculing or expelling members who deviate from group rules or expectations. Some may therefore object to this ideal type and again claim I am adding apples and oranges. If so, my comparisons are of fruit salads—because the many differences between conventional psychotherapies on the one hand and between various PSHPG's on the other, make strict comparisons and definitive conclusions impossible.

The observations that follow are based upon limited personal experience and not upon empirical research; and the conclusions derived from these observations may therefore not be justified. However, these conclusions are presented as a basis for understanding PSHPG's as a social movement and type of psychotherapy. My observations are not equally significant or equally valid; some are repeated because of a different emphasis in each comparison. The comparisons are presented under the following headings: A. Structural and Procedural Differences, B. Reciprocity between Therapist and Clients and between

Peers, C. Moral Attitudes of Therapists and Peers, D. The Psychological and Social Systems of Therapists and of Peers, E. Group Therapy with Therapists and with Peers, and F. Therapists' Professional Identification and Peers' Fellowship Identification.

Similarities and Differences between Conventional Psychotherapy and PSHPG's

A. Structural and Procedural Differences

CONVENTIONAL THERAPY	PSHPG
1. The therapist maintains authority and control.	1. Peers maintain authority and control.
2. The therapist sets the fee that is payment for his services; and he insures that it will be paid.	2. Peers solicit free-will offerings that support their group and the fellowship of which it is a part.
3. The therapist keeps case records (which are withheld from the client).	3. No records are kept.
4. The therapist schedules private appointments (known only to the therapist, the client, and the client's family—and to those whom any one of them may choose to tell).	4. Peers attend meetings that are almost always open to the public and to which visitors and observers are invited.
5. Therapy sessions are scheduled according to a timetable and for a definite period of time.	5. Each group in the fellowship meets according to a timetable; however, any member can attend meetings of any group in the fellowship. Group meetings are indeterminate in length.
6. Therapy sessions do not follow a prescribed order.	6. Meetings tend to follow a regular, predetermined order of business.
7. The therapist may be seen outside the regularly scheduled appointments on an emergency basis.	7. Peers may call special or emergency meetings or one may call upon other peers as he needs them.
8. Therapy is conducted in hospitals, clinics, offices, etc., specifically designed or established for this purpose and controlled by the therapist.	8. Meetings are conducted in halls, meeting rooms, homes, etc., not designed or established for psychotherapy purposes but controlled by peers.

9. The therapist is required to have completed a program of professional education including clinical training under appropriate supervision; he is also required to be licensed, certified, etc.

9. Peers are not required to have completed a program of professional education or to be licensed or certified; however, each fellowship or movement may have a training program that prepares its own members for greater responsibility within the fellowship.

10. The therapist determines therapy procedures and goals to help the client understand himself or to realize his fullest potential as an individual, as a precondition for solving his problems.

10. Peers determine therapy procedures and goals to help each other change specific behavior or solve a particular problem within the contest of their movement.

11. The therapist discourages his client from reading the scholarly or professional literature about his psychotherapeutic theories and methods.

11. Peers are encouraged to read the literature about their fellowship, which is displayed, distributed and sold at meetings, to learn its history, principles, effectiveness, and impact upon the community.

B. *Reciprocity between Therapist and Client and between Peers*

CONVENTIONAL THERAPY

1. A hierarchal or differential status exists between therapist and client; the therapist is the leader because of his socially defined and institutionalized role based upon his training, license, etc.

2. The therapist does not fulfill role prescriptions that have been established by his clients.

3. The therapist (in contrast with the client) is successful, normal, healthy, mature, wise, etc.

4. The therapist does not have to experience the problem or behavior that defines the client: alcoholism, drug addiction, obesity, neuroticism, etc.

5. The therapist does not reveal himself to the client.

6. The therapist, not having experienced and overcome the client's problem, is not a role model for his client.

PSHPG

1. A peer status exists in the fellowship's therapy activities; leaders are those who help others achieve their therapeutic goals.

2. Peers become therapists when they encourage and support others' efforts to change according to the principles of their fellowship.

3. Peers acknowledge to each other that they are failures, abnormal, neurotic, immature, stupid, etc.

4. All members of the fellowship have experienced the problem or behavior that defines them as peers: alcoholism, drug addiction, obesity, neuroticism, etc.

5. Peers reveal themselves to each other.

6. Peers, having experienced and overcome the same problem, are role models for each other.

7. Because the therapist has not experienced and overcome the client's problem, the client may not identify with the therapist but may question his ability to understand him or help him change; the therapist does not become an instrumental significant other.

7. Because peers have experienced and overcome the same problem they do identify with each other; they know that each understands the other and can help the other change; peers become instrumental significant others.

8. The therapist's "difference" from the client prevents him from establishing "gut"-level interaction with the client, which is postulated as necessary for liberating insight and change.

8. The members' common problem encourages the establishment of "gut"-level interaction between them, which is postulated as necessary for liberating insight and change.

9. The therapist tends to regard the client as responsible for his lack of progress; the client's inability to achieve his asserted goal is his failure.

9. Peers tend to regard themselves as responsible for each other's lack of progress; a member's inability to achieve his goal as defined by the group's purpose is failure by the fellowship.

C. *Moral Attitudes of the Therapist and Peers*

CONVENTIONAL THERAPY

1. The therapist professes moral neutrality and is nonjudgmental, because he regards the client's deviant behavior as a medical problem that must be understood and not judged.

2. The therapist does not make the client feel guilty, ashamed, sinful, etc.

3. The therapist does not punish deviant, irresponsible, self-defeating behavior.

4. The therapist labels the client "sick," instead of expressing a moral judgment. The label may permit the client to deny responsibility for his behavior.

5. The therapist considers the client "sick" and thereby justifies the client in his sick role. The client, playing the sick role, stays sick.

6. The therapist is areligious and tends to negate the importance of "spiritual" and "inspirational" activities.

PSHPG

1. Peers profess a moral position and are judgmental, since behavior that is deviant, self-destructive, irresponsible, stupid, etc. should be changed even if it is a medical problem.

2. Peers may make each other feel guilty, ashamed, sinful, etc.

3. Peers may punish deviant, irresponsible, self-defeating behavior.

4. Peers' moral judgments about each other do not permit them to deny responsibility for their behavior.

5. Peers may consider each other "sick," but they expect "well" behavior of each other. Peers, playing the well role, get well.

6. Peers consider religious attitudes important and utilize "spiritual" and "inspirational" activities.

D. *The Social and Psychological Systems of Therapists and Peers*

CONVENTIONAL THERAPY

1. The psychodynamically oriented therapist has a diagnostic approach. He reviews the client's past to discover the causes of present problems.

2. The therapist offers "insights" and "interpretations" on the basis of free associations, dreams, fantasies, slips of the tongue, etc., that reveal the client's unconscious processes or that are revealed through the discussion of genetic and developmental material.

3. The therapist seeks the "underlying causes" of the present problems, which he regards as symptoms, to preclude possible "symptom substitution" or greater problems such as depression, psychosis, or suicide.

4. The therapist may foster psychological regression and evoke a transference neurosis as a therapeutic technique.

5. The therapist regards any behavior that prevents the client from discovering the underlying cause of his problem as conscious or unconscious "resistance."

6. The therapist regards "symptomatic" or "acting out" behavior as evidence of the client's inability to control his instinctive impulses, his imperfect self-understanding, or his resistance to change because of the gratification gained from such behavior.

7. The therapist keeps out of the therapy experience whatever may disturb the exploration of unconscious material.

8. The therapist develops and manipulates the "transference" relationship; he plays one role (or one role at a

PSHPG

1. Peers tend to be diagnostically oriented and review each other's past to discover the cause of present behavior and problems.

2. Peers offer insights and interpretations on the basis of unconscious processes and genetic and developmental material.

3. Peers seek the underlying causes of the present problems, which they regard as symptoms; they are not concerned with symptom substitution or with greater problems if these causes are not discovered.

4. Peers do not foster psychological regression or evoke a transference neurosis.

5. Peers regard any behavior that is not in accord with the member's asserted goal and therefore not in accord with the principles and goal of the fellowship as evidence of his unreadiness or unwillingness to accept the philosophy and discipline of the fellowship.

6. Peers regard deviant behavior as evidence of the member's irresponsibility, immaturity, lack of will power, or lack of desire to change.

7. Every aspect of the peer's functioning in the real world is subject to group review and evaluation.

8. Peers interact with many others who play real life roles that are open to examination, and they experience

time), principally a parental or authority figure.

9. The therapist regards the client's problems to be due to "unconscious conflicts," "death instincts," etc., or to factors in his personal history that formed the client and over which he has no control; thus a client may believe that the therapist absolves him from responsibility for his problems.

10. The nondirective therapist responds to his client in the here-and-now and attempts to develop an effective therapeutic relationship based upon unconditional positive regard.

11. The therapist attempts to enhance the client's self-attitudes to achieve self-actualization and the realization of his human potential.

12. The psychodynamic and nondirective therapists tend to be passive in their relationship with the client. Each assumes that through their procedures and techniques they will either help the client understand his intrapsychic processes or help him gain enhanced self-attitudes; in this way each will enable the client to solve his specific problems.

13. Neither therapist ridicules the client or expresses their hostile feelings toward the client.

14. Both therapists give and the client receives, support (Dean, 1969).

15. Both therapists assume that gains in the psychotherapy setting will be

various "transference" relationships directly.

9. Peers hold each other responsible for their behavior, regardless of its causes; they reject excuses that do not help the movement achieve its goals for them and may harm others. They urge responsibility for each other; require appropriate behavior in accord with the purpose of their movement. Their primary concern is with their own land others' behavior, and they support others' efforts and effective functioning by example, encouragement, "spotting," "endorsement," exhortation, ridicule, etc., to achieve day-to-day goals.

10. Peers respond to each other in the here-and-now and develop therapeutic relationships based upon honest confrontation in which they express negative as well as positive views.

11. Peers attempt to help each other solve specific problems or deviant behavior; and by the successful accomplishment of these goals they help each other achieve self-actualization and the realization of each member's human potential.

12. Peers are active in their relationship with each other. They focus on the presenting problem, emphasize activity, and assume that by following the principles and practices of their movement they will help the member solve his specific problems and thereby cause intrapsychic changes and enhanced self-attitudes.

13. Peers may ridicule and attack each other with great hostility, and they may provoke aggressive and hostile feelings. However, peers regard such attacks and provocations as others' expressions of concern and care.

14. Peers give as well as receive support.

15. Peers assume that the fellowship experience will be transferred into the

transferred to the client's everyday life experiences.

16. Neither therapist offers substitute satisfactions for inappropriate behavior and may regard such substitutes as defeating the goal of therapy.

17. Neither therapist offers the client material or nonmaterial recognition and rewards to undertake and continue therapy.

18. Neither therapist observes ceremonials and rituals about special dates or activities associated with the individual's own life cycle or the therapy experience to reinforce the therapy.

19. Neither therapist utilizes texts, slogans, creeds, "prayers," readings, or other prepared material as part of the therapy experience.

20. Both therapists give periodic support during the scheduled appointments.

21. Neither therapist gives the client advice.

22. Neither therapist involves the client's family.

23. Neither therapist assists the client in the development of social skills.

24. Both therapists have limited concern about the client's everyday problems and do not actively help him function more effectively in his daily life.

25. Both therapists' scheduled appointments are part of a series in which the client is removed from his real-life experience.

member's everyday life which is the fellowship or includes many members of the fellowship.

16. Peers attempt to find substitute satisfactions for inappropriate behavior and may regard such substitutes as effective change devices.

17. Peers continually motivate and support each other's expressed desire to change by various material and nonmaterial recognition and rewards.

18. Ceremonials and rituals about special dates or activities are used to reinforce the purpose and value of fellowship.

19. Peers utilize texts, slogans, creeds, "prayers," readings, or other prepared materials, which they apply to their own situation as part of the therapy experience.

20. Peers are always available to support one another if they appear committed to the fellowship and want to maintain their affiliation.

21. Peers give each other advice.

22. Peers tend to involve the families of fellowship members and offer the member and his family a common cause with which to identify.

23. Peers help each other develop social skills; they also assist each other as members of a communications grapevine through which they share information about jobs, rentals, bargains, etc.

24. Peers are concerned about each other's everyday problems and help each other function more effectively in their daily life.

25. Each meeting of the fellowship involves the member in activities and relationships that become part of his real-life experiences.

26. Both therapists may be the only supporters of the client's effort to change.

26. Peers are members of a community, each member of which supports the others' efforts to change.

27. Each client is one among others of the therapists' clients.

27. Each member is a peer among others who participate in a fellowship or movement.

28. The therapy experience encourages self-involvement.

28. The fellowship experience encourages involvement with others.

29. The client's preferred or desired behavior occurs randomly, and both therapists reinforce it haphazardly.

29. Peers give each other periodic support in accordance with a meeting schedule and continuing support by their availability to each other. Appropriate behavior is defined and required by membership in the fellowship; such behavior is encouraged but not planfully reinforced.

30. Both therapists learn and keep their clients' secrets private.

30. Peers disclose their secrets in public.

31. Both therapists, as "significant others," represent "generalized others" and symbolically accept the clients for the community, despite their harmful behavior toward others.

31. Peers' knowledge of each other's secrets is "punishment" for behavior that may be associated with present problems and serves to expiate their guilt feelings. Thus peers do not represent significant others, they are significant others; each one's acceptance of the other is not symbolic but real.

32. Neither therapist encourages the client to make restitution to those whom he has harmed in some way.

32. Peers encourage each other to make restitution to those whom they may have harmed in some way.

33. Both therapists determine which clients they will accept and tend to select those who are younger, intelligent, educated, verbal, attractive, and able to pay for private psychotherapy and to function despite their deviance or problem.

33. Peers do not select each other; anyone who has the problem that defines their fellowship is eligible for membership, and they have a hopeful attitude about helping anyone who joins their movement. At the same time they will not jeopardize their movement because of a peer's deviant behavior, which may threaten the well-being of others or of their movement. They may expel such a member.

34. The client has no impact upon the community and no status in the client role.

34. Peers encourage involvement with others by participation in a social movement. As members of this social movement, which has novelty and positive aspects, peers make an impact upon the community, have status as members of their fellowship, and thereby gain self-esteem.

35. The client does not have an opportunity for mobility to various positions in the therapy setting.

35. Peers have an opportunity for mobility to various positions within the fellowship.

36. The client never achieves the status or performs the role of the therapists.

36. All peers are considered therapists.

37. Neither therapist organizes community groups to support the therapeutic ideology with which they are identified; however, clients may do so.

37 Peers organize community groups to support their movement and publicize it in every way they can.

38. The client continues to live in a setting that constrains him in his established behavior, and the therapists return the clients with whom they have been successful, as well as those with whom they have not been successful, to this setting at the conclusion of therapy.

38. Peers who have had an unsuccessful experience in the fellowship drop away (and are not known to new members), while those who have solved their problems maintain a place in the social system of their movement and are responsible for aiding and training others to whom they serve as role models.

E. Group Therapy with Therapists and Peers

CONVENTIONAL THERAPY

1. Therapy is primarily individual, and group therapy is one modality used by the therapist.

PSHPG

1. All therapy occurs in groups; individuals may form shifting therapeutic dyads within the structure of the fellowship.

2. The therapist always controls the group because of his status gained prior to and outside the group.

2. Group leadership develops and is assumed by different members as they help others achieve the movement's purpose and thereby solve their problems.

3. The therapist's consideration is "What is in the best interests of each individual member ?"

3. The peers' consideration is "What is in the best interest of the movement?" In this way each member serves himself and the others best.

4. The therapist regards the client's inability to fit into the group as an aspect of his problems, which he does not complicate by denying him admission or rejecting him from the group.

4. Peers regard another's inability to fit into their movement not only as an aspect of his problem but also as a threat to the movement. They may deny admission or reject from the fellowship anyone who may damage or destroy it.

5. Clients tend to be similar in many ways: race, education, economic level, etc.

5. Peers tend to be different in many ways, other than their common problem: race, age, education, economic level, etc.

6. Clients with different problems and histories, who are not role models for each other, may participate in the same group.

6. Peers with similar problems and histories, who are role models for each other, are members of the fellowship.

7. The client's achievements gained prior to and outside the group—his profession, wealth, how well known he is—may affect his status in the group.

7. A member's achievements gained prior to and outside the movement—his profession, wealth, how well known he is—affect his status in the group. He may be treated more severely if he attempts to use his achievements to impress others.

8. Clients achieve status in the group by emulating the therapist's activity and assuming an "associate therapist" role in relation to him.

8. Peers achieve status in the movement by indicating the contrast between their former and present behavior, by helping others, by serving as "sponsors," and by undertaking greater responsibility in their movement.

9. The client's observed behavior in group interaction is assumed to be a sample of his "real" characteristic behavior.

9. Members continually interact so all know each other's "real," characteristic behavior.

10. Clients may withhold information about themselves and still maintain a place in the group; clients therefore have limited knowledge about each other.

10. Peers must and do share all information about themselves and have complete knowledge about each other.

11. Clients may interact on the basis of group norms during the group meeting; however, they may behave on the basis of deviant norms outside the group meeting.

11. Members' interaction continues before and after meetings so members observe each other's behavior and exert pressure to make it conform with fellowship norms.

12. Since groups meet once or twice a week, the group offers limited opportunities for clients to experience self-examination, self-assessment, behavior change, etc., and to attempt to change real-life behavior and attitudes.

12. Peer interaction is a continuously available opportunity for self-examination, self-assessment, peer assessment, and behavior change. The fellowship offers opportunities for peers to have real-life meaning for each other and to change real-life behavior and attitudes.

13. Group members do not have real-life meaning for each other; they are self-concerned individuals who are incidentally concerned with others as they attempt to solve their own problems and change their behavior. They are not interdependent in their efforts to change problem behavior.

13. Peers have real-life meaning for each other and assist each other to change real-life behavior and attitudes. Peers are aware of their interdependence, and they are concerned about their own and the others' efforts to solve their problems, to change their behavior, proving the validity of the movement to which they have committed themselves.

14. Clients resist imposing on other group members outside of scheduled group meetings. At the same time the therapist discourages clients' contacts outside the group because of possible damaging contact, mutual exploitation, etc.

14 Peers are always and immediately available to each other and being called upon by another for help is a mark of esteem that is highly regarded and reinforces the value of the movement.

F. Therapist's Professional Identification and Peers' Fellowship Identification

CONVENTIONAL THERAPY

PSHPG

1. The therapist's professional status ascribes to him the ultimate source of wisdom in the therapist-client interaction.

1. Different members are regarded as a source of wisdom as they function characteristically in various situations to help their peers achieve their goals. Where professional therapists participate in the fellowship, they play an auxiliary role and are dominated by the group members.

2. The therapist's professional status and his identification with a specific psychotherapeutic ideology and technique may restrict experimentation and inhibit creativity.

2. The peers' identification is with their movement, they are not concerned about functioning as therapists, so they may introduce innovations in psychotherapy.

3. The therapist's economic dependence upon his clients may make him vulnerable to their manipulation.

3. Peer relationships have no economic aspect, and peers are not vulnerable to manipulation on this basis.

4. The client may participate in psychotherapy activities that he questions, because the therapists' authority is imposed upon him, because of his dependent status, or because the therapist's function is institutionalized and societally accepted.

4. Members participate in the fellowship voluntarily and accept the helping activities of their peers only as long as they want to.

5. The therapist represents and accepts the community and its authority, values, etc.

5. The fellowship represents and accepts the community and its authority, values, etc., which the peers accept.

6. The client may not have the means for mobility and success in the therapist's world because of his deviant behavior or psychological problems.

6. Peers are members of a movement that encourages mobility within the fellowship itself; peers become successful according to the ways and values of their movement.

7. The client becomes dependent upon the therapist, which is just like being dependent upon his addiction (if this is his problem), or it becomes a substitute problem (Ross, 1963).

7. A member may become dependent upon the movement, which is just like being dependent upon his addiction (if this is his problem), or it becomes a substitute problem.

8. The client has faith in the therapist on the basis of his status and reputation in the professional community, his own knowledge of the therapist's helpfulness, and the status of the referring person.

8. Peers have faith in each other because of the success of their movement in aiding others with problems like their own.

9. The client may not regard the therapist as someone with power greater than his own, which could create an expectation of help and thereby become a source of help to the client.

9. Peers encourage each other to acknowledge that there is a power greater than themselves that they can call upon for help and that is a source of help to them.

10. Community attitudes to conventional therapy range from unfriendly to active support; in general they are tolerant and accepting.

10. Community attitudes to the fellowship range from hostility to active support; in general they are skeptical and resistant.

The PSHPG Model and Some Propositions about Psychotherapy

What is the significance of these postulated similarities and differences between the constructed models of conventional psychotherapy and PSHPG's? Do they suggest the source of psychotherapeutic effectiveness of the self-help movement? The following propositions are presented for consideration. They may also be phrased as hypotheses to be investigated to help develop a more effective theory and practice of psychotherapy:

Psychotherapy should be offered without fees. If psychotherapy is essentially a human relationship that cannot be bought, charging a fee for psychotherapy is a contradiction in terms.

Psychotherapy should be offered without such elements of a bureaucratic structure as fees, records, scheduled appointments, privacy, special settings, professional training, etc., except those that the participants themselves decide are helpful to them and that they want to assume to achieve their goals.

The client should know the therapist as another human being; the therapist should therefore be prepared to reveal as much about himself as he asks the client to reveal.

Therapists should be those peers whom the clients select on the basis or criteria they determine. This may include experience with the problem behavior they are attempting to overcome.

Spiritual and inspirational concepts and methods that are in accord with the client's preexisting values or that he is willing to assume as a member of a fellowship may be used effectively in psychotherapy.

Moral and judgmental attitudes can be used effectively in psychotherapy.

Psychotherapy does not require searching for and interpreting the unconscious or the developmental sources of present behavior; if such a search is useful, it can be conducted by untrained personnel.

Members of PSHPG's "analyze" each other, offering "insights" into and "interpretations" of each other's behavior, thoughts, and feelings. Although many believe that this activity is the cause of psychological change, it more likely occurs because each member is expected to conform with behavior the fellowship has defined as appropriate. His conformity is secured by his desire to meet the expectations of other group members whose approval he values and seeks.

Psychotherapy that modifies behavior and attitudes without discovering "underlying causes" does not cause "symptom substitution."

Psychotherapy does not require the creation or analysis of the "transference neurosis."

The therapist's "unconditional positive regard" for the client is not a necessary or sufficient condition for psychotherapeutic change.

Therapists can help their clients define and achieve their psychotherapeutic goals by using recognition and reward for their clients' efforts and desirable behavior and attitudes, and punishment for their clients' lack of effort and undesirable behavior and attitudes.

Psychotherapeutic goals should be explicitly stated in the form of a contract, and all therapeutic activities should be regularly evaluated in relation to how well they help the client achieve the stated goal.

Public rather than private sharing of experiences considered responsible for problem behavior, public rather than private acknowledgment of damage or harm done to others, and efforts at restitution to those damaged or harmed are effective psychotherapeutic procedures.

Negative and hostile behavior and attitudes such as ridicule and forms of punishment and expulsion from the group may help a client change his behavior. This is so when he knows that others who express such behavior and attitudes toward him have fully revealed themselves to him and fully entered the therapeutic relationship with him.

Therapists and clients may develop rituals that have significance for them and foster identification and commitment to therapy goals.

Therapists should offer substitute satisfactions for their clients' inappropriate behavior.

Advice giving may be used constructively in psychotherapy.

Psychotherapy should be concerned about the client in his real-life activities, in relation to all members of his family, and in relation to all others who play an important part in his life.

Therapists are effective to the degree that they model or "teach" new ways of behaving to their clients by their own example.

Psychotherapy should encourage people to become involved with others and participate with them in common activities and endeavors.

The continued participation in the fellowship of those peers who have been helped in the fellowship supports the expectations of new members that they will receive the kind of help they need and serves as a self-fulfilling prophecy.

Psychotherapy should be conceived of and practiced as social interaction (social learning) between peers, instead of as intrapsychic exploration (analysis or relationship) between therapist and client.

Although members of PSHPG's profess the "medical model," they function in accord with the learning model.

PSHPG's develop new significant others, a new reference group, and a new culture with its own norms of role-performances and role-expectations. The group defines a new style of living for members of the fellowship. The members of the fellowship simultaneously enable and constrain each other to behave in ways they have agreed are desirable and appropriate for them (Lewin, 1948).

Peers gain self-esteem not only from the "therapeutic" activities conducted by the fellowship but also from the impact of the fellowship upon the community.

PSHPG's enable the individual to redefine his problem from one in which he needs professional help from others to one in which he can help himself and others. His participation in the PSHPG is also positively regarded by his significant others and by the larger community. The redefinition of the problem and the positive regard expressed by others enables the individual to develop a more enhancing self-concept, which is psychotherapeutically valuable apart from any other benefits that may be gained from participation in the PSHPG.

Group therapy should be the principal therapeutic modality.

Therapists should arise out of group interaction to achieve the members' defined goals.

Individuals with the same problems serve as most effective role models for each other.

The therapy group or setting should offer the client opportunities for mobility within it.

Psychotherapists should encourage clients with problems to join and/or form PSHPG's.

PSHPG's are most effective when they do not have enthusiastic community support and have not been infiltrated by professionals.

Psychotherapy as a PSHPG movement is—or has the potential to be—more effective for more people with more and different problems and for much less money than conventional psychotherapy, regardless of its guiding psychological theory and the auspices through which it is offered.

The psychotherapist should accept the responsibility to assist in creating a society in which the therapeutic activities conducted in PSHPG's are practiced as the basic relationship between people in the society as a whole.

It should be pointed out that PSHPG's achieve their goals without the application of specific behavior-modification techniques, without an existential search for identity, without the exploration of human potential, without psychodrama, without creative fighting, without screaming, without mind-expanding drugs, without marathons, without feeling each other up, without taking off clothes, and without sexual intercourse between therapist and clients (McCartney, 1966).

PSHPG's are fellowships whose members have a common problem and who establish relationships with others in which they fully reveal themselves. Within such a community of relationships, and in the presence of members who acknowledge the help they received through the fellowship, the peers make it possible and desirable to modify their own and others' behavior and solve their own and others' problems. The procedures and techniques utilized within the fellowship to modify behavior are those long identified with learning theory.

The Implication of PSHPG's for Psychotherapy and Society

The asserted effectiveness of PSHPG's in helping many people to overcome problems that are presently defined as psychological has a number of very significant implications for psychotherapy, and also raises questions about the social function of psychotherapy under professional auspices:

1. The PSHPG model indicates that the theories and practices of neither of the two prevailing psychotherapeutic approaches in America are necessary or sufficient for psychotherapeutic change.

2. Although PSHPG's appear to accept the medical model of mental illness, they are not aware that their success denies its validity. PSHPG's have played an important part in changing the label of the deviant as someone who is immoral to someone who is sick (Trice and Roman, 1970b). Both concepts, however, are based upon the principle of "possession": The immoral individual was possessed by evil spirits; the sick individual is possessed by disease. Both require the intercession of someone who meets certain criteria and who is sanctioned by the community to exorcise the evil spirits or to extirpate the cause of the disease. In PSHPG's all the members sanction each other's efforts to change their own and the others' behavior by their membership in the fellowship. PSHPG members do not recognize that their inappropriate, deviant, distressing behavior may be defined in terms of rules that have been broken, and that there is a constant interaction between members of the community and changing rules. When PSHPG members achieve this understanding they can better appreciate the social change rather than the psychiatric world view they presently hold (Reissman and Miller, 1964).

3. The theory of inappropriate behavior as the expression of unconscious conflicts proposes that humans function on the basis of inherent biological drives or instincts. The social order does not permit the expression of these drives which, under certain circumstances, appear as symptoms. Alleviating the symptom is considered to be a superficial way of dealing with it, since the psychic energy will express itself in another way; another symptom will pop out, "symptom substitution" will occur. However, alcoholics who overcome their alcoholism, addicts who overcome their addiction, and neurotics who overcome their neuroticism without exploring the presumed unconscious motives for their behavior do not display other symptoms. On the contrary, the alcoholic, addict, neurotic and others—the criminal, obese, psychotic—all who overcome their specific problem in PSHPG's become more effective total persons.

4. The basis upon which problem or deviant behavior is defined is questioned. Human beings behave in many different ways and believe many different things, some of which are

defined as inappropriate or deviant in particular situations (Becker, 1963, 1964). Many people considered sane in our society believe that their god intercedes on their behalf when they pray to him (?), that stars determine human events, that reincarnation enables an individual to fulfill his Karma, that social institutions are the concretization of unconscious instinctual urges, that one can communicate with the dead, etc. Few people seriously challenge such beliefs. Thus, it may be proposed that deviance is the label given to behavior that is offensive or disturbing to those in authority and who have the power to impose such a definition.

Associated with this issue is who defines deviant behavior. When gambling, for instance, is considered the expression of moral weakness, the clergy deals with it; when it is considered a legal problem, attorneys deal with it; when it is considered a problem of public order, police deal with it; and when it is considered a sickness, physicians deal with it. Each labeling group—or profession—has vested economic and status interests in defining deviance so it falls within its area of expertise and function. The effectiveness of Gamblers Anonymous for some gamblers, compared with those who now have the authority to label it, suggests that a new, as yet undetermined, definition of gambling behavior may emerge. The ambivalence of some professionals about PSHPG's may stem from their concern that their definition of deviance will be rejected for one developed out of the PSHPG experience.

5. The value of diagnoses of alcoholic, addictive, neurotic, obese and other personality types is challenged by the fact that all are helped by the same kind of experience in different PSHPG's.

6. Not all PSHPG members may benefit from their participation in the fellowship because the same observable deviant behavior may arise from two different primary sources: biological or interactional. Individuals who are helped by PSHPG participation may be those whose problems have an interactional cause; individuals who are not helped by PSHPG participation may have problems with a biological cause. These "unsuccessful" members should be referred for medical treat-

ment with vitamins, psychoactive chemicals, and other drugs. On the other hand, individuals who are not helped by various drugs should be advised to join and participate in a PSHPG. Obviously, interactional strain can cause psychosomatic ailments and complaints that require specifically medical treatment.

7. Psychodynamic concepts may be more interesting and valuable as literary metaphors than as guides to why people behave as they do and what causes them to change. Such concepts, associated with the medical model, may actually inhibit necessary research (Taber *et al.*, 1969). Questions must also be raised about the relevance of studies that count the number of times the therapist says "uh huh" or "uh uh," how often the therapist and client blink their eyes, the length of silent periods during a therapy session, or whether the personality types of the client and therapist form a compatible therapeutic dyad.

8. The value of psychotherapy that does not attempt to change the social systems of which the client is a member must be challenged. This issue must be seen on two levels: First, an individual's problems or deviant behavior and negative self-concept are learned and expressed in a particular family or work setting in which he interacts with significant others. Psychotherapy may help him understand himself better, become more open, attempt more appropriate behavior, etc. However, if he remains in or returns to his family or work setting following psychotherapy, his problems or deviant behavior will persist because his significant others, who have not changed, will constrain him to behave in his characteristically inappropriate ways and to maintain his negative self-regard. This situation is often found in marital problems following psychotherapy with one spouse (Hurvitz, 1967). Thus, it is necessary to change the social system, which includes the client's significant others. Second, the larger society must also be changed. It has a characteristic impact upon the members of the more intimate family system and creates the situations that foster problems or deviant behavior. A less competitive and individualistic society may prevent some of the problem and deviant behavior in our society, although it may generate problems unique to it.

The success of PSHPG's that utilize group confession does not prove that group confession is, in it self, the necessary or sufficient condition for psychotherapeutic change. The PSHPG experience does suggest that in our society group confession creates affective bonds between group members who thereby become significant others. While confession may be cathartic, it is not usually the cause of behavior change in itself. Nevertheless, all experienced psychotherapists can report instances in which private confessions to them about masturbation, a single homosexual experience, a premarital pregnancy, or death wishes toward someone who subsequently died relieved guilt feelings and anxiety and enabled more appropriate behavior to follow.

It may be that the individual, under the pressure of guilt and shame, learned to behave in ways defined as problem or deviant. Relieving him of his guilt and anxiety is but the first step in helping him to achieve psychological competence. Once he has confessed and been relieved of his guilt and shame he must learn to behave in "appropriate" ways. Those members of the group who have helped relieve him of his guilt become significant others. Their expectations now motivate him to change because he wants to maintain a place in the fellowship, which has become important to him. These changes are reinforced in various ways by fellow group members, primarily by their acceptance of him as a good member of the group. In this way the interaction of PSHPG members approximates that of kibbutz members (Darin-Drabkin, 1963; Leon, 1969; Weintraub *et al.*, 1969) and of members of the collectives established by Makarenko in Russia (Baker, 1968).

PSHPG's apparently effect psychological change in their member because of two elements in the group experience:

1. PSHPG's stimulate and maintain emotionally involving relationships between members by encouraging them to reveal information about themselves not usually disclosed in public. The emotionally charged group interaction facilitates the new member's acceptance of his peers as significant others, his identification with the group, and of the fellowship of which it is a part.

2. The new member then meets his peers' expectations and

responds to their constraints, which are modeled and expressed verbally and nonverbally. He thus participates in a continuing learning process, behaving in the way the fellowship defines is appropriate to achieve a desired goal.

Each member may play a different role in these two processes with other members: One may establish and maintain the appropriate emotional climate, another may foster the learning process, and others may perform both roles simultaneously or at different times.

These two processes exist in all psychotherapy and may be the necessary and sufficient conditions for psychotherapeutic change activities:

1. The therapist conducts expressive activities, creating and fostering an emotionally charged atmosphere and establishing a unique working relationship, in order to become a significant other to the client.

2. The therapist then conducts various instrumental activities that he utilizes to effect behavior change. These are based upon his socially defined role, the client's expectations in relation to this role, and the client's acceptance of the therapist's theoretical–logical framework.

If the foregoing observation is valid, all psychotherapeutic systems can be spotted on a grid with "expressive" and "instrumental" axes marked, for instance, from 1 to 10. Relationship therapies, religious conversion "cures," and cures based upon charisma and chutzpah are 10 on the expressive axis and 1 on the instrumental axis; behavior-modification methods are 1 on the expressive axis and 10 on the instrumental axis. Other psychotherapeutic systems can be similarly spotted on such a grid. Psychotherapy may be more effective if "diagnosis" also considers the particular balance of expressive and instrumental roles the therapist should play with a particular client and whether and how this balance should change in the course of therapy.

PSHPG experiences can also be identified with the socialization process in primary groups. The fellowship becomes an

extended "family" for each member, and the peers with whom
he interacts becomes his immediate "family." Some peers play
instrumental or expressive roles; others may play both (Parsons
and Bales, 1955). An emotionally close but growth-encouraging
environment is created, which fosters resocialization in accord
with the values of the movement.

The "family" function of PSHPG's has fostered the establishment of communes by young people that serve as a voluntary
therapeutic community for them. Many of these young people
had family problems and sought surrogate family relationships
to resolve these problems. These young adults do not feel comfortable in existing PSHPG's, most of whose members are older
than they are; they cannot afford to participate in the play-
therapy centers, although they park their vans and tents near-
by; and as members of the counter-culture are looking for an
alternative life-style. Some of these young people participated
in Synanon, Alanon, or similar programs, others may have
received help at communal Free Clinics or lived in half-way
houses or other self-help establishments under professional
direction, and others may have heard or read about these programs and recognized their potential value for them. Several
elements were involved in young adults' joining or forming
therapeutic communes; these include: their dissatisfaction with
city life and the romanticization of rural communes as an aspect
of the ecology movement; the failure of their radicalism and
their personal inability to participate in organized radical
activities; the sexual experimentation permitted in communes;
the permissiveness toward drug use; the opportunity to explore
the occult, mysticism, Eastern religions, and other esoteric
phenomena without requiring much information; and the
prevailing psychologization of behavior with the opportunity to
participate in confrontations, sensitivity sessions, marathons,
etc. Although the communes obviously serve as an extended
family of peers and as a therapeutic community, the members
may not recognize or acknowledge it as such.

Despite resistance to social activism and community involvement by the "anonymous" groups, the largest PSHPG movement with a common philosophy, the members of some other
PSHPG's have helped initiate various projects and activities on

behalf of "mental patients." For instance, the Fortune Society, an organization of ex-convicts, has an aggressive advocacy program on behalf of former prisoners. Members and former members of various PSHPG's are challenging professionals whom they accuse of treating them with indifference, incompetence, and ignorance. Their activities are associated with the development of the American Association for the Abolition of Involuntary Mental Hospitalization, and the Patient Advocacy Service (PALS) established at the Washington University Law School in St. Louis. The "mentally ill" have participated in many informal discussions and organized conferences about "The Rights of Persons Labelled Mentally Disabled." The "Mental Patients' Liberation Project" planned a conference with workshops on Economics and Psychiatry; The Insane Experience; Psychiatry: Science, Medicine, or Bullshit; Crisis Center; Psychiatric Totalitarianism and the Legal Rights of Mental Patients, and Modalities of Psychiatric Treatment: Future Shock. These discussions became the basis for proposed legislation and community action. A recent development in some communities is the organization of former patients, now board and care home residents, into residents' councils to discuss services, facilities, etc., and to fight their exploitation by some home operators. News about these activities is reported in "Constructive Action" published by Shirley Burghard.*

The effectiveness of PSHPG's challenges traditional definitions of psychotherapy and the value of conventional theories and practices. Some psychotherapists who acknowledge the effectiveness and value of PSHPG's in changing behavior and feelings of people with psychological problems prefer to consider these "Peer Self-Help Groups" – omitting "Psychotherapy." They do so by referring to the authority of "standard definitions" of psychotherapy. It apparently does not occur to these critics that the effectiveness of PSHPG's requires modification of these traditional definitions. The attempt by some professionals to define psychotherapy only in relation to what they do is an attempt to deny the value of significant others and the role they play in the real life experiences of an individual with

*Copies may be obtained by writing to "Constructive Action," 710 Hickory St., Syracuse, N. Y. 13203.

psychological problems. The most important contribution of PSHPG's to our understanding of psychotherapy may be the increased awareness that these groups foster through constructive human interaction in the daily environment. On this basis, the professional therapist should regard his primary responsibility to determine and support these constructive forces rather than become involved in an intimate relationship with a single client. Continued support for other psychotherapeutic activities of questionable value suggests that these have a latent function that is more important than the manifest one (Merton, 1957). The writer suggested that this function is to serve as a means of social control (Hurvitz, 1973).

In conclusion, it is necessary to point out that only because of our status-centrism as professionals do we regard our activities as heralding the "Third Revolution" in mental health (Hobbs, 1964). It more likely began in Akron when Bill W. and Dr. Bob met and formed what later became AA, setting the general model for the PSHPG movement. Professionals will gain and not lose in stature when they recognize this fact (Hurvitz, 1971). It is now necessary to study PSHPG's with more precise instruments than one clinician's impressions to determine more precisely just what it is about PSHPG's that makes them "work"—and what makes them more effective for some people with problems, deviant, distressed, or disabling behavior than conventional psychotherapy.*

References

Albee, G. W. (1959), *Mental Health Manpower Needs*. New York: Basic Books.
Albee, G. W. (1968), Conceptual models and manpower requirements in psychology. *Am. Psychol.*, 23:317–320.
Alcoholics Anonymous World Services, Inc. (1965), *Twelve Steps and Twelve Traditions*. New York: Alcoholic Anonymous World Services, Inc.
————(1970), *World Directory*. New York: Alcoholics Anonymous World Services, Inc.
Andriola, J. (1956), Letter. *Am. J. Psychiatry*, 113:467.
Anonymous (A Member of Alcoholics Anonymous) (1949), The A. A. program of recovery. In *Rehabilitation of the Handicapped: A Survey of Means and Methods*, ed. W. H. Soden, 234–245. New York: Ronald Press.

*The writer's recent application to NIMH for a small grant to study PSHPG's was denied.

Arnhoff, F. N. (1968), Reassessment of the trilogy: Need, supply, and demand. *Am. Psychol.*, 23:312–316.

Bagley, C. (1968), The evaluation of a suicide prevention scheme by an ecological method. *Soc. Sci. Med.*, 2:1–14.

Baker, B. (1968), Anton Makarenko and the idea of the collective. *Educ. Theory*, 18:285–294.

Bales, R. F. (1944), The therapeutic role of Alcoholics Anonymous as seen by sociologist. *Q. J. Stud. Alcohol*, 5:267–278.

Bassin, A. (1968), Daytop Village. *Psychol. Today*, 2:48–68.

Becker, H. S. (ed.) (1963), *Outsiders: Studies in the Sociology of Deviance*. New York: Free Press.

———(ed.) (1964), *The Other Side*. New York: Free Press.

———, and Geer, B. (1957), Participant observation and interviewing: A comparison. *Hum. Organ.*, 16:28–32.

Beers, C. W. (1948), *A Mind That Found Itself*. New York: Doubleday.

Berger, P. L. (1965), Towards a sociological understanding of psychoanalysis. *Soc. Res.*, 32:26–41.

Berzon, B., and Reisel, J. (1970), For personal growth. *Encountertapes*. Atlanta: Human Development Institute.

———, and Solomon, L. N. (1966), The self-directed therapeutic group: Three studies. *J. Couns. Psychol.*, 13:491–497.

Bierer, J. (1951), *The Day Hospital: An Experiment in Social Psychiatry and Synthoanalytic Psychotherapy*. London: Lewis.

Billington, B., Munns, J. G., and Geis, G. (1969), Purchase of conformity: Ex-narcotic addicts among the bourgeoise. *Soc. Prob.*, 16:456–463.

Bion, W. R. (1961), *Experiences in Groups*. New York: Basic Books.

Blanck, G. (1970), Letter. *Health PAC Bull.*, 3:14.

Blum, E. M., and Blum, R. H. (1967), *Alcoholism: Modern Approaches to Treatment*. San Francisco: Jossey-Bass.

Burghard, S. M. (1970), Constructive Action (for good mental health). Syracuse, N. Y.: American Conference of Therapeutic Self-help/Self-health/Social clubs (ACT) (Mimeograph).

Carter, C. V., Dalsimer, J. S., Morrison, A. P., and Breggins, P. R. (1962), *College Students in a Mental Hospital*. New York: Grune & Stratton.

Casriel, D. (1963), *So Fair a House: The Story of Synanon*. New York: Prentice-Hall.

Chafetz, M. E., and Demone, H. W., Jr. (1962), *Alcoholism and Society*. New York: Oxford University Press.

Cherkas, M. S. (1965), Synanon Foundation: A radical approach to the problem of addiction. *Am. J. Psychiatry*, 121:1065–1068.

Clark, W. H. (1951), *The Oxford Group*. New York: Buchman Associates.

Co-Founder (1957), *Alcoholics Anonymous Comes of Age*. New York: Harper and Brothers, by arrangement with Alcoholics Anonymous Publishing, Inc.

Collier, P. (1967), The house of Synanon. *Ramparts*, 6:45–54.

Connecticut Association for Mental Health, Inc. (1968), *Proceedings of the Institute of Social Clubs for Former Psychiatric Patients*. Hartford, Conn.: Connecticut Mutual Life Insurance Company.

Cook, J. A., and Geis, G. (1957), Forum Anonymous: The techniques of Alcoholics Anonymous applied to prison therapy. *J. Soc. Ther.*, 3:9–13.

Cumming, J., and Cumming, E. (1962) *Ego and Milieu*, New York: Atherton Press.

Darin–Drabkin, H. (1963), *The Other Society*. New York: Harcourt, Brace and World.

Davis, K. (1949), Mental hygiene and the class structure. In *A Study of Interpersonal Relations*, ed. P. Mullaby, 364–385. New York: Grove Press.

Dean, S. R. (1969), Self-help group psychotherapy: Mental patients rediscover will power. Paper presented before the World Mental Health Assembly, Washington, D. C., November 18, 1969. Reprinted in the *Congressional Record*, 91st Congr. 1st Sess., Vol. 115, No. 191, November 19.

de Tocqueville, A. (1835), *Democracy in America*. New York: New American Library, 1961.

Dewey, J. (1925), *Experience and Nature*. LaSalle, Ill.: Open Court Publishing Co.

Drakeford, J. W. (1967), *Integrity Therapy*. Nashville: Boardman Press.

———(1969), *Farewell to the Lonely Crowd*. Waco, Tex. : Word Books.

Eckhardt, W. (1967), Alcoholic values and Alcoholics Anonymous. *Q. J. Stud. Alcohol*, 28:277–287.

Egelson, J., and Egelson, J. F. (1961), *Parents without Partners*. New York:Dutton.

Eglash, A. (1958), Adults Anonymous: A mutual help program for inmates and ex-inmates. *Journal of Criminal Law, Criminology and Police Science*, 49:237–239.

Ellsworth, R. E. (1967), *Nonprofessionals in Psychiatric Rehabilitation*. New York: Appleton-Century-Crofts.

Endore, G. (1960), *Synanon*. New York: Doubleday.

Eysenck, H. J. (1960), The effects of psychotherapy. In *Handbook of Abnormal Psychology*, ed. H. J. Eysenck, 697–725. New York: Basic Books.

Fleischl, M. F., and Waxenberg, S. E. (1964), The therapeutic social club, a step toward social rehabilitation. *Int. Ment. Health Res. Newsl.*, 6:2–6.

Fagin, B. (1968), The Seventh Step Foundation at Preston. *Youth Auth. Q.*, 21:35–42.

Fox, R. (1957), Treatment of alcoholism. In *Alcoholism, Basic Aspects and Treatment*, ed. H. E. Himwich, 163–172. Washington, D. C.: American Association for the Advancement of Science.

Frank, J. D. (1963), *Persuasion and Healing*. New York: Schocken Books.

Gellman, I. P. (1964), *The Sober Alcoholic: An Organizational Analysis of Alcoholics Anonymous*. New Haven, Conn.: College and University Press.

Gordon, W. W., and Babchuk, N. (1959), A typology of voluntary associations. *Am. Sociol. Rev.*, 24:22–29.

Graziano, A. M. (1969), Clinical innovations and the mental health power structure. *Am. Psychol.*, 24:10–18.

Grob, S. (ed.) (1963), *The Community Social Club and the Returning Mental Patient*. Revere, Mass.: R. Novin.

Grosser, C., Henry, W. E., and Kelley, J. G. (eds.) (1969), *Nonprofessionals in the Human Services*. San Francisco: Jossey-Bass.

Group for the Advancement of Psychiatry (1966), *Psychiatry and Public Affairs*. Chicago: Aldine.

Grosz, H. J. (1972), *Recovery, Inc. Survey, A Preliminary Report*. Chicago: National Headquarters of Recovery, Inc.

Guerney, B. G., Jr. (ed.) (1969), *Psychotherapeutic Agents: New Roles for Nonprofessionals, Parents, and Teachers*. New York: Holt, Rinehart and Winston.

Hayman, M. (1956), Current attitudes to alcoholism of psychiatrists in Southern California. *Am. J. Psychiatry*, 112:485–493.

———(1966), *Alcoholism: Mechanism and Management*. Springfield, Ill.: Charles C. Thomas.

Hill, M. J., and Blane, H. T. (1967), Evaluation of psychotherapy with alcoholics; a critical review. *Q. J. Stud. Alcohol*, 28:76–104.

Hobbs, N. (1964), Mental health's third revolution. *Am. J. Orthopsychiatry*, 34:822–833.

Holzberg, J. P., Knapp, R. N. and Turner, J. (1966), Companionship with the mentally ill: Effects on the personalities of college students. *Psychiatry*, 29:395–405.

Holzinger, R. (1965), Synanon through the eyes of a visiting psychologist. *Q. J. Stud. Alcohol*, 26:304–309.

Hook, S. (ed.) (1960), *Psychoanalysis, Scientific Method, and Philosophy*. New York: Grove Press (Evergreen Books).

Hurvitz, N. (1967), Marital problems following psychotherapy with one spouse. *J. Cons. Psychol.*, 31:38–47.

———(1970), Peer self-help psychotherapy groups and their implication for psychotherapy. *Psychother. : Theory, Res. Pract.* 7:41–49.

———(1971), Peer self-help psychotherapy groups. *Radical Ther.*, 1:5.

———(1973), Psychotherapy as a means of social control. *J. Cons. Clin. Psychol.*, 40:232–239.

James, W. (1925), *The Philosophy of William James*. Drawn From His Own Works; With an Introduction by Horace M. Kallen. New York: Modern Library.

Johnson, H. K. (1956), Letter. *Am. J. Psychiatry*, 113:36.

Jones, M. (1953), *The Therapeutic Community*. New York: Basic Books.

Kadushin, C. (1966), The friends and supporters of psychotherapy: On social circles in urban life. *Am. Sociol. Rev.*, 31:786–802.

Katz, A. H. (1970), Self-help organizations and volunteer participation in social welfare. *Soc. Work*, 15:51–60.

———, Husek, J., MacDonald C. J. (comps.) (1967), Self-help and rehabilitation, an annotated bibliography. Los Angeles: University of California, School of Public Health (Offset).

Koegler, R. R., and Brill, N. Q. (1967), *Treatment of Psychiatric Outpatients*. New York: Appleton-Century-Crofts.

Kramer, R. M. (1969), *Participation of the Poor, Comparative Community Case Studies in the War on Poverty*. Englewood Cliffs, N. J.: Prentice-Hall.

LaPiere, R. (1959), *The Freudian Ethic*. New York: Duel, Sloan & Pearce, Inc.

Larrabee, E. (1960), *The Self-Conscious Society*. Garden City, N. Y.: Doubleday.

Lee, D. T. (1966), Recovery, Inc.: A well role model. *Q. Camarille*, 2:35–36.

———(1971), Recovery, Inc.: Aid in the transition from hospital to community. *Ment. Hyg.*, 5:194–198.

Leon, D. (1969), *The Kibbutz: A New Way of Life*. Oxford: Pergamon Press.

Lewin, G. W. (ed.) (1948), *Resolving Social Conflicts*. New York: Harper and Brothers.

Low, A. A. (1945), The combined system of group psychotherapy and self-help as practiced by Recovery, Inc. *Sociometry*, 8:332–337.

———(1950), *Mental Health through Will Training: A System of Self-Help in Psychotherapy as Practiced by Recovery, Incorporated*. Boston: Christopher Publishing House.

———(1959), Recovery, Inc.: A project for rehabilitating post psychotic and long term neurotic patients. In *Rehabilitation of the Handicapped: A Survey Of Means and Methods*, ed. W. H. Soden, 213–226. New York: Ronald Press.

Maier, H. (ed.) (1965), *Group Work as Part of Residental Treatment*. New York: National Association of Social Workers.

Mann, M. (1958), *Marty Mann's New Primer on Alcoholism*. New York: Holt, Rinehart and Winston.

———(1970), *Marty Mann Answers Your Questions about Drinking and Alcoholism*. New York: Holt, Rinehart and Winston.

Maxwell, M. A. (1962), Alcoholics Anonymous: An interpretation. In *Society, Culture, and Drinking Patterns*, ed. D. J. Pittman, 277–585. New York: Wiley.

McCall, G. J. (1969), *Issues in Participant Observation: A Text and Reader*. New York: Addison-Wesley.

McCarthy, R. G. (1958), Alcoholism: Attitudes and attacks, 1775–1935. In *Understanding Alcoholism*, ed., S. D. Bacon, 12–21. Philadelphia: American Academy of Political and Social Science.

McCartney, J. (1966), Overt transference. *J. Soc. Res.*, 2:227–237.

McKinney, J. (1966), *Constructive Typology and Social Theory*. New York: Appleton-Century-Crofts.

McNeill, J. T. (1961), *A History of the Cure of Souls*. New York: Harper and Brothers.

Merton, R. K. (1957), *Social Theory and Social Structure*. Rev. enlarged ed. Glencoe, Ill.: Free Press.

Millman, L. I., and Chilman, C. S. (eds.) (no date), Poor people at work. An annotated bibliography on semi-professionals in education, health, and welfare services. Washington, D. C.: U. S. Department of Health, Education, and Welfare.

Moreno, J. L. (1960), *The Sociometry Reader*. Glencoe, Ill.: Free Press.

Mowrer, O. H. (1964), *The New Group Therapy*. Princeton, N. J.: Van Nostrand.

———(1966), Integrity Therapy: A Self-help approach. *Psychother.: Theory Res. Pract.*, 3:114–119.

———(1969), Integrity Groups Today. Paper originally presented under the title, Group therapy and therapeutic communities examined in the light of behavior modification principles, at the First Southern California Conference on Behavior Modification, Los Angeles, October.

Mueller, E. E. (1964), Rebels with a cause: A report on Synanon. *Am. J. Psychother.*, 18:272–284.

National Association of Social Workers (1960), *Use of Groups in the Psychiatric Setting*. New York: National Association of Social Workers.

Nelson, N. (ed.) (1957), *Freud and the 20th Century*. New York: Meridian Books.

Parsons, T. (1951), *The Social System*. Glencoe, Ill.: Free Press.

———, and Bales, R. F. (1955), *Family, Socialization and Interaction Process*. Glencoe, Ill.: Free Press.

Patrick, S. W. (1965), Our way of life: A short history of Narcotics Anonymous Inc. In *Drug Addiction and Youth*, ed. E. Harms, 148–157. Oxford: Pergamon Press.

Piette, M. (1936), *John Wesley and the Evolution of Protestantism*. London: Sheed and Ward.

Poser, E. G. (1966), The effect of therapist's training on group therapeutic outcome. *J. Cons. Psychol.*, 30:283–289.

Rangel, L. (1968), Broadcast No. 7934-E.E. 2047, University of California (Sunday, October 20).

Rausch, H. L., and Rausch, C. L. (1968), *The Halfway House Movement: A Search for Sanity*. New York: Appleton-Century-Crofts.

Reiff, P. (1961), *Freud—The Mind of the Moralist*. Garden City, N. Y.: Doubleday (Anchor Books).

———, and Riessman, F. (1965), The indigenous nonprofessional: A strategy of change in community action and community mental health programs. *Commun. Ment. Health J. Monog.*, 1:3–32.

Riessman, F. (1965), The "helper" therapy principle. *Soc. Work*, 10:27–32.

———, and Miller, S. M. (1964), Social change versus the "psychiatric world view." *Am. J. Orthopsychiatry*, 34:29–38.

Rioch, M. J. (1966), Changing concepts in the training of therapists. *J. Cons. Psychol.*, 30:290–292.

———,Elkes, C., Flint, A. A., Usdansky, B. S., Newman, R. G., and Silber, E. (1963), National Institute of Mental Health pilot study in training mental health counselors. *Am. J. Orthopsychiatry*, 33:678–689.

Ripley, H. S., and Jackson, J. K. (1959), Therapeutic factors in Alcoholics Anonymous. *Am. J. Psychiatry*, 116:44–50.

Rogers, C. R. (1951), *Client-Centered Therapy*. Boston: Houghton Mifflin.

Ross, L. (1963), *Vertical and Horizontal*. New York: Simon and Schuster.

Ruitenbeek, H. (ed.) (1962), *Psychoanalysis and Social Science*. New York: Dutton.

Sagarin, E. (1969), *Odd Man In :Societies of Deviants in America*. Chicago: Quadrangle Books.

Sands, B. (1964), *My Shadow Ran Fast*. New York: Prentice-Hall.

Sargant, W. (1964), Psychiatric treatment, here and in England. *Atl. Mon.*, 214:88–95.

Schofield, W. (1964), *Psychotherapy: The Purchase of Friendship*. Englewood Cliffs, N. J.: Prentice-Hall.

Schorer, C. E., Lowinger, P., Sullivan, T., and Hartlaub, G. H. (1968), Improvement without treatment. *Dis. Nerv. Syst.*, 29:100–104.

Scodel, A. (1964), Inspirational group therapy: A study of Gamblers Anonymous. *Am. J. Psychother.*, 18:115–125.

Seeley, J. (1967), *The Americanization of the Unconscious*. New York: International Science Press.

Shelley, J. A., and Bassin, A. (1965), Daytop Lodge—A new treatment approach for drug addicts. *Corr. Psychiatr. J. Soc. Ther.* 11 : 186–195.

Sills, D. L. (1957), *The Volunteers : Means and Ends in a National Organisation*. Glencoe. Ill.: Free Press.

Simmel, E. (1948), Alcoholism and addiction. *Psychoanal.*, 17 : 6–31.

Smith, P. L. (1941), Alcoholics Anonymous. *Psychiatr. Q.* 15 : 554–562.

Sobey, F. (1969), Volunteer services in mental health: An annotated bibliography, 1955 to 1969. Chevy Chase, Md.: National Institute of Mental Health.

Sobey, F. (1970), *The Nonprofessional Revolution in Mental Health*. New York: Columbia University Press.

Stein, M., Vidich, A. J., and White, D. M. (eds.) (1960), *Identity and Anxiety*. Glencoe, Ill.: Free Press.

Stewart, D. A. (1955), The dynamics of fellowship as illustrated in Alcoholics Anonymous. *Q. J. Stud. Alcohol*, 16:251–262.

Sutherland, J. (ed.) (1959), *Psychoanalysis and Contemporary Thought*. New York: Grove Press.

Szasz, T. S. (1961a), The uses of naming and the origin of the myth of mental illness. *Am. Psychol.*, 18:59–65.

——— (1961b), *The Myth of Mental Illness; Foundations of a Theory of Personal Conduct*. New York: Harper and Row.

Taber, M., Quay, H. C., Mark, H., and Nealey, V. (1969), Disease ideology and mental health research. *Soc. Prob.*, 16:349–357.

Tiebout, H. M. (1944), Therapeutic mechanisms of Alcoholics Anonymous. *Am. J. Psychiatr.*, 100:468–473.

Thigpen, C. H., and Cleckley, H. M. (1964). Some reflections on psychoanalysis, hypnosis, and faith healing. In *The Conditioning Therapies*, eds. J. Wolpe, A. Salter, and L. J. Reyna, 96–111. New York: Holt, Rinehart and Winston.

Toch. H. (1965), *The Social Psychology of Social Movements*. New York: Bobbs-Merrill.

Torrey, E. F. (1969), The case for the indigenous therapist. *Arch. Gen. Psychiatr.*, 20: 365–373.

Trecker, H. B. (ed.) (1956), *Group Work in the Psychiatric Setting*. New York: Whiteside, Inc., and William Morrow.

Trice, H. (1958), Alcoholics Anonymous. In *Understanding Alcoholism*, ed. S. D. Bacon, 108–116. Philadelphia: American Academy of Political and Social Science.

—— (1959), The affiliation motive and readiness to join Alcoholics Anonymous. *Q. J. Stud. Alcohol*, 20:313–320.

——, and Roman, P. M. (1970a), Sociopsychological predictors of successful affiliation with Alcoholics Anonymous. *Soc. Psychiatr.*, 5:51–59.

——, and Roman, P. M. (1970b), Delabeling, relabeling, and Alcoholics Anonymous. *Soc. Prob.*, 17:538–546.

Trow, M. (1957), Comment on "Participant observation and interviewing: A comparison." *Hum. Organ.*, 16:33–35.

Verinis, J. S. (1970), Therapeutic effectiveness of untrained volunteers with chronic patients. *J. Cons. Clin. Psychol.*, 34:152–155.

Volkman, R., and Cressey, D. R. (1963), Differential association and the rehabilitation of drug addicts. *Am. J. Soc.*, 69:129–142.

Wagonfeld, S., and Wolowitz, H. M. (1968), Obesity and the self-help group: A look at TOPS. *Ame. J. Psychiatr.*, 125:249–252.

Weber, M. (1947), *The Theory of Social and Economic Organization*, Trans. A. M. Henderson and T. Parsons. New York: Oxford University Press.

Wechsler, H. (1960), The self-help organization in the mental health field: Recovery, Incorporated, a case study. *J. Nerv. Ment. Dis.*, 130:297–314.

Weinberg, M. S. (1968), The problems of midgets and dwarfs and organizational remedies: A study of the Little People of America. *J. Health Soc. Behav.*, 9:65–71.

Weintraub, D., Lissak, M., and Amzon, Y. (1969), *Moshava, Kibbutz, and Moshav*. Ithaca, N. Y.: Cornell University Press.

Wilbur, G., and Muensterberger, W. (eds.) (1951), *Psychoanalysis and Culture*. New York: International Universities Press.

Wilder, J. R. (1963), Self-help in mental illness. *Med. Practition.*, 11:14–18.

Williams, R. M., Jr. (1960), *American Society, A Sociological Interpretation*. 2nd ed., rev. New York: Knopf.

Wintrob, R., and Wittkower, E. D. (1968), Witchcraft in Liberia and its psychiatric implications. In *An Evaluation of the Results of the Psychotherapies*. ed. S. Lesse, 305–317. Springfield, Ill.: Charles C. Thomas.

Wright, C. R., and Hyman, H. H. (1958), Voluntary association memberships of American adults: Evidence from national sample surveys. *Am. Sociol. Rev.*, 23: 284–294.

Yablonsky, L. (1965), *The Tunnel Back: Synanon*. New York: Macmillan.

PART II

SOCIOLOGISTS
AND PSYCHOTHERAPISTS

INTRODUCTION

PSYCHOTHERAPISTS make up a professionalized occupation and share numerous characteristics with members of other occupations. Their professionalism intermingles with degrees of occupational identity, images, and commitment and career patterns. Typically, they must adapt to some form of organizational life, as well as to new occupations that emerge and compete with them. Sociologists share these common features of an occupation with psychotherapists but have an additional characteristic that is particularly relevant: one branch of sociology specializes in the study of occupations and thus brings to its interaction with psychotherapy a frame of reference for examining occupations in general, and professionalized ones, in particular.

The authors in Part II approach psychotherapists from this frame of reference, seeing them as occupants of dynamic occupational roles that are much in flux. Professors Dommermuth and Bucher, for example, examine the rather unique situation in which a new occupational specialization within psychiatry—community psychiatry—is fitfully emerging. In their article "The Psychotherapist in Community Mental Health," based on their observation and field experiences with two psychiatric residencies and two Community psychiatry programs, they sketch out two types of training programs that have emerged in response to trends in social psychiatry, civil rights, and poverty demands. One type, the elective model, continues to be based in dynamic psychotherapy, but trainees are exposed to a variety of treatment methods in which they deal primarily with other mental health professionals, and not directly with patients. These training experiences are optional for the trainee and supplement a traditional psychiatric education.

A second type, however, is a formally designated subspecialty with its curriculum, entrance requirements, and an academic timetable. Courses are sharply oriented to the nature of community processes, to organizational life, and to intervention procedures within these contexts. The authors conclude that the later career patterns of those who come from subspecialty training experience differ sharply from those who experience the eclectic type. The former produce those strongly committed to the new occupation; the latter tend to either "dabble" in community psychiatry or practice in both traditional or community psychiatry at the same time.

The subspecialty training patterns would logically emerge as the logical process for training of the new occupation. But the authors conclude that vulnerabilities in the community psychiatry movement strongly suggest that the eclectic, or elective, model will continue to thrive in training those who practice community psychiatry. From this assessment, the authors discern a third trend: training community psychiatrists in inter and intrapersonal phenomena but emphasizing the use of this knowledge in a range of community contexts.

The authors stimulate basic research questions: What are the social and psychological processes that operate to produce a new occupation? How does this new occupation sustain its identity vis-a-vis the parent occupation from which it springs? What other socialization patterns exist in the welter of community psychiatry activities? How does the interaction between a recently spawned occupational role (community psychiatrist) and the training organization within which it is nurtured shape the resulting identity, commitment, and subsequent career pattern?

Professor Tucker, in "Therapeutic Sociology in a Mental

Health Service" focuses on his experience as a sociologist in a metropolitan hospital. His chief theme is the struggle he experienced in maintaining his occupational identity, even in a relatively congenial work environment. He also comments in detail on research problems in maintaining rapport while entering into the hospital setting. Using careful participant–observation he documents his efforts to install a record-keeping system and its manual in the mental health services unit and to mount and sustain sociological research in a large and complex hospital organization. Defining "therapeutic sociology" as a "sociologists' developmental participation, involvement, and examination of therapeutic activities," Tucker presents a detailed narrative of what happened as he pursued his occupation. Despite initial cooperation and acceptance of the need for accurate record keeping about the therapeutic processes, his efforts to establish a system that he, as a sociologist, could direct largely failed. Over a year and a half his role was "limited to follow-up research with the sociologist serving in a technical role rather than a professional one." His occupational role, as he saw it, was threatened. Tucker developed intraservice research, but organizational support within the unit waned steadily. Consistently the service unit reacted to pressures from outside groups who insisted on evidence of the unit's effectiveness, while at the same time showing little understanding of the complexities and difficulties of research.

Much of the same theme prevails when Tucker assesses his overall experiences as one who engaged in "therapeutic sociology." His effect on the "doing of therapy" was minor; his role as a sociologist was sharply altered by the organization in that he shaped his activities to therapeutic activities, foregoing research interests in developing records, for example. Furthermore he found that he had to engage in negotiations in order to remain in the "stream of therapeutic activities" at all. Tucker advises sociologists who wish to do "therapeutic sociology" to reorder their priorities to more harmoniously match those of therapy personnel. This means they must put research last and adapt to therapeutic activities, rather than the reverse.

Clearly the most basic questions raised by Tucker for further consideration are: What factors account for one occupational member retaining his occupational identity in one situation while others lose theirs in varied settings? What threats do the sociologist consistently pose in working with psychotherapists? To what extent do professionals in various occupations conform to their alleged ethics when pressed by organization forces to violate them?

In the article "What Troubles the Trouble Shooters?" the focus shifts from the sociologist to a sociological examination of the psychiatrist. Professor Daniels concentrates on those occupation-based concerns and anxieties that psychiatrists express as they react to the content of their professional roles. Her data does not support the hypothesis that these worries vary between psychiatrists in private practice and those employed by formal organizations such as hospitals and clinics, although those in military life tend to be somewhat different. Her work does point, however, to some of the ingredients in a psychiatrist's occupational self-image that may be disturbing to him. Using a sentence-completion device for collecting data, she analyzes self-descriptions of psychiatrists to isolate these negative aspects of the profession's self-image. Apparently dominating these concerns is the loneliness inherent in practice. Although it seems that those in organizational practice would feel less isolated, her data does not show this. Psychiatric practice, regardless of setting, seems to generate loneliness. In contrast, psychiatrists are not very concerned about their effectiveness, even though it is a widely discussed question in many circles: they believe they have a powerful, almost God-like image. They clearly deplore such a perception of them by patients, but attribute to fellow psychiatrists characteristics that are consistent with patients' views.

Less prominent, but none the less revealing, are other features of the occupation: psychiatrists are very critical of colleagues, feeling they are often arrogant and unfriendly and show a need for security. A small minority even believe many of their professional peers suffer mental illness. Another interesting theme is the feeling by a minority that the occupation exposes them to temptations such as using patients to satisfy their needs to seduce women.

Since Daniels focuses exclusively on negative aspects of the occupations the question arises: What are the positive aspects of the psychiatrist's self-image? What is there about military life that produces differences in self-concern when contrasted to therapists working in more traditional settings? Since occupational identity is related to occupational commitment, how committed to the *practice* of psychiatry are psychiatrists? Finally, are there specific types of organizational structures, such as collegial ones, where the sense of isolation tends to significantly decline?

Finally, a recent occupational development, not only in psychiatry but across many other health-delivery systems, is examined. Both Professor Ritzer in "Indigenous Nonprofessional in Community Mental Health: Boon or Boondoggle?" and Professor Albrecht in "The Indigenous Mental Health Worker: The Cure-All for What Ailment?" explore nonprofessionals from distinct subcultural minorities who supplement and often replace the professional and paraprofessional health worker. Ritzer places this development in proper perspective by observing that it is part of the far-ranging conflict between clients and professionals. This "revolt of the client" is largely a resistance of minority-group members—Blacks, students, women—against the power and authority vested in professionals. One method for meeting the demands of these minority groups, and producing new jobs as well, has been the use of indigeneous nonprofessionals. Theoretically this new breed of mental health worker would be in a position to understand the emotional needs of minority-group members, acting as their representatives among mental health helping agencies. It was assumed that mental health professionals would welcome additional manpower, especially from a source that would be no threat to them. Ritzer concludes, however, that the movement has been far more a boondoggle than a boon, that the new careers movement, including the indigenous mental-health worker, has been largely coopted by the present system, eliminating it as a source of much-needed change in health-delivery systems. Ritzer offers many reasons for the "boondoggle": the new occupations actually act to pacify neighborhoods rather than produce meaningful change; they merely reinforce a focus upon the individual as "sick," ignoring institutional aspects; jobs performed by indigenous workers are meaningless and lacking in a "career" potential. "Indigenous nonprofessionals were doomed to lives as 'marginal men' acceptable to neither professionals nor clients." According to Ritzer, they have become merely "a part of the problem rather than part of the solution." He argues that the role is impossible to fill, beset by a myriad of intense contradictions.

Albrecht agrees with Ritzer's criticisms but concludes that such an ideological position blinds him to many facets of the movement that do not fit into a blanket assessment of it as a failure. That is, Ritzer's judgment "is based more on ideological position than on empirical data." Such a position is not appropriate for scientific endeavors Albrecht points out, citing evidence that shows the movement has been relatively successful where it has been assumed that the major goal was to increase the effectiveness of therapy and service. If, however, one uses, as Ritzer does, a variety of ideological goals such as enhancement of political power or the reduction of the "revolt of the client," then the movement is bound to be a failure.

This exchange between Ritzer and Albrecht points out provocative aspects of this highly controversial subject. Should the new careers movement be evaluated by a systems, rather than a goal-attainment, model? What temperamental demands does the occupational role make on its occupants? Can the concept of cooptation be operationalized so that these criticisms of the program can be tested objectively? What have been the range of responses by professionals to the recent rapid development of paraprofessionals and nonprofessionals in their areas of expertise? Lastly, and ironically, has the movement resulted in the opening of upward mobility channels for members of minority groups so that they leave behind an even more depowered and segregated group than before the movement was inaugurated?

From the standpoint of occupational sociology the entire

discussion focuses attention on the question of occupational *mandate* and *license*. An occupation possesses a societal mandate that gives it the exclusive right to perform certain tasks. What effect have the entire paraprofessional and nonprofessional movements had on the societal support for mental-health professionals to "do therapy?" For that matter, has there ever been a conclusive societal mandate among them to "treat" the mentally ill?

Chapter 4

Paul R. Dommermuth
and Rue Bucher

THE PSYCHOTHERAPIST IN
COMMUNITY MENTAL HEALTH

AMONG medical specialties, psychiatry has long been conspicuous for its segmentalization. The visibility of various segments in psychiatry may have come about because they have tended to be organized along ideological lines, they represent different responses to the central questions of the field: What is the nature of mental illness? How should it be approached? The members of these groups take up polemical positions with regard to these issues, which become loosely organized as coherent professional ideologies (Strauss *et al.*, 1964). The latest segment to emerge in the area of mental health is known as "community psychiatry."

We are concerned with assessing the current development of community psychiatry and the stages through which it passes, particularly how it approaches the recruitment and social-ization of new members. An emerging segment, like an emerging specialty or profession, moves through a series of successive, but overlapping, stages.*

The first of these stages involves a great deal of definitional activity on the part of the members of the new segment. They spend much time discussing the need for new perspectives or foci, proffering definitions of what it should be like, and

---

*The elucidation of the developmental stages in professions is the focus of R. Bucher, *The Natural History of Professions*, a monograph in preparation.

debating what sorts of activities it should and can undertake. The object is to map out professional territory and stake claims to the area. (Hughes, 1958)

Second, the emerging segment weights the requirements to develop these new activities. What institutional conditions are necessary to carry out the projected work of the segment? Can these be found in existing institutional settings? Must institutions be modified or must new institutions be created? At this stage there is generally a good deal of empirical testing of institutional settings with these questions in mind.

The next stage to emerge, if the segment is to progress, involves the validation of the segment's claims by significant publics (other professional groups, various lay publics, numerous governmental agencies, or perhaps all of these). Here the emerging segment must begin to concern itself with the problem of generations: how to recruit new members, and how to train and socialize them into carrying out the mission of the segment. As these problems are worked through, the segment may be said to be entering another, advanced stage of development: *consolidation*. We believe that socialization processes must be worked out in order for consolidation to occur.

The above model bears considerable resemblance to the processes characteristic of occupations undergoing professionalization, about which there exists a vast literature within the sociology of occupations. There is, however, one major and highly consequential difference. The people involved in the emergence of a new segment or specialty are already accredited professionals. No one is questioning their status, since they generally come out of existing, established professional bodies.

This is significant because the relationship of the emerging group to the established groups that fostered it constitutes one major focus of conflict during and often beyond the emergent stage. For example, persistent conflict has been observed in the relationship of surgical specialities to the parent group, general surgery. The phenomenon is not associated only with the ideological cast of psychiatric segments.

Community psychiatry can be taken as illustrative of this model of emerging segments. In this case, however, we have more information on the conditions leading to its emergence than is available on most other professional groups. Two independent sets of developments, one within psychiatry and related disciplines and the other growing out of political movements in America and elsewhere, virtually propelled community psychiatry into being.

Two major developments in and around psychiatry paved the way for the growth of community psychiatry among the mental health professions. One, undoubtedly, was the series of epidemiological studies, beginning with the pioneering work of Faris and Dunham (1939) and continuing through the work of Hollingshead and Redlich (1958) to such studies as the Midtown Manhattan series (Srole *et al.*, 1962). These studies raised a number of basic questions about the need, distribution, and quality of the present systems of mental-health care. Despite the nagging methodological hassles that still plague such works, the consistency of the findings makes it difficult for mental-health professionals to ignore the clear implications: People in the lower strata of our society have the greatest need for these services and receive the least, and, at times, possibly damaging, care.

In the fifties came the movement known variously as "social psychiatry," "milieu therapy," or "therapeutic communities." These groups attacked the organization of the institutions in which those labeled "mentally ill" were incarcerated. The object was to reform these institutions and thereby lessen the damage their inmates suffer. A psychiatric ideology emerged that placed the etiology of mental illness in interpersonal and social arrangements and the alleviation of it in the manipulation of interpersonal relations. During the past decade many state facilities throughout the nation have undergone some measure of reform, although in our view, it has not been sufficient.

In many places the urgency of getting patients out of these large, custodial hospitals counteracted somewhat the inevitable process of institutionalism that accompanies prolonged hospitalization. However, where the cycle of hospitalism is broken, there remain serious problems. Prior questions emerge: How do we keep patients from landing in hospitals in the first place?

How do we keep them from returning? Thus, the tenets of social psychiatry logically pointed toward what today is termed community psychiatry. The next step was to work within communities to prevent patients from coming to hospitals and to aid them in not returning once they were released.

In this sense social psychiatry might be characterized as a child of the fifties. Community psychiatry developed in the sixties, in conjunction with some striking social movements within our society, namely, the civil rights movements and the "discovery" of poverty in America. Out of the convergence of these movements and the resulting political pressures much of the current validation of community psychiatry arose. These groups drew glaring attention to facts that some professionals had acknowledged for years: Our health professions and institutions remain notoriously unresponsive to demonstrated need and are highly unimaginative when asked to develop innovative approaches to such problems.

In this climate of criticisms, federal and other levels of government moved to make funds available for large-scale community-oriented psychiatry efforts. In so doing these agencies were validating the turf staked out by community psychiatry and its claim that there is a demonstrable need to develop new means for treating mental illness in a mass society. By providing such funds, these agencies were indirectly saying that this segment of the professional community does possess the expertise to carry out this mission. Unfortunately, the professional community was still embroiled in that controversy.

When various governmental agencies moved in, community psychiatry was in the throes of definition, though there had been a few forays into institutional testing (Caplan, 1965). A number of the lively debates of this period are to be found in the writings of such spokesmen as Sabshin (1966), Diesenhaus (1968), McGee and Wexler (1969), Dunham (1965), and Kubie (1968). The issues remain unresolved, but this offers small comfort to those who wish to meet the social challenge or who are faced with the immediate necessity of using federal funds. They have had to proceed on the basis of the current theories with only a modicum of empirical testing. (This accounts for the fact that today we observe the operation of a number of models of "how-to-do" community psychiatry.)

It is more important however, that community psychiatry is faced with the necessity of recruiting and training people. How is this developmental process evolving? We would expect differences in the development of socialization processes to manifest themselves in the form of different types of training programs. But this situation is further complicated by another, highly significant, observation. Psychiatry, for some time, has been pursued by its allied health professions. We use the term "pursued" deliberately. The development of the social psychiatry movement effected a drastic realignment of relations between psychiatrists (MD's) and "auxiliary" mental health professions. These new treatment modalities tended to diminish the importance of professional (in particular, medical) credentials, and many allied mental health professionals—clinical psychologists and social workers—succeeded in pressing claims for equal expertise in these new therapeutic techniques (Schatzman and Bucher, 1964).

Thus, at the same time that community psychiatry fitfully moves towards institutionalizing its socialization processes in the form of training programs, other mental health disciplines, such as psychology, also have been on the move, presenting a challenge to the authority and autonomy of psychiatry as a medical specialty and leading to interprofessional conflicts over psychiatric supremacy. The thrust of community psychology, the major source of this challenge, must be taken into account; it is making strong claims in this area, and "it isn't letting any grass grow under its feet" (Diesenhaus, 1968; McGee and Wexler, 1969).

The following observations are not the result of specific research projects dealing with the types of socializing programs psychiatrists and psychologists have developed in community mental health; instead they are the by-product of two intensive studies directed toward other highly related issues. The first was conducted by Strauss and his colleagues (1964) and dealt with psychiatric ideologies and institutions. The second is a longitudinal study of professional socialization that included two different psychiatric residency programs (Bucher *et al.*, 1969). In addition, the authors have been participant–observers as faculty, research preceptors, and consultants in several of the programs cited.

The Response of Traditional Programs

In approaching these questions our perspective has been comparative. By this we mean that the new developments of community psychiatry are more clearly understood when compared with the benchmark data of traditional programs.

Since World War II the dominant segment in American psychiatry has been the psychodynamic, one-to-one therapeutic model developed by Freud and his disciples. During this period psychiatry moved away from a view of mental illness rooted in a biological etiology toward one firmly established and rooted in psychological factors (Smith, 1952; Strauss *et al.*, 1964). In the past two decades this segment of psychiatry has been responsible for training the vast majority of the country's psychiatrists. This type of training clearly spells out what treatment activities are right and proper for psychiatrists, as well as other mental health professions; the conditions under which the activities are optimally performed (and conversely those under which it is impossible to practice); and the ideal sets of social structural and interactional relationships that must accrue if therapeutic efforts are to be successful.

The logical outgrowth of institutionalizing these ideas in training programs is the emergence of patterned career lines for the products of such programs. At the individual level this approach not only spells out what trainees learn about where and how they should practice; it structures the career alternatives from which they may choose and eventually accounts for the career lines they follow. Collectively this produces a distinctive pattern or flavor to the mental health care dispensed by these professionals.

For example, completion of training under this traditional

model usually leads to a career line that revolves around the private practice of psychiatry in office settings. For variation, this may be coupled with practice in a variety of in-patient settings dealing with limited ranges of mental illness or with choices from an array of subspecialty-like areas of treatment modalities: child, adolescent, forensic, academic, geriatric, group, and family practice. Most often these additions to private practice are conducted within a Freudian framework, the work of neo-, pseudo- and anti-Freudians notwithstanding. For purposes of comparison, consider how these patterns emerge within the socialization program of one such traditional institution.

PPI is a psychiatric institute and an integral part of a large general medical complex. It has 80 beds subdivided into five wards. The residency is a well-established program, the aim of which is to produce a general psychiatrist well grounded in analytically based, insight-oriented psychiatry. This goal is achieved by providing ample opportunity and exposure to a specific range of mental illness in multiple settings. Compared to other programs with which we have had contact, this training comes under the careful and intensive supervision of a large staff comprised of psychoanalysts or analysts-in-training. The experiences are reinforced by extensive formal and informal links to the local analytic institute.

Residents undergo a variety of training experiences, but the bulk of these—which clearly establish the core of the program and for which residents are rewarded—involve one-to-one activities in traditional settings dealing with traditional problems amenable to this mode of therapy.

Thus, it is not surprising that most of the trainees, upon completion of their training and military obligations, enter the local psychiatric community as private practitioners. (Bucher, 1965; Bucher et al., 1969) A majority remain in the metropolitan area during the early stages of their careers, which is partly explained by the high proportion who enroll in analytic training locally.

That such a program is successful is beyond doubt. It is not uncommon for trainees to have their time completely booked shortly after leaving the program. The question is not one of success, but how it will incorporate the thrust of the community mental health movement into its own traditional approach. Observations over the past three years suggest that change is coming, but from the viewpoint of those outside the system it is much too slow.

Alternatives to the Traditional Model

In contrast to traditional programs are four developing programs in psychiatry and psychology. (Our observations are based on two psychiatric residencies, where we were participant–observers over a period of four years, and two community psychology programs, where we served as either faculty member or research consultant for three years.) Although these programs are still quite new, it is safe to predict that they eventually will differ considerably from traditional programs in terms of the nature, scope, distribution, and quality of care they seek to provide.

The programs may be separated into two distinct types: the elective model (at times are tempted to call this the "hit-and-miss" model) and the elaborated or "subspecialty" model.

The elective programs are loosely structured, and, at times, chaotic. The goals of the two programs we observed are stated in general terms; organizational conflict was aroused most often when efforts were made to make these goals explicit and operational.

Both psychiatric programs started with an expressed interest in the mental health problems of specific neighborhoods in the city. Prolonged negotiations were opened with neighborhood groups about the kinds of services they lacked and the priorities they placed on meeting these needs. This resulted in a pattern which seems to hold in other parts of the country: in the development of some type of affiliated programs in an agency through which trainees may rotate for various lengths of time. The training experiences *attempt* to provide new approaches, but differ from the traditional only insofar as they offer genuinely different opportunities to make therapeutic interventions. Our observations suggest that opportunities where insight-oriented, dynamic psychotherapy is not automatically the treatment of choice, are not prevalent. Trainees are, however, asked to become involved in an array of treatment modalities, including crisis intervention, a variety of group therapies, marital counseling, family therapy, and case and agency consultation in which the responsibilities of the trainees are with other mental health professionals and not directly with individual patients. This latter point has important, direct career consequences.

All too often trainees of other types are later hired to administrate and plan these innovative attempts, a situation for which they are little prepared and in which their chances of survival are slim. The positions often require responses of a political nature and are beyond the capabilities of these young professionals. Furthermore, they are often asked to act using conceptual armamentarium they do not fully understand, such as the sharp delineation of mental health care for a specific catchment area using public health concepts of primary, secondary, and tertiary treatment.

The consequences of such involvement is often undesirable and unanticipated for both the mental health staff members and the community needing their services. It can result in value shifts that restrict freedom in terms of treatment choices and the autonomy of the young professionals involved. It may eventually lead to a stress on political skills to the relative neglect of service skills. Lastly, it is conceivable that such practices may perpetuate differential treatment patterns, an evil most community mental health practitioners hope to eliminate. These two programs, and the community psychiatry movement in general, have failed to grapple seriously with the political implications of their work.

All of these experiences are elective or optional; they are taken in conjunction with the rest of the training program. In one program with a strong psychoanalytic flavor trainees were subjected to considerable pressure to forego these experiences. In a few cases failure to do so led to interpretations that the trainees were "resisting learning."

The dominant term for this type of program seems to be *eclecticism:* Trainees are not forced into a lock-step sequence; they have alternatives to the dominant professional identity produced by the training institution. The products of this type of program usually emerge with the traditional bag of tricks plus a new perspective on the profession as it relates to community mental health problems.

The training staffs do not expect this new frame of reference to be fully developed. Instead, it is hoped that the trainee's appetite has been whetted and that these new concerns will blossom into some serious commitment, expressed by some formal and explicit efforts to fulfill the mission of community psychiatry and fill in knowledge gaps in its theoretical foundations. We found people starting courses about the nature of communities, the use of social systems analysis, and the social structure of complex organizations in the health area. At times these were offered with the help of outsiders or by a staff member with serious interest in the area.

One must ask what happens to those who complete such programs and how they differ, if at all, from those trained in the elaborated or subspecialty type. As expected, the trainees of such loosely organized programs vary considerably in the development of their commitment to community psychiatry, which often leads critics to prophesy an early death for the movement. However, our tracing of the early career lines of graduates of these two residencies reveal two reasonably distinct career patterns.

The first consists of those who maintain interest in the area but are employed and involved primarily outside it. They work "at it" in a somewhat dilettantish fashion and are best characterized as "dabblers." While our observations may have ended too soon, it appears that this group will not follow serious careers in community mental health.

In contrast, the second group starts off with considerable interest, taking full- or nearly full-time positions in the area of relatively high salaries. Gradually, some of this group shift their time commitments to private practice and correspondingly devote less time to community psychiatry; they are the "pragmatists."

The Elaborated or Subspecialty Alternative

The elaborated programs differ considerably from the elective: They are organized separately and experiences within them are arranged as integrated wholes. As formal programs, in contrast to optional sequences within a formal program, they are housed in a university center and a large medical complex, where considerably more freedom to experiment with training professionals usually existed. In addition, a varied staff with the additional background necessary for consultation is readily available.

These programs are designed around an academic calendar with a formalized curriculum for a year in one case and two years in the other. Entrance requirements, which are separate from those necessary to enter such adjacent programs as psychiatric residencies or clinical psychology, include a stipulation that trainees enter after having completed some regularly accredited professional training. This feature may be an attempt to negate the oft-heard criticism of traditionalist colleagues, who claim that "program X is trying to produce community mental health professionals when they haven't yet acquired the skills of the parent profession!"

The early career projections of trainees are consistent with the high interest and commitment required for entry into these programs; most of them plunge into community mental health immediately. Serious doubts about a future in the field are not evident, although some are concerned with making a living while developing the related skills necessary for community work. A few trainees feel concerned about leaving "the mainstream of psychiatry," by which they seem to mean the world of private practice and individual insight-oriented psychotherapy. These same trainees usually carry a few private patients, to "make ends meet" and to keep their "therapeutic skills sharp."

This group, and a small proportion of students from the elective programs, might be called the "committeds." They embark on significantly different career patterns and career projections from the "dabblers" and "pragmatists." Does the future of community health depend on their energy, endurance, creative thinking, and innovative skill?

When we compare these two local programs with what is happening in a number of nationally-known programs, a number of similarities are found, which encourage us to think that these formulations may generally be valid (Caplan, 1965; Hume, 1964a and 1964b; Bernard, 1964). These observations are further supported by the formation of a new division of the American Psychological Association, Division 27 specializing in Community Psychology.

Some Possible Outcomes

The crucial questions at this point revolve around where these groups are going and what they will encounter. The development of training programs is inextricably bound to these issues. If community psychiatry is to move forward, training programs must be further institutionalized. On the other hand, community psychiatry and its training programs are highly vulnerable in several critical ways more so than most emerging segments within professions.

First, community psychiatry makes an easy target for a rising band of critics who assert that it has no basis in theory and tested practice. There is a paucity of research in the field that might lead to the development of theory and rational practice. Some proponents of community psychiatry acknowledge the seriousness of these charges (Sabshin, 1969) but so far have made minimal strides in overcoming them.

Second, the community acceptance required by community psychiatry differs somewhat from that required of other specialties and segments in medicine. The relation of psychiatry to its various publics has always been an issue in the field, but as long as psychiatrists practice in private offices or large public hospitals their publics sift and sort themselves out. Community psychiatrists, though, present themselves to a specific community with the dual message: You need us and we are here to help you. In the lower-class and ghetto communities that are the particular target of community psychiatry, this message is received with considerable conflict. On one hand, leaders protest that their people have the greatest need and receive the least services. On the other, they resent the implied stigma of this position. They say that they need help but then insist that their best hope, and the position of greatest dignity, is to help themselves. As a consequence, community psychiatrists have achieved a precarious foothold in these communities at best. Indeed, a number have suffered rejection by communities and have almost literally been ejected from the scene.

Finally, community psychiatry is particularly vulnerable in that its support comes overwhelmingly from governmental sources and slightly from private philanthropy. No other medical specialty except public health is in such a position. The whole ethos of American medicine clamors against dependence on government, and in this instance, even an ideological opponent of the American Medical Association can see the danger. The usual vagaries of government support are insecure enough, but in a political climate where the major ideological thrust behind community psychiatry programs, the "War on Poverty," is being steadily dismantled, proponents of the field have reason for anxiety. Its vulnerability in terms of scientific credentials and community acceptance provides ammunition for the enemies of the community psychiatry movement, in and out of government.

It is conceivable that community psychiatry may pass from the scene. Nonetheless, we are emboldened to believe that developments in the relationship between society and organized medicine may make it difficult for government to totally reject the *mission* of community psychiatry: to provide psychiatric services to the mass of citizens who otherwise would promptly clutter the public hospitals. Programs may be cut back, or discontinued, but it seems likely that something in this area will continue.

Given this guarded optimism, what can we foresee for the recruitment and socialization of community psychiatrists? We would expect the "elaborated" type of program to be predominant. A significant variant on this model would involve creating an independent specialty. The presence of different types of professionals around community psychiatry provides some support for this possibility. Such a development could lead to new alignments and the building of training programs specifically for community mental health workers, programs that would recruit from a variety of professional and semiprofessional backgrounds. At the moment, there is scant evidence that any such movement is under way, and if it were to emerge it conflicts with the precedence of the elaborated programs and the support they have enjoyed.

However, we suspect that the "elective" type programs, with all their shortcomings, will not disappear soon. For one thing, these provide a recruiting ground, enticing some proportion of psychiatric residents into a more intensive experience with community psychiatry. If psychiatry as a whole accepts the *mission* of community psychiatry, the elective types of program are likely to be incorporated as regular portions of a psychiatry residency, much as child psychiatry or in-patient psychiatry are incorporated today.

A further argument for the persistence of elective programs lies in the vulnerability of community psychiatry. Support for psychiatric residents exposed to the elective programs is part and parcel of the support for the general psychiatry residency. Support for the elaborated programs consists of specific grants for the training of community psychiatrists. If the latter support is cut back, it is unlikely that new elaborated programs will appear or that current ones will be expanded. Thus, community psychiatry may have to depend upon general psychiatry funding and use the elective format until the political and professional situation is more hopeful.

One other model, similar to the elective model but with significant departures, is discernable. First, its proponents accept the concept that the mission of community psychiatry should apply to psychiatry. Most important, a psychiatrist in this model is defined as a person who has expertise in interpersonal and intrapsychic matters but *who can apply* this knowledge appropriately in *a variety of community settings*. Thus, we envisage an integration of traditional psychiatry and community psychiatry:

This is the psychiatrist of the future. To implement this, a great deal more experience, with proper organization and supervision, is needed, than is characteristic of the elective-type program.

We offer the above predictions with a trepidation appropriate to the fragility of our sociological crystal ball. Some activities, though, will certainly follow whatever directions training in community psychiatry takes. (See Dommermuth, 1970; and Bucher, 1962.) Until specific types of programs are well institutionalized, definitional activity will continue. Assuming that some research will begin to feed into this, together with other kinds of reports from the field, the format of training programs will remain highly labile for an indefinite period. There will be struggles over eligibility for recruitment and membership in new associations. The nature of the ties between the new segment's official bodies and those of the parent organization will be at issue, depending on whether community psychiatry continues to develop along the lines of a subspecialty or whether it makes significant inroads into psychiatry as a whole. There will be national power struggles over this. A related problem, for example, is whether the new group will depend on establishing its own journals or fight for significant representation in general ones. In all of this, the proper format for training in community psychiatry will be a central issue.

References

Bernard, V. (1964), Education for community psychiatry in a university medical center. In *Handbook for Community Psychiatry and Community Mental Health*. ed. L. Bellak, 82–123. New York: Grune & Stratton.

Bucher, R. (1962), Pathology: A study of social movements within a profession. *Soc. Prob.*, 10:40–51.

——— (1965), The psychiatric residency and professional socialization. *J. Health Hum. Behav.*, 6:197–206.

———, Stelling, J., and Dommermuth, P. (1969), Implications of prior socialization for residency programs in psychiatry. *Arch. Gen. Psychiatr.*, 20:395–402.

Caplan, G. (1965), Community psychiatry: Introduction and overview. In *Concepts of Community Psychiatry*, ed. S. E. Goldston, 3–18. Washington, D. C.: Department of Health, Education, and Welfare.

Diesenhaus, H. I. (1968), Community psychology: Foreseeable needs and relations to the academic world. Paper presented at the spring meeting of the Illinois Psychological Association, Chicago, 1968.

Dommermuth, P. (1970), Adolescent psychiatry: A sociological perspective. In *Training and Learning Adolescent Psychiatry*, ed. D. Offer and J. F. Masterson. Springfield, Ill.: Charles C. Thomas.

———— and Bucher, R. (1969), Some observations on community psychiatry and implications for professional recruitment and socialization. Paper presented at the annual meetings of the Society for the Study of Social Problems, San Francisco, 1969.

Dunham, H. W. (1965), Community psychiatry: The newest therapeutic bandwagon. *Arch. Gen. Psychiatr.*, 12:303–313.

Faris, R. E. L., and Dunham, H. W. (1939), *Mental Disorders in Urban Areas.* Chicago: University of Chicago Press.

Hollingshead, A. B., and Redlich, F. (1958), *Social Class and Mental Illness.* New York: Wiley.

Hughes, E. C. (1958), *Men and Their Work.* Glencoe, Ill. : Free Press.

Hume, P. B. (1964a), Community psychiatry, social psychiatry and community mental health work: Some interprofessional relationships in psychiatry and social work. *Am. J. Psychiatr.*, 121:340–343.

———— (1964b), Principles and practice of community psychiatry: The role and training of the specialist in community psychiatry. In *Handbook of Community Psychiatry and Community Mental Health*, ed. L. Bellak, 344–363. New York: Grune & Stratton.

Kubie, L. S. (1968), Pitfalls of community psychiatry. *Arch. Gen. Psychiatr.*, 18:257–267.

McGee, T., and Wexler, S. (1969), The evolution of municipally operated, community-based mental health services. Paper read at the annual meetings of the American Orthopsychiatric Association, New York, April, 1969.

Sabshin, M. (1966), The boundaries of community psychiatry. *Soc. Serv. Rev.*, 40: 247-254.

———— (1969), The anti-community mental health "movement". *Am. J. Psychiatr.*, 125:1005–1012.

Schatzman, L., and Bucher, R. (1964), Negotiating a division of labor among professionals in the state mental hospital. *Psychiatry*, 27:266–277.

Smith, H. L. (1952), *New Roles for Psychiatry: A Sociological Study.* Unpublished manuscript.

Srole, L., *et al.* (1962), *Mental Health in the Metropolis.* New York: McGraw-Hill.

Strauss, A., *et al.* (1964), *Psychiatric Ideologies and Institutions.* New York: Free Press.

Chapter 5

Charles W. Tucker

THERAPEUTIC SOCIOLOGY IN A MENTAL HEALTH SERVICE *

THERAPEUTIC sociology," as it is used here, is not "engineering sociology" or "clinical sociology" (Gouldner, 1965, pp. 18–21). Nor is it exclusively the application of social research methodology to "clinical data" as Lennard and Bernstein (1969, p. 3) have defined "clinical sociology." The meaning of "therapeutic sociology" is similar to Lee's definition of the "clinical study of society" (1966, pp. 330–331):

the clinical study of society is the concerned, objective, intimate, continuing, and thoughtful observation, critical evaluation, and absorption into evolving theory of spontaneous social responses to corrective or manipulative efforts.

Therapeutic sociology is a sociologist's developmental participation, involvement, and examination of therapeutic activities. The sociologist who engages in therapeutic sociology

*I thank the following persons for their comments on previous drafts: Gary Albrecht, Dick Brymer, Jo Chandler, Arlene Daniels, Norman Denzin, Betty Nash, Jerry Manis, Peter Manning, Larry Reynolds, Douglas Skelton and Robert Stewart. The editors of this volume made several suggestions that served as the basis for revising this chapter; their efforts are appreciated. One person who required special recognition is Hal Chandler. Without him Chapter 5 could not have been written. Naturally, none of these persons is responsible for the data, interpretations, opinions, and conclusions contained in this chapter.

may become implicated in a wide range of activities from informal conversations to controlled experimental studies. He examines his own actions as they relate to therapeutic activities and attempts to discern their consequences.*

Perspective, Methods, and Background

This account spans about three years (September 1968–June 1971). To collect the data I used participant–observation, interviewing, questionnaires, and psychiatric records; most of the interviews were tape recorded and most of the data from the psychiatric records were processed by computer. For this account I rely most heavily on participant–observation notes. Thus, a word on their "reliability" is relevant.

For each of my daily transactions I wrote who was involved and what had occurred. I also took notes of other transactions that were reported to me in informal conversations. After one year I distributed the notes to the two persons who had been implicated in the majority of the transactions and who had reported observations to me. I asked them to "correct" all of the "mistakes" they found. Neither person found "mistakes," but instead they added some observations and interpretations. I used this same procedure for all of my participation notes and obtained similar results. I also asked several other persons who were involved in these activities to read and judge the accuracy of my account; they did not disagree with my description. If one considers "reliability" to be intersubject agreement, my participant–observation notes are reliable.

Rather than present the activities as they actually occurred I have separated them into units or sets. Although this is a distortion of the actual historical process, it gives a clearer and more detailed account of each major activity. This distortion is

---

*I will not review the previous research in therapeutic sociology but it seems that the studies by Strauss *et al.* (1964) and those reported in Bucher and Stelling (1969) "fit" this definition. Although many studies are done in medical settings (Hyman, 1967, pp. 119–155 and Coe, 1970, for a review) very few use this type of approach.

justified on the basis that the focus of this chapter is the sociologist's activities within a larger set of therapeutic activities.

My work took place in a southern metropolitan hospital, controlled jointly by several counties and the city in a standard metropolitan statistical area of nearly two million people. It is one of the largest hospitals of its type in the country, containing about 1000 beds and serving over 30,000 patients annually. It is the only hospital in the area that serves indigent patients.

The institution also serves as a major training hospital for a private university medical school. Although it is not the only facility used by the medical school for training, all of the medical students and residents rotate through it during their training, some several times (e.g., during the first and third year of their residency). Though the hospital has a dual function—medical training and patient care—the emphasis is usually on the latter from the hospital's perspective.

In the early sixties the hospital had a small in-patient psychiatric unit operated by the university.* The personnel for this unit were hired by the university and did not follow the rules of the hospital. For example, the nurses on the unit did not wear uniforms and they did not follow the vacation or salary schedule of the other hospital nurses. Furthermore, though the hospital was racially segregated and had a policy of treating males and females on separate wards, the psychiatric unit did not adhere to either of these policies. Eventually, although the results with the patients were generally good, the services provided by the psychiatric unit were judged to be inadequate by the hospital, the university, and the community, and the unit was discontinued.

In November 1965 the hospital assumed the responsibility for the operation of an in-patient service and established an out-patient drug clinic. The administration established liaison with legal authorities and arranged for mental patients who were arrested as "Possibly Demented" to be transferred from the jails to a locked in-patient unit guarded by a police officer. The hospital hired all the nursing and clerical personnel, the university psychiatry department provided the medical services in the

*This historical account was obtained from persons who were working in the hospital during that period of time.

form of one half-time psychiatrist, one third-year psychiatric resident, and four first-year psychiatric residents. The hospital controlled all nonmedical personnel—area clerks and secretaries—and the nurses. Thus, the university had little control over the nonmedical and paramedical personnel in the psychiatric service.

This psychiatric service was typical of those found today in most general hospitals. Residents evaluated those persons referred from the medical emergency clinic by the intern on duty, the police, or other-referral sources. Those cases considered non-emergencies were sent home with medications or continued treatment through the out-patient drug clinic. The majority of the persons referred were admitted to the in-patient unit where they stayed until they could be transferred to the only mental hospital in the state. There were very few other agencies or clinics that could be used for disposition or after-care, and less than a third of the patients were sent home from the hospital in-patient unit. Although there is little systematic information about the operation of the service during this time, it has been estimated that 70 percent of the persons evaluated by the residents in the Medical Emergency Clinic were admitted to the in-patient unit, and, of those, nearly 70 percent were sent to the state mental hospital.

As part of their three-year training program the psychiatric residents spent six months in this service, concentrating on diagnostic decision making and the management of a patient's behavior within the in-patient unit. Due to the case load and limited external resources, the residents' training in out-patient treatment was generally reserved for rotations in other hospitals used by the university for training.

In 1968 the university department, because of a number of demands to expand the hospital psychiatric service, altered the focus of these services. It acquired funds for an additional 18-bed in-patient unit, but rather than using these funds for that purpose, negotiated with the hospital to add other services. These included an emergency psychiatric clinic to replace the medical emergency clinic for psychiatry, an additional out-patient clinic related to the present drug clinic, and a day hospital. Although not designated as one officially, this complex amounted to a comprehensive mental health center within the hospital.

One service was an outgrowth of the psychiatric emergency clinic and was called the crisis intervention service (CIS).* Every person requesting aid or referred to the psychiatric services was evaluated by this service, whose primary purpose was to provide immediate crisis intervention and treatment for all persons requesting aid within two hours of their request. It operated in a general systems framework: all acting units—a person, dyad, triad, or family—are viewed at any given moment as a product of a variety of biological, psychosocial, and environmental influences. A crisis was defined as a temporal situation in which, due to various internal or external stresses, an acting unit can no longer continue to function without change. It was seen as a "dangerous opportunity" for all concerned and defined a situation in which change will occur. The change might be good or bad from a number of perspectives—those of the identified patient, the family, or the therapist. In intervention, ideally, some mutually satisfactory agreement involving all concerned parties could be reached, a meaningful relationship could be established, and treatment could proceed in the direction of the acting unit's increased capacity to relate to a variety of other acting units in a mutually satisfactory manner. The aim of psychotherapy, then, was to intervene in a crisis so as to achieve the maximal benefit for as many as possible.

The CIS was staffed by a psychiatrist, a psychologist, a sociologist, a secretary, three clerks, one third-year resident, six first-year residents, four psychiatric social workers, and two psychiatric nurses. These persons were divided into two teams consisting of three co-therapist pairs—a resident and a social worker or nurse as a pair, a male and a female composing a pair. The co-therapists were mutually responsible for evaluating and treating the acting unit that requested aid. The "treatment of choice" was out-patient family crisis therapy, which consisted of two to six treatment sessions. Emphasis was on the establish-

*This conception of the crisis intervention service, definition of crisis, and crisis therapy was developed by Harold M. Chandler (1970). Similar notions, along with a review of crisis therapy, can be found in Langsley and Kaplan (1968). For the literature in crisis intervention, see Parad (1965).

ment of a therapeutic relationship, providing external sources of support for the family, establishing definite goals for treatment, resolving the crisis, and obtaining a meaningful, effective, and permanent termination. In general, the treatment aimed to provide a meaningful therapeutic experience that increased the adaptive potential for the acting unit.

As a faculty member of the university psychiatry department I was able to enter the service, in September 1968, without any special explanation. I was not labeled a "researcher" or a person working on a special project; I was designated as "our sociologist" by several members of the staff. In the beginning I attended teaching conferences, staff meetings and took part in most of the activities. I spent the next two months looking, listening, and asking questions. Even though I was involved as a staff member in most of the activities, I still maintained an antipsychiatric and social-behavioristic orientation to these activities (see Tucker [1966, 1969] for an elaboration of the orientation). Looking back now, it seems that I was attempting to see if my observations were consistent with my orientation.

Much of what I saw then seemed to be in accord with my orientation rather than in conflict with it. Short term and family therapy were emphasized, with a focus on behavior rather than psychodynamics. The theoretical orientation was "eclectic," (Abroms, 1969) "community psychiatry" (Rubin, 1969). There was a concern for research as well as providing quality service and training. The traditional ideological conflicts, especially those involving medical versus nonmedical professionals, were not evident. Some of the critical assessments of psychiatry, e.g., Goffman and Szasz, were accepted as accurate for much of psychiatry but not applicable to "our psychiatry." In sum, I was accepted initially into the service without question and found that my orientation was similar to those in the psychiatric services.

The Sociologist's Activities

For nearly three years I engaged in a variety of activities ranging from "counseling" potential patients to typing and mimeographing record-keeping forms. For descriptive purposes this range of actions will be collapsed into two major sets: developing a record-keeping system and accompanying procedures manual, and undertaking a number of intraservice research studies.

Record-Keeping System and Manual

Amid a discussion of organizational problems in a weekly staff meeting, one member of the staff suggested that we develop a computerized record-keeping system and a manual. Although there was a manual and some minimal recording procedures, these were judged to be inadequate for the total complex of services. The staff saw this as one way to organize the services; I saw it as an opportunity to become involved in the operation of the services.

We began by drawing a flow chart, the purpose being to outline the path a person should take to get into and out of the service complex. It served as a guide for the manual and the record-keeping system. The manual was written from a process, rather than a static, perspective. A set of procedures, always involving record-keeping forms, was prescribed for each phase, emphasizing the processes involved in treatment rather than the formal structure of the services.

We investigated systems used in a variety of other mental health services, and decided that most of these systems were inadequate for the CIS. They contained very little systematic information about the person's condition (e.g., presenting complaint), previous history of events regarding present condition (e.g., events occurring in last 24 hours), or the therapist's assessment of the person (e.g., attitude toward patient). Most of the records required lengthy handwritten descriptions but contained inadequate directions for writing them. We found that most of the record systems were clearly biased in the direction of the "sick role" (i.e., they only asked for negative information about the person); this was a major inadequacy from our point of view. Thus, we began to develop our own record-keeping system.

We constructed a form where most of the information items were precoded. The major sociodemographic "variables"—age, sex, religion, ethnic group, marital status, income, and occupation—were on the form, along with household composition. We asked for the presenting complaint, referral source, and a series of items on previous treatment history. Then we asked the evaluators to describe the person's primary stress along with their assessment of the person's reaction to that stress. The remainder of the form contained items regarding suicide, homicide, diagnosis, and disposition. The complete form—one page and one IBM card of information was put into operation in November 1968, along with a manual.

The staff, as well as the secretary of the service, responded negatively to these procedures, which were seen as additional and unnecessary work. The secretary, who had to post, label, and file each record complained and requested some additional clerical assistance. The social workers were usually given the task of obtaining all the sociodemographic information; they said this task inhibited their involvement in evaluation interviews. Consequently, most of the record-keeping forms were not completed, filed, or labeled; the manual was not read; and most of the procedures were not followed. Several members of the senior (non-CIS) staff did not consistently demand that the records be completed, and when the sociologist did, some residents complained of his "research project."

My response to these events was mixed. In part, I saw it as my failure, but I also realized that some of the senior staff members did not support these changes. Timing was also important. We had introduced this new system toward the end of the residents' June–December rotation. Some CIS members were critical of the residents for not having a sense of "medical responsibility" toward their patients. In addition, complaints about the system reached other members of the university department, and they inquired about the situation. They were sensitive to such complaints because the CIS was established outside the mold of traditional psychiatry; some were skeptical about its merits. I responded by disengaging from the service at first; after several discussions with the CIS staff, we decided to develop a new record-keeping system and manual and to introduce it at the beginning of the new rotation on January 1, 1969.

The new system increased the total amount of coded information obtained from the person being evaluated, whom we designated as an identified patient (IP). The form used by the co-therapists, i.e., resident and social worker pair, was expanded. We developed a new questionnaire, a Social Activities Schedule, to be completed by the IP. The questions on this form, which could be answered with "Never," "Rarely," "Sometimes," "Often," or "Very Often"—were about the performance of household tasks, the performance of work tasks, previous experience with doctors and hospitals, the occurrence of certain "symptoms", and the occurrence of certain "stress" events (see Tucker and Smith, 1971). This questionnaire was to be answered by the IP *before* being interviewed by the co-therapists. Along with these forms a new procedures manual was written that described all of the psychiatric services and emphasized the record-keeping system as a crucial part of evaluation and treatment. The manual and the record-keeping system were introduced after the rotation began on January 20, 1969. The initial response was negative, but we decided to keep this system for several months to evaluate its effectiveness.

For the first time we requested a new clerical position from the hospital to assist with the new system. We had already selected a person for the position and intended to ask the hospital to hire her on our recommendation. Because the position had the title of "Statistical Clerk" (a new title in the list of hospital positions), a job description was written to indicate how this position related to hospital operations. We discovered, at that moment, that the hospital preferred to make its own selection of personnel for positions and that our approval, but not our recommendation, was all that was required. After six weeks of negotiating we finally succeeded in hiring the person we had recommended.

At the same time we discovered something about the hospital's approach to out-patient clinics. I was appointed to represent the service on the institution's Medical Records

Committee. The concern at this time was the establishment of records for the patients that were not admitted to the hospital. There were no records for most of the patients who were being seen on an out-patient basis. In fact, they had no hospital records on the persons seen by the CIS. No record-keeping system for out-patient clinics had been devised, and the CIS records were considered by the hospital to be incomplete and unofficial. This problem with out-patient records affected my relationship with the hospital throughout these activities.

Some of our earlier activities began to affect the ongoing operation of the CIS and its relationship to other psychiatric services. There was an increase in the percentage of completed records. The staff began to discuss the records in conferences and used the information from the records in the supervision of the psychiatric residents. Each day a meeting, called debriefing, was held between the co-therapists going off duty and the senior CIS staff members. The purpose was to have the co-therapists describe the people they had seen during the previous eight hours, indicate the type of treatment they prescribed for those persons, and justify that treatment. The records were utilized extensively in debriefing, and the co-therapists were often reminded of the utility and importance of this information for treatment. There were times when I emphasized the records to such an extent that the co-therapists asked about my "research project with the records." I then deemphasized the research aspects of the record-keeping system and reemphasized the system's relevance to treatment.

There were still many complaints about the system. Some senior staff members claimed that these were to be expected while others considered them an indication that the record-keeping system should be altered. At a staff meeting it was decided that I should interview the co-therapists to discover their problems with the system. The results from this investigation would be used to alter the system, which would be put into effect before the new rotation in July.

In general, the co-therapists found the records to be useful to their work. But there was consensus among the co-therapists as to specific changes that should be made in the forms: Some of the precoded items should be open-ended questions. They wanted to be able to write some information about each identified patient in their own words. Also the sociodemographic "variables" should appear first in the record form so they could be completed by a clerk, if necessary.

When I began to develop a final version of the new intake form, I discovered several areas of conflict among the senior staff psychiatrists: A few staff members emphasized medicine, while others distinguished psychiatry from medicine—a difference between a biological and interpersonal orientation. This disagreement was partially resolved by designating the new form as the "Psychiatric History and Evaluation," "psychiatric" identifying the service, "history" indicating the medical and hospital aspects of the form, and the "evaluation" showing the part this form played in determining the IP's treatment.

The only other major disagreement dealt with the mental status examination section of the form. This examination is traditionally used by a psychiatrist (and only by a psychiatrist) to determine the extent of a person's pathology. It is a major diagnostic tool that usually includes such items of information as appearance, psychomotor activity, affect, type of speech, orientation to time and place, and thought content. The staff psychiatrists disagreed over certain labels for "moods," the correct characterization of "thinking," and the notion of intelligence. One insisted that a judgement regarding intelligence be included. One psychiatrist said the "moods"—"happy," "content," and "fearful" should be eliminated because he thought no patient would have them. After much discussion they remained on the form. Finally, one psychiatrist proposed we label the item regarding thinking as "thinking deviations," though this would not allow a person to be judged as thinking properly. This was partially resolved by calling the item "cognitive mechanisms" and including both "normal" (e.g., concentration) and "abnormal" (e.g., denial) items. The new form was typed and put into effect on June 2, 1969, so it could be pretested before July.

During the pretest period we only found a few problems with the new form, mainly typing errors. When the new forms and manual were introduced in July, several other changes occurred regarding my relationship with the service. I was placed on the budget of the CIS and became involved in the planning, i.e., the orientation sessions for new staff. I also became involved in a number of negotiations with the hospital over the clerical assistance and funds necessary to operate the record-keeping system.

A person for coding was previously obtained from the hospital, but due to other clerical tasks in the CIS she was unable to perform the coding. She spent her time "filling in" for the other clerks on the service. I pointed out to the other members of the staff that the coding was not being done because the clerk's activities deviated from her job description. In response, I was told that the task of coding would be done when we solved all the other problems in the CIS. Finally, the clerk resigned because she was unable to do the coding along with the other tasks.

The record system required not only a new clerk for coding but an additional clerk to interview persons who requested psychiatric aid, and we began to negotiate with the hospital for this new position, which would make it possible for the records to be coded. These data could be used for a descriptive analysis of the CIS as well as a basis for evaluating its effectiveness. I disagreed with some staff members regarding the relative importance of coding the records; service and training were considered the top-priority tasks. I also became aware of a lack of agreement with the psychiatric services regarding the priority of tasks.

The staff continued to complain about patient overload, and this was brought to our attention in the weekly staff meetings. Other complaints included the lack of supervision and lack of office space. For the first time, the co-therapists complained about the difficulty of finding their records. They considered these records important for treatment, but they were useless if they were not readily available. One senior staff member who considered the information from the records to be invalid and completing the records to be bothersome suggested that the current record-keeping system be eliminated and a new one devised. We argued against the proposed change and interpreted the complaint as positive evidence that the system was working. The co-therapists had begun to employ the records as a significant part of their treatment. Another senior staff member finally agreed with this interpretation and asked for our recommendations. We said that we needed an additional clerk and that we had been negotiating for this position with the hospital. We were told to continue the negotiations.

When the new clerk was hired I attempted to rearrange the working schedule of the clerks to increase the amount of time for coding. This schedule was rejected, and I was told that the records would be coded later. Finally, there was a compromise schedule for the clerks but it still did not allow enough time to code records. I was reminded again, that the record coding was a low-priority task.

The problems within the psychiatric services were now becoming more evident to the university department, and several were discussed informally. A few of the senior staff members were complaining that the CIS was attempting to control the other services. To correct this situation the senior staff sent out some new directives: All budget requests were to be cleared by a senior staff member before the money could be spent; the request for funds to analyze the record data was denied; all negotiations with the hospital for any purpose were to be channeled through a new administrative assistant, and I was informed that funds to support a full-time sociologist might not be available for the next fiscal year (July 1970–June 1971). I responded with a progress report detailing some of the problems the CIS had encountered with the hospital and the other psychiatric services. In addition, the CIS staff wrote a memo to the senior staff detailing several problems and requesting assistance in solving them. The senior staff members agreed.

Most of the problems within the CIS continued, however. We continued to have trouble with the clerks and secretaries. There was no agreement between myself and the CIS staff as to how much time was to be devoted to records and research. Moreover, a new mental health law was to become effective in January, and this law required that separate clinical records be maintained, emphasizing their importance in spite of the senior staff's intention to reduce their effectiveness. The hospital requested that some data be gathered to indicate the effectiveness of the new mental health law. Although some funds were given to the psychiatric services to implement it, none were allocated to the coding of data. My requests for funds were ignored, and I obtained volunteer workers to code the records.

During the orientation of the new residents in January 1970, there was a discussion of the new mental health law and the variety of forms that were to be completed for each IP. The staff disagreed as to how to apply the law in the case of a so-called "voluntary admission." This was resolved by having the IP sign a voluntary admission form. The Psychiatric History and Evaluation form was discussed in detail, and the disagreements about the mental status examination section recurred.

From January–June 1970 I spent most of my time doing research attempting to keep the record-keeping system coordinated. I became less and less implicated in administrative-type activities within the CIS, and this was called to my attention by the CIS staff. But I did have an opportunity to observe or receive reports about a number of activities within the psychiatric services.

The new mental health law was a problem not to the new residents but for the social workers, who were to implement it. They were given the task of having all the new forms completed, but it was difficult for them to do this and establish a relationship with their residents so they could work as co-therapists. Because the new law emphasized in-patient or hospital activities, the residents spent more of their time in the in-patient service than with the CIS. This reduced the number of cases being treated as "crisis cases" or "out-patient cases." It also reduced the amount of time that the residents and social workers spent as co-therapists.

Problems continued in the relationships between the CIS and the other psychiatric services. Our requests for more assistance for the growing clerical tasks of our service were either ignored, denied, or complied with after a continuing series of requests. The psychiatrist in charge of the CIS was told that he would be transfered to a new mobile crisis service. This service was to work outside of the hospital by evaluating persons in their homes to see if it would be necessary to send them to the hospital for further evaluation or treatment. The service was to be established in July, and it was the first clear indication that we had that there would be several overall changes made in the psychiatric services.

Another sign of change came when a senior staff member asked me to make several extensive changes in the record-keeping system. First, it was to be a separate entity in the total complex of services, no longer directed by me as part of the CIS but, instead, as someone under the direction of the psychiatrist in charge of all the psychiatric services. Secondly, we decided to revise the record forms on the basis of data that had been analyzed for the first four months of 1970. This resulted in reducing the intake record form to half the size of the previous form. Finally, the emphasis would be on research within the psychiatric services. Not all of these changes had been approved by all the senior staff members, and we entered a period of negotiation regarding them.

The new intake form was approved, but it was noted that the existing record showed that many items were not completed on the previous forms. I argued that "no information" responses to items were very useful, because knowing the circumstances under which the co-therapists would not complete an item is as useful as a series of completed items. This argument was rejected. The separate record-keeping system for the psychiatric services was to be eliminated and made part of the hospital's medical records.

The separation of the record-keeping system and emphasis on research were approved with several modifications. Without special psychiatric records the job of the sociologist became a part-time one, and the budget was changed to cover only half of the sociologist's salary. Next, the emphasis on research was limited to follow-up research with the sociologist serving in a technical, rather than a professional role. It was implied that the sociologist's previous research activities were of little utility to the service and that greater control over his subsequent activities would be exercised. Finally, the follow-up research would only be considered useful if it would show that the service was fulfilling its stated goals. In other words, the data was to be analyzed so as to indicate the service's success and not its failures. To this I strongly disagreed, and I told a senior staff psychiatrist that I would not take part in any research designed to confirm the biases and previous conclusions of the staff. This, of course, reduced my utility to the service even further, and I was told that the prospect for future employment was in doubt.

After a series of negotiations I became half-time in the psychiatric services —where I limited activity to doing follow-up research and analyzing data that had been heretofore collected —and half-time in a new service for methadone treatment— where I devised a record-keeping system and took part in the organization of the program. This experience was not similar to the one I had in the psychiatric services (see Tucker, 1971a, for a description). It appeared that the sociologist's activities were reduced to a minimum in the psychiatric services.

Intra-service Research

After the initial tasks with the record-keeping system were completed in July 1969, I began several intra-service research projects. Because of the service's emphasis on co-therapeutic decision making, my first research project dealt with the residency training process. This was the only mental health service known to operate with co-therapeutic relationships, so I wanted to investigate the consequences of these relationships for residency training.

I designed my study from a processual perspective and planned to interview each resident as he came into the service, in the middle of his rotation, and during his last week. In addition, I would interview the social workers in the middle and at the end of the rotation. I had also designed a questionnaire that each resident and social worker would complete before each interview.

The study focused on several variables and their change

during the training process: for example, self identification (Tucker, 1966) and psychiatric treatment ideologies (Armor and Klerman, 1968). Another interest was the effect of prior socialization (Bucher, *et. al.* 1969) on the shape of the residency process (Bucher, 1965). Finally, the study considered the effect of supervision and the changes in the organization of the service on the residency-training process.

As I began this study my position within the system was accepted by both the residents and social workers. They did not question the purposes of the study, were extremely cooperative, and said it was not necessary to remind them that the information was confidential; they trusted me. Therefore, I did not see the necessity of obtaining informed consent. Throughout the study all seemed to answer my questions honestly, even when they involved personal information, and they thanked me for the opportunity to be involved in the study.

A preliminary analysis of the data from this set of residents and social workers indicates several interesting findings. First, self-identification did not alter dramatically. The designations of physician and social worker were maintained throughout. Second, attitudes toward ideologies seemed to become more eclectic from this training experience; they did not emphasize any *one* type of ideology—psychiatric, somatic, or social. The residents and social workers questioned whether there was anything like a "cure" for mental illness. Finally, as was expected, the organizational difficulties encountered in the psychiatric services affected the training process. The co-therapists noticed and took into account most of the inter-personal conflicts that occurred, and felt them to be detrimental to their training.

This same study design was repeated for the residents and social workers of the January–June 1970 rotation. The responses to my questions were quite different than those I had encountered in the previous study. According to the residents, the inconclusiveness on the part of the staff and social workers regarding the new mental health law was a problem. The social workers could not decide how to enact the new law, and their residents, who were responsible for its enactment, had difficulty making decisions. Many of their decisions were called into question but few solutions were offered. The residents responded to these events with anger and disengagement. They were less cooperative in answering my questions. For the first time I found that several of the residents refused to let some of their answers be tape-recorded, it was difficult to make appointments for interviews. In spite of these difficulties I proceeded as usual and obtained the data, concluding that these events were mainly the result of organizational problems rather than the nature of my research. The conclusion was confirmed by sub-sequent observations.

As a matter of procedure I applied to the university depart-ment to make this research an official project. The committee reviewing the project noted that I had failed to obtain informed consent from the residents and social workers. Several second-hand reports indicated that the committee was very concerned about the fact that the residents were being studied without the department's knowledge or approval. When I started to obtain signatures from the residents and social workers on a consent form I had devised, they began to question my research and asked what I intended to do with the information. I told them that I had always considered it as confidential, and they signed the forms without further questions. The university department had no further criticisms of my research.

The results from this research were similar to those obtained from the previous group of residents. The self-identification data showed very little alteration over time, attitudes toward ideol-ogies were eclectic, and the organizational problems inhibited the establishment of a relationship between the residents and the social workers. These residents were critical of the psy-chiatric services and the lack of organization that prevailed. In addition, they said that their learning was hampered by the lack of supervision and adequate teaching conferences. In general, this second group of residents was far more critical of the psychiatric services.

Another research project started during 1970 was a follow-up study using the intake data as the basis for the follow-up interview schedule. In attempting to design this study several problems were encountered: The 1969 records were not coded and it would be impossible to compare the intake data with the follow-up data. There were no funds available to hire interviewers for the research. Finally, some of the staff members were uncertain about the value of this research. A few wanted a well-designed study; others wanted a "service-oriented" study. Given these problems, a number of compromises were made.

We decided that the 1969 records must be coded; a random sample from each month was selected for the study. Without funds we were limited to a mailed questionnaire or a telephone follow-up study, but this still required an assistant in the research project. We decided to do 200 telephone contact follow-ups and 400 mailed questionnaire follow-ups. The telephone calls could only obtain minimal information, while the mailed questionnaires could be matched with the intake data, i.e., questions that were answered by persons at intake were asked in the mailed questionnaires.

In the meantime my view's about the staff and the psychiatric services altered. The interest in research that I had detected during my entrance into the service had either been eliminated or greatly diminished. This was partly the result of the demands of "outside" groups, e.g., legislature, health department, voluntary associations, who wanted some "proof" of success. Moreover, there appeared to be very little understanding within the staff regarding the complexities of doing research. In addition, several staff members were dissatisfied with the operation of the CIS and made it clear that research results would not assist in solving these fundamental problems. In all, the situation was less than ideal.

I obtained volunteers to do the research and coding. From the mailed questionnaire study we received a 30 percent return. However, the senior staff decided that money was not available for the analysis of these data, and they were not analyzed.

In the telephone surveys we were able to contact 75 percent of the sample. By hand-tabulating the information we found that over 85 percent of the respondents were satisfied with the service they had received from the CIS. Further, those who obtained subsequent treatment did so from the CIS rather than elsewhere.

Some Consequences Regarding Therapeutic Activities

It is difficult to determine, in a systematic manner, how my activities shaped the activities of those doing therapy. I made only a few observations of actual therapy activities, and I have no reports of how the therapists performed therapy prior to my entrance into the service. Finally, it would be difficult to determine whether any change resulted from my activity or the activities of others in the serivice. The "answer" to this question, therefore, is quite impressionistic.

The aspects of the organization described in the manual along with the record-keeping system emphasized certain therapeutic procedures. Mutual decision making by the residents and their co-therapists was prominent and seemed to increase as the service developed. But the manual was ignored by most of the senior staff, residents, and social workers. Second, the "treatment of choice" emphasized in the manual was "outpatient family crisis therapy." There was an increase in the number of these dispositions. Last, obtaining systematic information for decisions was emphasized. There was a great deal of discussion regarding the ways to determine the correct treatment, and this had some effect on the types of treatment given in the CIS.

I would estimate that my overall effect on the "doing of therapy" was minor. The therapeutic activities within the CIS were determined mainly by the therapists' experiences with their cases. Professional training and experience played a part as did the supervision of the therapists by the staff psychiatrist.

To understand the effect of the therapeutic activities on the sociologist's activities I turn to my participant observation notes. I entered the service as a member of the university department and spent the first few months observing. In developing the record-keeping system and the manual, we took the therapeutic activities into account, designing the organization to fit these therapeutic activities. Thus, the record-keeping system and manual were directly related to the therapeutic activities.

My activities were consequently altered in several ways. First, I did not insist that the records be seen as a research project. We decided to integrate the record-keeping system into the therapeutic activities. Second, the type of information obtained was not determined by research interests. Therapeutic activities were prominent in deciding the composition of the records. Last, the shape of the therapeutic activities determined the shape of my work. When the record-keeping system appeared to alter the therapeutic activities, records, not the therapeutic activities, were changed. When problems occurred, my activities were altered for the sake of the therapeutic activities.

To remain within the "stream" of therapeutic activities required a wide variety of negotiating activities. Initially, I had to negotiate the design of the record-keeping system within the staff of the psychiatric services, and they were consulted at every stage of the system's development. Additional clerical assistance means negotiations with the staff and the hospital administration. To develop the manual for the psychiatric services there was a continuous series of negotiations with the staff. Every time a section was rewritten by one staff member, all the others had to be consulted about this alteration. Finally, the intra-service research involved negotiations with some of the CIS staff.

Some of the constraints placed on my research within therapeutic activities have been mentioned previously. I was seldom told not to begin a particular research project because I seldom asked permission. On the other hand, I was told to do research that I did not consider either applicable to sociology or well designed. I was asked to gather information that would justify the existence of the psychiatric services. A few senior staff members felt only politically relevant research should be undertaken, by which they meant research data that indicated that the psychiatric services were effective.

Finally, if one considers control by others a constraint, the

responses to the record-keeping system by certain staff members
were constraining. The system was seen as my technique of
gaining some control over my own activities as well as the activities of others in the psychiatric services. To counteract this
some of the senior staff members demanded that the record-
keeping system be changed; during the first 18 months I was
asked to change the record-keeping system four times. This
involved the construction of several new forms, changes in
previous forms, and the construction of completely new code-
books. The record-keeping system was finally reduced and subsequently eliminated, in spite of the fact that it was required by
the new mental health law.

The majority of the constraints I experienced were in my
relationships with senior staff members responsible for the total
complex of services. By contrast I found that my research
activities were not as restricted within the Crisis Intervention
Service. Some of the staff members in the CIS were aware of
my research activities and seldom prohibited me access to information. I tape recorded meetings, debriefings, and a few
therapy sessions. Most of my personal interviews were done with
the staff members of the CIS. With a few minor exceptions, my
interviews were open, honest, and quite frank. But the CIS
was not considered to be "in tune" with the other psychiatric
services. It eventually was eliminated in name, function, and
purpose, if not in conception.

The "sociological skills" utilized in therapeutic activities—
questionnaire construction, interview schedule construction,
sampling, research design, interviewing, administration of
research activities—are determined to some extent by the type
of therapeutic activities. If those who are engaged in therapeutic
activities consider the enactment of these skills to be "disruptive," then the sociologist will have little success.

Specifically, questionnaire and interview schedule construction, along with knowledge about data coding and analysis,
were helpful in the design of the record-keeping system. An
overall perspective of organizational processes and their administration was lacking in the service until a flow chart was designed
and a manual of standard operating procedures for the total

complex of services written. Finally, there was minimal understanding of research activities. The discussion of research and the
enactment of several research projects added to the staff's com-
prehension (see Tucker, 1971b for elaboration and comment).

The extent of interdisciplinary cooperation or conflict in
therapeutic activities is very difficult to determine: There are
not many activities involved in interpersonal relationships
that can indicate cooperation or conflict. I believe this issue
mainly involves interpersonal transactions, not the differences
between the disciplines. Others see the "intrinsic" differences
between disciplines as problem-producing. They emphasize
the conflicts between persons of different disciplines, the medical
doctor–psychiatrist and sociologist relationship, for example
(Hyman, 1967). However, no relationship involving human
beings is ever limited to cooperation or conflict; each one involves an emergent mixture of these behaviors and a multitude
of others (Blumer, 1969). Thus, the transactions emphasize
human relationships.

In all the activities described above, a wide variety of relationships were established. These involved persons with no
professional training as well as those with very specialized
professional backgrounds. In a majority of transactions there
was no mention of professional or disciplinary differences. The
relationships were established on the basis of the occurring
activity, and, when the transaction was concluded, another
relationship was initiated based on another activity. Agreement
and disagreement was mixed within each activity. Many transactions were terminated "for the moment" without acts of agreement or disagreement.

In retrospect, I am more aware of conflict than cooperation,
but neither activity was restricted to disciplinary relationships.
In fact, if I could quantify these behaviors precisely, I would
find that the conflict between those of similar disciplines was
greater than conflict between those of dissimilar disciplines.
But a final judgement on interdisciplinary cooperation or conflict
cannot be made.*

*This does not mean that one's discipline is unimportant. We can observe
instances where a medical doctor introjects in the transaction the statement: "You
are not allowed to do that; I am the doctor here." In this transaction the discipline

Finally, how may these activities aid our understanding of organizations? The above account contains several examples of the principles of organization evident in the studies of Strauss *et al.* (1964) and Bucher and Stelling (1969). Weick states one such principle: "Processes in organizing must continually be reaccomplished" (1969, p. 36). When the service developed there were negotiations between the university department and the hospital, the hospital and the legal authorities, the university department and the community agencies, as well as the psychiatric services with all of these acting units. In addition to the yearly budget negotiations, these relationships were continually being renegotiated. To obtain personnel for the system required negotiations with the hospital at one time and, at another, with the university department. Changes in personnel and operating procedures required negotiations among the psychiatric system, the university department, and the hospital. Each time these processes were reaccomplished the outcome was in doubt. As Weick points out "processes are repetitive only if this repetitiveness is continuously accomplished" (p. 36). To make them work out this way is problematic rather than routine.

Also applicable is Weick's (1969) principle: "Control is a prominent process within organizations, but it is accomplished by relationships, not by people" (p. 37). The record-keeping system and the manual were efforts at controlling the organizing processes. My experience supports the notion that it cannot be done by people but must be done through relationships. Similarly "attentional processes are a crucial determinant of human organizing" (Weick, 1969, p. 38). Again, the record-keeping system was considered an attempt to focus attention on certain aspects of behavior. Disagreements became apparent in the discussions regarding the mental status examination, one of the essential tools for decision making about diagnosis. Problems occurred when attempts were made to alter the traditional form.

Finally, several features of client-centered organizations

---

or profession is relevant. My thought is that we must have evidence of such behaviors before we can consider the discipline or profession to be consequential transactionally. I observed very few behaviors of this sort.

mentioned by Mechanic (1968) and by Coe (1970, pp. 264–288) are found in this account. The importance of so-called "lower participants" mentioned by Mechanic (1968) became evident in many of the negotiations regarding secretaries and clerks.

Most of the problems that occurred involving the hospital made evident the "dual authority system" that exists in most general hospitals (Coe, 1970, pp. 276–277). The hospital has control over the nursing service and, thereby, all nonmedical and paramedical personnel. These persons are necessary for the operation of any service. Furthermore, to operate a service within the hospital it is necessary to either follow their policies, negotiate changes in policies, or violate them. In most instances, the service staff chose to negotiate policy modifications, which usually required several months.

Summary and Conclusions

In general, it appears that the therapeutic activities determined the sociologist's activities to a greater extent than the sociologist's activities determined the therapeutic activities. The main effect of the sociologist's activities was to increase the staff's attention to the organizational aspects of therapeutic activities. The record-keeping system and the research pointed up the systematic collection of information. The sociologist "made a place" for himself in the service through a series of negotiations. There were several constraints on the sociologist's behavior relative to the larger complex of psychiatric services, but he was allowed to do research.

On the other hand, the therapeutic activities altered the sociologist's activities to a great extent. Compromises were required to stay within the "stream" of activities (Trice, 1956). The character of the record-keeping system was determined, in the main, by the therapeutic work. I was aware of several different responses to research: Research data were to be used for political purposes (i.e., to obtain operating funds); research was a threat to the organization, because it might reveal the failures and problems of the psychiatric services; service and training could not be assisted by research. Then, research was the lowest-priority task. Clerical assistance for the record-keeping system was diverted into service activities. Whatever research was accomplished in the psychiatric services was done as special projects with the support of a few CIS staff members. The therapeutic activities determined to a large extent what the sociologist did; it clearly set limits on his activities.

These experiences also illustrate some principles of organizing that may aid in understanding organizational behavior: Continual negotiating and renegotiating, the importance of control, similarities between the problems in this hospital and other hospitals.

Finally, I would suggest that the "therapeutic sociology" done in this mental health service is similar to that done in other therapeutic settings. On that basis some conclusions can be drawn on the future of "therapeutic sociology."

With the development of community mental health centers there will be an increased opportunity for "therapeutic sociology," which will be determined by what is allowed in these settings. The sociologist will be forced to put aside some of his "textbook" notions about research, particularly about the importance of research.* The demands for service and training are predominant; research must take last place. If a sociologist understands this, it will prepare him to handle the situation, which, I think, will exist for some time.

If a sociologist decides to proceed with 'therapeutic sociology" in a mental health setting in spite of this situation, it can be a beneficial learning experience. He can learn his own limitations, understand the complexities of doing sociology in a therapeutic setting, obtain some information about therapeutic activities, come to know some very interesting and personable people, and discover a "new world" outside the confines of academia. There are very few experiences that can offer more than doing "therapeutic sociology."

---

*A study by Glasscote and Gudeman (1969) of the major mental health centers in the U.S. shows that less than 4 percent of the time spent by all staff members is spent in research. By comparison, 57 percent of the time is spent in patient care and 16 percent of the time is spent in staff meetings.

References

Abroms, G. M. (1969), The new eclecticism. *Arch. Gen. Psychiatr.*, 20:514–523.

Armor, D. J., and Klerman, G. L. (1968), Psychiatric treatment orientations and professional ideology. *J. Health Soc. Behav.*, 9:243–255.

Blumer, H. (1969), *Symbolic Interactionism.* Englewood Cliffs, N. J.: Prentice-Hall.

Brymer, R. A., and Farris, B. (1967 , Ethical and political dilemmas in the investigation of deviance: A study of juvenile delinquency. In *Ethics, Politics and Social Research*, ed. G. Sjoberg, 297–318. Cambridge: Schenkman.

Bucher, R. (1965), The psychiatric residency and professional socialization. *J. Health Soc. Behav.*, 6:197–206.

———, and Stelling, J. (1969), Characteristics of professional organizations. *J. Health Soc. Behav.*, 10:3–15.

———, *et al.* (1969), Implications of prior socialization for residency programs in psychiatry. *Arch. Gen. Psychiatr.*, 20:395–402.

Chandler. H. M. (1970), The emergence of a crisis intervention service. Norman: University of Oklahoma Medical Center (Mimeo).

Coe, R. M. (1970), *Sociology of Medicine.* New York: McGraw-Hill.

Glasscote, R. M., and Gudeman, J. E. (1969), *The Staff of the Mental Health Center.* Washington, D. C.: The Joint Information Service.

Gouldner, A. W. (1965 , Explorations in applied social science. In *Applied Sociology.* ed. A. W. Gouldner and S. M. Miller, 5–22. New York: Free Press.

Hyman, M. D. (1967), Medicine. In *The Uses of Sociology*, ed. P. Lazarsfeld *et al.*, 119–155. New York: Basic Books.

Langsley, D. G., and Kaplan, D. M. (1968), *The Treatment of Families in Crisis*, New York: Grune & Stratton.

Lee, A. M. (1966), *Multivalent Man.* New York: George Braziller.

Lennard, H. L., and Bernstein, A. (1969), *Patterns in Human Interaction.* San Francisco: Jossey-Bass.

Mechanic, D. (1968), Sources of power of lower participants in complex organizations. *Medical Sociology*, Appendix I. New York: Free Press.

Parad, H. J. (ed.) (1965), *Crisis Intervention.* New York: Family Service Association of America.

Rubin, B. (1969), Community psychiatry. *Arch. Gen. Psychiatr.*, 20:497–507.

Strauss, A., *et al.* (1964), *Psychiatric Ideologies and Institutions.* New York: Free Press.

Trice H. M. (1956), The "outsider" role in field study. *Sociol. Soc. Res.*, 41:27–32.

Tucker, C. W. (1966), Some methodological problems of Kuhn's self theory. *Sociol. Q.*, 7:345–358.

———(1969), Marx and sociology: Some theoretical implications. *Pac. Sociol. Rev.*, 12:87–93.

———(1971a), A sociologist in a methadone treatment program. Paper read at annual meetings of Ohio Valley Sociological Society, Cleveland.

———(1971b), Sociology within psychiatry. Paper read at annual meetings of the Society for the Study of Social Problems, Denver.

———, and Smith, A. E. (1971), Life events, symptom reports and social attributes Paper read at annual meetings of the Southern Sociological Society, Miami.

Weick, K. E. (1969), *The Social Psychology of Organizing.* Reading, Mass.: Addison-Wesley.

Chapter 6

Arlene Kaplan Daniels

(With the Assistance of Lauren
B. Chaitkin and Josephine
S. Thornton)

WHAT TROUBLES
THE TROUBLE
SHOOTERS*

THE difficulties or problems that concern psychiatrists were
discovered in this study by analyzing the responses of 152 psychiatrists to a sentence-completion list.†
Preliminary suggestions of what these problems might be
came from several sources. The medical and behavioral science
literature on psychiatrists point to difficulties arising from
countertransference, the inconclusive evidence for positive
results in psychotherapy, and questions about the future of psychiatry. Common sense and familiarity with the literature in
both social psychiatric research and research in the professions
brings up other areas : How do psychiatrists get along with one
another and with other professional colleagues ? What kind of

*I am particularly indebted to my friends and colleagues Rachel Kahn-Hut
and Joan P. Emerson who participated in the initial stages of conceptualization
and categorization of the data; in addition Rachel Kahn-Hut has edited every one
of the endless drafts of this paper with a patience and helpfulness far above the
ordinary call of friendship. I should also like to thank several other friends and
colleagues for their helpful suggestions in how best to organize and complete this
presentation: Eliot Freidson, Fred Goldner, Dorothy Miller, Thomas Scheff, and
Charlotte Green Schwartz.

†We are grateful to Dr. Morris J. Daniels of San Diego State College for the use
of this instrument which he devised.

pressures develop for these psychiatrists as they engage in practice? In addition, results of a pilot test suggested that statements about problems of isolation might be expected.

In a previous paper (Daniels, 1972) it was argued that there are major differences between private-office practice and practice where the psychiatrist is an agent of an employing organization. The differences warrant the view that divergencies in definition of responsibility to client, type of work, and structure of work day are sufficient to consider organizational practice a distinct subspecialty within psychiatry. With these considerations in mind, three types of problems were selected around which comparisons could be made between private and organizational psychiatrists: (1) feelings of isolation; (2) concern over the image status of psychiatry; and (3) concern over the effectiveness of psychiatric treatment.

Isolation

Private practitioners spend the better part of their working time (half or more) in individual or group therapy sessions, because therapy traditionally involves a lengthy session (45 to 50 minutes) with each patient (Frank, 1963). Usually the psychiatrist spends much of his productive time in such sessions conducted on a regular and continuing basis with each patient. The psychiatrist's professional life and working time are tied to the exigencies of his appointment book. Telephone calls are made and received in the 10- or 15-minute intervals between patients; hours are "free" or "booked" according to the patient schedule maintained. A successful therapist can be quite literally cut off during the course of his working day from any social contact except with patients. Private practice permits independent and autonomous work, but it also creates many pressures. One may be a sense of isolation from colleagues and the larger world.

Many organizational practitioners do not structure their day into a series of hour-long sessions with patients; nor is there as much concern with the long-term arrangement. Thus they can, if and when they wish, engage in discussions with colleagues and other professional staff about the general nature of their work, interesting cases, and problems. They have more freedom to rearrange their schedule, even though they may be expected to appear at their offices or on hospital grounds from the start of the work day until its end. We would therefore, expect psychiatrists in private practice to express more concern about isolation than the practitioners in organizations.

Image Status

Private practice provides the "ideal type" image of psychiatry. When members of the lay public (or potential recruits into the field) envision a psychiatrist, they are usually thinking of someone in this type of work. The picture includes voluntary patients who seek out the psychiatrist because they accept the idea that he can help them. This is indicated by their willingness to pay a fee for this service, but is also related to their prior education or knowledge about the psychiatrist's frame of reference (Kadushin, 1969).

If the psychiatrist is an analyst or an analytically oriented practitioner, he may have a steady and reliable income from a group of long-term analysands. Such practices require that patients be drawn predominantly from the prosperous or even extremely wealthy classes. And where patients are not wealthy, they show by their willingness to make sacrifices that the services of the psychiatrist are very important to them and that similar values are held between psychiatrist and patient. Generally, the office arrangements reflect tastes that accommodate such a patient population. Waiting rooms and offices are comfortable and tasteful, sometimes even luxurious.

The practitioner in organizations is usually a full-time employee, paid at a fixed salary irrespective of the number of patients interviewed a day or the length of time each patient is seen. While regular and predictable, such salaries do not compare favorably to the income potential of private practice. The types of patients are also different. They may be difficult cases to manage; they may be involuntary or at least reluctant inmates; and they may also question the value of treatment and the motives of the psychiatrist. And so the relationship may be an uncomfortable one in which the psychiatrist is forced to exert some control over the patient. The context in which therapist and patient meet is also less attractive. Offices are severely utilitarian, impersonal, small, spartan, and unrelieved by personal touches: often the bookcase is bare.

These differences in type of practice all tend to produce invidious distinctions between highly rewarded, high-status work (with rich or responsive patients) and less highly rewarded and low-status work (with poor or unappreciative patients in organizations). It is not surprising, then, that organizational practitioners tend to see themselves with lower status than private practitioners (and private-practice psychiatrists concur in this view.)* Under these conditions, one might expect practitioners in relatively low-status organizations like state hospitals to express considerable doubt about their prestige and worry about their professional image, while private practitioners should be relatively free from such doubts and worries.†

Effectiveness of Treatment

The many difficulties that the field of psychiatry has faced in justifying techniques and assessing results have raised serious theoretical and empirical questions for the practitioners. For the private psychiatrist, a serious question is: What should a patient legitimately expect as benefit from his expensive course of treatment (Frank, 1963)? The organizational practitioner may worry about this problem also. But, in addition, he must be concerned about making decisions with serious or even fateful consequences for the patient based on questionable expertise (Scheff, 1966; Hakeem, 1955; Miller and Schwartz, 1966; Szasz, 1963). These may include diagnoses affecting involuntary

---

*In a recent study (Problems in Social Change and Control in the Professions—NICHHD Grant HD 0277601) we found that in a forced ranking of types of practice, the average ranking by both organizational and private-practice psychiatrists indicated full-time organizational practice held the lowest prestige.

†Of course, psychiatrists in high-status organizations (e.g., Austen Riggs) would be more likely to resemble private practitioners in professional self-assurance. Such positions are, however, relatively few in number. For these observations I am indebted to R. Bucher and C. Schwartz.

commitment, prison (and even death) sentences, employment, security clearances, and military service. These decisions are made doubly difficult when the expertise on which they are based is debatable. Thus, doubts about effectiveness of treatment and attendant difficulties are problems that exist equally for psychiatrists in private or in organizational practice, even though they may involve somewhat different problems in each case. We therefore expected little difference between the groups over concern in this area. Since these problems are well recognized in the literature, and since they may be problems for both groups, overall mention of this theme was expected to be very high.

Study Design

In order to test and elaborate these preliminary speculations, a series of respondent samples were collected. The sample includes 81 private practitioners and 71 practitioners in organizational settings: 36 in state hospitals and 35 in the military.

The list of 18 phrases was designed to elicit responses about the profession. The incomplete sentences included some general or neutral items as: "My colleagues...," "In psychiatry it is best to be thought of as...," "Being a psychiatrist is like..," "They also included items designed specifically to elicit dislikes: "What annoys me about psychiatry..," "The trouble with most psychiatrists...," "One thing you never get in psychiatry...." (See the Appendix for the complete list). Respondents were asked to give spontaneous responses in completing the sentences and were assured that the study was designed to elicit information about professional rather than personal or private matters. Except for a pilot of 11 psychiatrists in private practice, all sentence completion lists were administered to informants at the end of lengthy interviews (one and a half to four hours). The majority of these interviews (122) were collected as part of a larger comparative study of professional groups.* This group of psychiatrists was divided almost equally between organizational and private practitioners. The sample of private practitioners

*Problems of Social Change and Control in Professions.

was selected by using introductions and referrals from psychiatrists already known through prior studies. These referrals, in turn, were asked to suggest further references. In addition to the "snowball" technique of sampling, direct solicitation by mail and phone of every psychiatrist in the phonebook of one large metropolitan city in California was used. Eliminating those who did not meet sample requirements (board certification or eligibility plus a private-practice schedule of approximately 25 hours a week or more), 50 percent of the psychiatrists contacted were pursuaded to participate in the study.

A second group of psychiatrists in private practice in a metropolitan area of the eastern United States were contacted as part of a dissertation project (Rachel Kahn-Hut, Ph. D. dissertation in progress, Department of Sociology, Brandeis University, Waltham, Mass.). Members of this group were all affiliates of a private teaching hospital. In this group 19 of the psychiatrists (50 percent of those contacted) agreed to participate.

The sample of organizational practitioners was selected somewhat differently. The entire number of career military psychiatrists (those who serve in some branch of the U.S. Armed Forces for a minimum of seven years and who hold regular commissions) is quite small at any point in time (usually around 200). Many of these military psychiatrists (70) had already participated in prior studies we had conducted. Therefore, the psychiatrists not yet included and serving within the Pacific Northwest were asked to participate. All consented. A few additional career psychiatrists who became accessible (by meeting at conventions or on field trips) during the course of the study were interviewed; they brought the sample to 35.

The remaining sample of organizational practitioners was selected by contacting state hospitals in a Western state and requesting permission of each individual psychiatrist for an interview. Of those meeting the study criteria (board certified or board eligible) 36 (57 percent of those contacted) participated in the study.

Such sampling methods as those described above are not systematic; but they are required by the difficulties of engaging the participation of psychiatrists who are often busy and difficult to reach. We were fortunate in having the help of prominent psychiatrists in the areas studied both to effect introductions and to give considerable informal help in urging other psychiatrists to cooperate.

Although there is reason to feel that we had good rapport with most subjects (they tolerated a long interview, returned questionnaires, and expressed interest in the study) some problems of interviewing or administering projective items to psychiatrists arose that seemed related to their professional training or experience. They have a "trained capacity" for evasiveness and non-committal responses to questions. Even in nontherapy situations, they may be guarded, if not actually suspicious and fearful of openness. Many informants answered the sentence completions only after long pauses, gave measured or evasive replies, or left some of the statements unanswered. Throughout the interviews it was common for one or two responses to be blocked. (In the total sample 40 percent of the respondents couldn't or wouldn't complete one or more of the sentences. This lack of response seemed to come fairly equally from all portions of the subsample: 38 percent from the private practitioners, 49 percent from the military psychiatrists, 33 percent from the state hospital psychiatrists.)

Perhaps this finding is a commentary about how these professionals feel about revealing information to an outsider. If the field were more cohesive with well-accepted and understood standards of practice, individual practitioners might feel more secure and so behave less cautiously. In addition, psychiatrists may feel uncomfortable about *role reversal*: i.e., responding to a sociologist who asks *them* to free associate. Learning about secrets through this technique is part of their stock in trade, their special prerogative; psychiatrists may thus be understandably reluctant to accept being studied in this manner by a sociologist. These data, then, cannot tell us what psychiatrists really "feel" about their profession. Rather, the themes culled from their responses may indicate what these professionals are publicly willing to admit or what they think suitable for the interviewer to know about them.

Findings: General Themes of Complaints

As we expected, the themes of isolation, image status, and effectiveness of treatment were all mentioned by the majority of those interviewed. In addition, two further themes emerged: Personal strains created by the nature of work and perception of negative personal characteristics among colleagues. Our belief that worries over effectiveness of treatment would be shared by all the population subsamples was also borne out. However no other expectation was realized. Effectiveness of treatment was the least frequently mentioned of all the major themes, rather than the most. And *no* themes differentiated between the two subsamples; respondents in all groups sampled showed the same overall responses in the five thematic areas analyzed. (See Table 1–5) However, close examination of these responses does explain in greater detail what worries or concerns psychiatrists express.

Effectiveness of Treatment

More than half of all respondents specifically mentioned worry about the effectiveness of treatment. This concern was expressed in three rather distinct subthemes: lack of standards and techniques, ambiguity of results, and pretending to possess expertise.

LACK OF STANDARDS AND TECHNIQUES

Thirty-five percent of all informants mentioned some problem relating to this subtheme. Psychiatry is "more an art than a science." Being a psychiatrist is like "being a painter." "it takes a great deal of mental work all the time as contrasted to surgery...where there are clear guidelines." The most important thing for the future of psychiatry "would be more research, more tools." "There are very few standards, very little that is definitely right or wrong, and roles very poorly defined." Further, a general uncertainty hovers over the entire field; there is not enough knowledge. Being a psychiatrist is like "someone in the dark searching for light." One thing you never get in psychiatry "is a clear cut formulation of anything."

"...we don't have enough knowledge." Being a psychiatrist is like "playing a piano in a whorehouse. You don't really know what's going on upstairs." "...we are dealing with so many unknowns that its almost impossible to have a cookbook."

AMBIGUITY OF RESULTS

Thirty-one percent of the respondents also indicate that results of treatment are hard to assess. There is uncertainty about what effective results should be, how long therapy should take. "I don't know if I am helping people." "...hard to learn from your mistakes." "...We can't tell whether or not patients get better," "...you never get to know what really happens to patients after they leave."

PRETENDING TO POSSESS EXPERTISE

In such circumstances, while it is surprising that so few of them do so, it is not surprising that psychiatrists (16 percent) also worry about overselling their product. A psychiatrist should be careful "of promising more than he can deliver." What annoys me about psychiatry "...an attitude that all answers are known and they are not." "...they overestimate the level of achievement of psychiatry and offer too much that is unrealistic to the patient." This problem arises not only in relation to the public but in interprofessional contacts. "I don't feel that (colleagues) are altogether open about what happens in their relationship with their patients...there's a tendency...when they talk among themselves, to talk primarily about successes." What annoys me about psychiatry "are the flimsily trained people who act as if they are trained and really are not and don't know the difference." "...they're inbred, are testy when confronted with objective or scientific data that fails to support bias or personal prejudice...."

Isolation

Two-thirds or more in each group of respondents made at least one complaint about feeling isolated. These feelings can be separated into three subthemes. The first includes any feelings of confinement or separation as well as remarks simply stating "too isolated." The second focuses on isolation from professional colleagues, medical and nonmedical. The third, communication difficulties, includes any more general problems of social distance that might encourage or enforce isolation.

STRUCTURED ISOLATION

The practice is physically isolated or isolating (38 percent mention this problem) because the hours and the nature of practice confine practitioners to their offices. The trouble with most psychiatrists ... "they are cloistered." Psychiatrists would perhaps be better off "if they'd leave the office more often." "...if the field were not so restrictive." There is a need for more personal contacts, broader and more enriching experiences outside their work, "...they become intellectually isolated." "...they don't have enough interests outside of the profession." Psychiatrists would perhaps be better off "if they had a wide range of interests in cultural matters in the arts and so forth." "...if they had a broader training in religion, philosophy, biochemistry." "I think probably most psychiatrists are naive to people in general. I think psychiatrists frequently get a very skewed view of the world." "...is isolated from the community which they serve." "I think it is so easy for a psychiatrist to become cloistered with his 8 to 10 patients a day ... where he doesn't have too much contact with the world. If you can have some outside contacts... it makes you a better rounded person."

ISOLATION FROM COLLEAGUES

Psychiatrists (27 percent) also complain that they are too isolated from other medical doctors or from other professionals in related fields. Sometimes they focus specifically on medicine, sometimes they deemphasize medicine and focus on other fields. "...one should keep in communication with quite a few colleagues." "...one needs to talk to other psychiatrists and other people." "...more closely associated with sociologists and anthropologists, philosophers and people in the arts than they would be with the science of medicine." "...remoteness from the rest of the field." Psychiatrists would perhaps be better off "if they had more communication with their fellow practitioners, psychiatric and non-psychiatric." "...to mix with other doctors more." "...one should have as frequent as possible professional contacts."

COMMUNICATION DIFFICULTIES

Psychiatrists see themselves as isolated by lack of opportunity to communicate (13 percent mention this problem). They cannot actively participate. "...you don't have the interpersonal play with the patients which sometimes you get in other fields of medicine. For instance, my brother is a dentist. He can talk to his patients. Small talk. I cannot do that. I cannot socialize. Sometimes I would like to, certainly." "...they need to keep themselves pretty detached from their patients." "...is the isolation produced by knowing many secrets which you can't discuss with other people." And so the situation in therapy may appear intimate but actually it is not. "...you have pseudo intimacy... seemingly close to other people, but...really illusions." "...they don't allow patients to get close enough to them." Even when psychiatrists feel they may communicate if they wish, their work is too arcane for others to understand. "...difficulty about communicating satisfactorily about patients and about concepts." "...alone or relying on one's own judgment because it is very difficult to explain to another person what one sees." "...is the difficulty explaining to people who are not in the field or who have had no experience with it before but who are just... curious, nice ordinary people...what you do...they can't really understand, you can't explain it..."

Image Trouble–Status Problems

Difficulties facing psychiatrists in projecting the appropriate image of their profession were seen by three-fourths of all respondents. Here four types of problems arise. First, in patient image trouble, the psychiatrist is misperceived as too powerful by his patients. Second, psychiatrists have general image trouble with both patients and public. The public has no clear idea what to expect; psychiatrists mention that it is difficult for them to project *any* kind of understandable image. Third, psychiatrists also have problems projecting an appropriate image to their medical colleagues. Although this last category is somewhat related to isolation, here it focuses only upon statements that specifically refer to medical colleagues and includes only those remarks that somehow indicate that psychiatry does not receive the respect it deserves from other medical specialists. Finally, any statements suggesting that psychiatrists help to create their own image trouble are included as the fourth subtheme.

PATIENT IMAGE TROUBLE

Over half the psychiatrists mentioned that patients do not understand what the limitations of psychiatry are; they see the psychiatrist as omnipotent, mysterious, unreasonable or coercive. The most common single response on one item was: Most patients see the psychiatrists as "God" (18 percent of the total sample studied mentioned this term specifically). Some additional responses to this item are: "mind-reader," "priest," "magician," "authority figure," "head-shrinker," "man with all the answers," "superhuman," "much more powerful than he really is..." The main concern seems to be that what patients expect is impossible to deliver.

GENERAL IMAGE TROUBLE

Psychiatrists feel they are generally seen by both public or their patients (18 percent mention this problem) "as either omnipotent or impotent." "Education will be required to bridge the gap," but... "there's no really good way... to educate the public." Yet psychiatrists should keep trying to bridge that gap. "...if they concerned themselves more with their public image." "...spend more time in public relations."

STATUS PROBLEMS IN MEDICINE

At the same time, psychiatrists also see themselves (10 percent mention this problem) as terrifically underrated or unappreciated by other physicians who might be expected to be more understanding. One thing you never get in psychiatry "a true understanding on the part of medical colleagues of what psychiatry is about and sympathy to psychiatry." The most important thing for the future of psychiatry "is to improve its relations with other medical specialties." "It is important to be the kind of psychiatrist... that is respected by his medical colleagues."

PSYCHIATRISTS CREATE IMAGE TROUBLE

Psychiatrists also criticize their colleagues for not trying hard enough to project an appropriate image (15 percent mention this problem). ". . . is its willingness to keep an air of mystery about itself." At the same time, they do oversell the profession. Psychiatrists would perhaps be better off "if they avoided giving opinions about matters they are not objectively certain of." ". . . they have some tendencies to play God too." ". . . to avoid overselling his potential." They are also not as careful about their personal behavior as they should be and often give the field a bad name. ". . . must appraise what other people think of him and keep it in mind." ". . . are the large number of prima donnas in the field." ". . . that doesn't appear like a nut." ". . . have to treat other psychiatrists often as patients."

Personal Strains Created by the Work

There was considerable discussion of personal strains or pressures created by the nature of psychiatric practice. 1. The work of the psychiatrist is too hard. 2. It creates too much pressure. 3. The practice of psychiatry does not provide sufficient rewards. 4. It presents too many temptations. Three-fourths of the entire sample mentioned at least one of these four types of problems.

WORK IS TOO HARD

The most frequent response was that work is too demanding of the practitioner. Almost half of the total sample mention this problem. ". . . one has to invest a great deal of oneself." ". . . with most psychiatrists. . . they can't leave their work in the office when they go home." ". . . more frustrating than I bargained for." ". . . is the frequent unsolvable problems." And for state hospital informants only, what annoys me about psychiatry ". . . administration, staff-work, mechanics, drudgery, routine."

TOO MUCH PRESSURE

A related topic mentioned by a fourth of all respondents was that the work created a lot of pressures. A psychiatrist should be careful "because of the responsibility that they have for people's lives and emotions and things," that it was likely to exacerbate personal weaknesses, "...psychiatrists often become involved in areas where they shouldn't be involved" "...you had better resolve your own personal problems and conflicts very carefully or you are going to get into difficulties either in your practice or in your personal life." Such pressures account for emotional instability among psychiatrists. The nature of the psychiatric profession is such that "...we have a high suicide rate."

NOT ENOUGH REWARDS

Most responses of the 26 percent in this category came from replies to the item "One thing you never get in psychiatry...." The most frequently recurring responses were "rich" or "gratitude." Others were "kind thoughts," "paid enough," "is a lot of money," "people recognize and appreciate what you are trying to do," "you can only make a limited amount of money in your entire practice because of your time."

TOO MANY TEMPTATIONS

Finally, psychiatrists complain that the nature of the work puts temptations in their path to do things they know they ought not do. In the entire sample, 16 percent mentioned this problem. For example, "too many psychiatrists like to talk about patients and at times to identify patients particularly if they are well known people...it is very tempting," "using patients to satisfy his own needs," "to be sure what he's doing for his patients is primarily for them and not for him." There are also temptations to harm themselves by leading "too sedentary a life," "...you never get enough exercise." or by succumbing to women, "...at first, I was afraid and careful of certain kinds of patients like paranoids and seductive women."

Negative Personal Characteristics

The second unexpected theme that emerged from the data was that psychiatrists are quite critical of their colleagues:

Seventy-eight percent of all respondents complained about some unattractive or negative qualities they saw in the practitioners around them. Perhaps these complaints do not tell us about evaluations of the personal characteristics of colleagues but rather about the lack of agreement in the field about how psychiatry should be practiced. These negative remarks may also reflect the way in which invidious character terminology is used as a weapon in the factional debates between those with differing perspectives (Armor and Klerman, 1968).

Whatever the explanation for them, these complaints can be subclassified into three main types: Psychiatrists complain that colleagues are overly superior and somehow maintain entirely too much distance from patients, public, or fellow professionals. Psychiatrists are dependent and overconforming; they have a limited vision, preferring regular hours and salary; and they possess traits of security-mindedness, unimaginativeness, and laziness. Finally, psychiatrists sometimes label their colleagues with the terminology of mental illness and imply that colleagues are or seem to be crazy.

OVERLY SUPERIOR, TOO MUCH SOCIAL DISTANCE MAINTAINED

The most common remark is that psychiatrists are arrogant, unfriendly, and uncommunicative. Two-thirds of all respondents mentioned this problem. Some of the adjectives they used to describe their colleagues were: "self-satisfied," "self-righteous," "vain," "pompous," "hard-shelled," "uninterested in people," "secretive," "stiff." These characteristics are particularly resented when displayed before colleagues. What annoys me about psychiatry "...well, I think the arrogance and the pompousness of how psychiatrists behave to each other."

DEPENDENT AND OVER CONFORMING

The second most common derogatory classification (33 percent mentioned it) was that psychiatrists showed "a need for security," that they are "unimaginative," "inhibited," "lazy," and "timid." Virtually all of these responses (81 percent) came in answer to "One thing that psychiatrists practicing in institutional settings seem to have in common...."

MENTAL ILLNESS

Since a concern with diagnosis and pathology is so common in psychiatry, it is probably not surprising that psychiatrists sometimes use both lay and professional mental illness labels on themselves. This use of labels may also reflect something broader about the structure of psychiatry: the assimilation into the psychiatric framework of lay conceptions about mental illness (as well as vice versa). Such a blurring between professional and lay distinctions may be connected with the fact that there really is no agreed-on, delimited body of psychiatric knowledge (Garfinkel, 1956).

Sixteen percent of all respondents mention this category. They remarked that their colleagues are "masochistic," "odd," "crazy," "crack-pots," "depressed," "senile," "immature," "a screwy bunch," and "kooks," or that (in psychiatry it is best to be considered) "normal," "sane."

Analysis of Informant Responses for the Total Sample Population

Generally speaking, the concerns that appear through the sentence completions suggest the type of difficulties psychiatrists find in their working life. The existence of common perceptions of these problems is reflected both in the limited range of responses and in many identical or nearly identical patterns of responses. However, a few noticeable differences between subsamples—chiefly distinguishing the military psychiatrists from the others—exist.

As far as similarities, some of the themes discussed in this paper offer no surprises. Effectiveness of psychiatry is a much-debated topic, and perhaps the only surprise is that psychiatrists don't mention it even more than they do. (This may reflect our research method).

One of the more interesting results of administering a sentence completion list is the opportunity it affords to catch sight of fugitive themes through which a new descriptive picture of a profession may be formed. The general theme of isolation, frequently found in these data, for example, is not often discussed in professional journals, although the subtheme of improvement of relations with other professionals is well documented (Caplan, 1964; Riessman *et al.*, 1966). However, informal discussions with psychiatrists prior to this study indicated the importance of the general theme of isolation; they frequently mentioned the necessity for taking clinic, teaching, or research appointments—sometimes at little remuneration—as respite from the loneliness of practice. And for the military and state psychiatrists, the recurrence of this theme may indicate a wish to see more of their colleagues outside the employing institution. The sentence completion list provides some empirical evidence that the concern about isolation may be widespread throughout psychiatry.

Isolation may affect the concerns expressed as image trouble or status problems. The most frequently mentioned aspect of image trouble is the perception of the psychiatrist as too powerful or too important. This would reinforce any tendencies toward an unreasonably high opinion of himself that the psychiatrist himself might hold. And such tendencies, if encouraged in the office interview, would not motivate a psychiatrist to break out of his splendid isolation. This situation may encourage or produce the difficult, arrogant behavior psychiatrists complain of in their colleagues. The focus, which also arises in subthemes of image trouble and in effectiveness becomes clearly dominant in negative personality characteristics. A majority of all informants in all samples indicate that they find a number of their confreres difficult or even intolerable.

Let us consider this finding in the context of the three anticipated themes: isolation, effectiveness, and image. Negative personality characteristics are aggravated in a work context that is isolated from observation and in which adequate results are hard to define. Furthermore, the theory is ambiguous and provides rationalizations for failure, e.g., the patient wasn't "working" or was "resisting." Under these circumstances it is not surprising that psychiatrists may complain about the arrogance of their colleagues. And it is also not surprising that they may feel isolated both physically and in terms of opportunities for communication with others and that they have image problems. Arrogance is hardly attractive; combined with the natural conditions of isolation created by the nature of practice, it might well inhibit professional relationships or friendships with others.

These considerations lead to speculations about the most general sources of tension in psychiatry. The psychiatrist has to learn to use himself as the sounding board in the therapeutic situation. And so he will have to be involved and sensitive to his responses to the patient. But the psychiatrist must avoid the dangers of becoming too personally involved. However, once he embarks upon his practice he has no one to guide or check him in order to evaluate his degree of success. He must tolerate interpersonal pressures, and resist temptations. But there is no one, certainly not the patient (who sees the psychiatrist as God), who can tell him to "shape up" if he should prove weak or injudicious.

Analysis of Differing Responses
Between Sub-Populations in the Sample

Military psychiatrists show the highest number of concerns about the major themes; they lead the other psychiatrists in four of the five themes presented. And in three of these four (image, negative personal characteristics, and effectiveness) military psychiatrists are markedly above the average score for the entire population (by 16, 12, and 10 percentage points, respectively). In this difference they also show more variations from the mean than does any other subsample.

While the results are not conclusive, it does appear that it is not organizational psychiatrists per se who will differ from private practitioners, but it may be that certain subgroups— as those in the military—have a sufficiently different place in the profession to provide a different focus on problems from that of their colleagues. Previous research on military psychiatry does lend some support to the view that they may be a unique group in some respects. Many of their responsibilities and problems are quite different from those arising in civilian practice, (Daniels, 1972).

However, there are some interesting differences between the organizational and private samples that should be noted in the attribution of negative characteristics. A disproportionate number of the responses suggesting that institutional psychiatrists are insecure or overly concerned with security come from the *private* practitioners. Perhaps because such remarks might be considered self-derogatory, the organizational practitioners contribute fewer such responses. But if we consider another negative attribution—mental illness—we find an interesting reversal suggested between these two respondent groups. The organizational psychiatrists offer more disparaging remarks in this category than do the private practitioners. It seems likely that organizational practitioners associate these disparaging characteristics with private practitioners and not with themselves. This possibility is supported by examination of the completions to the sentence: "One thing that psychiatrists in orthodox analytic practice have in common...." In a sample of 98 private practitioners, 14 military psychiatrists, and 34 state hospital psychiatrists selected from the larger study, positive remarks were made by 22 percent of the private practitioners and 10 percent of the organizational men. Negative remarks were made by 28 percent of the private practitioners and 40 percent of the organizational men.

Conclusions

The original hypotheses have not been supported. Differences in structural position within the specialty do not affect focus of problems concerning the specialty. But this negative finding is somewhat moderated by considering what we have learned from examining the themes that have been presented. Psychiatrists have told us much about what they *don't* like in their profession when they complete the sentences offered. Perhaps these complaints are indicators of the price that is paid for maintaining the structure of psychiatric practice as it now exists. If we take isolation as an example we can see that it is the other side of the coin of nonobservability in work. Psychiatrists want the latter, insisting upon confidentiality and privacy. Unfortunately, isolation is one structural condition required for nonobservability. Belief in the necessity for restrictions on ordinary social interactions with patients is structurally related to the kind of psychiatric theory on which much practice is based: That is, the psychiatrist is the neutral object or screen against which the patient projects images. The psychiatrist may uphold this theory while deploring one of its consequences—his isolation. Finally, isolation is a consequence of lack of communication about the basic issues of his work. Psychiatric training encourages intellectual loneliness because it includes no tradition of mutual questioning and examination of collegial performances at work. Psychiatrists are then unwilling to examine these issues with their colleagues when they become active professionals. Thus they maintain the security of the general ideology at the expense of some self-imposed isolation.

The problems stemming from isolation are complicated and exacerbated by the problems arising from patient expectations and public awe of the psychiatrist. Marmor (1953) points out that the constant exercise of authority carries with it the occupational hazard of tending to create unrealistic feelings of superiority in the authority figure. Marmor argues that whether or not persons with a "God Complex" are attracted into psychiatry, the activities of the professional at his work will encourage the creation of this attitude. This problem arises for members of any occupation in some type of relationship of power over clients—doctors, lawyers, clergymen, teachers, political and military leaders. Here, the paradox may be that the exercise or assumption of authority may be necessary to perform the required service satisfactorily. Yet feelings of authority make it more difficult to cope practically with many real problems. Characteristics of arrogance or smugness, encouraged by responses of overawed patients and then nurtured in the isolated environment of a private practice, can create a battery of problems when a psychiatrist attempts to negotiate a disagreement with a colleague of equal prestige and power. New areas and problems in psychiatry—community psychiatry or conjoint family therapy—may require constant negotiation and personal effort from the psychiatrist to appease and compromise. It is not surprising, with such problems in mind, that the themes we have presented arise for the psychiatrists in this sample. And it is against such a background of analysis or interpretation that we attempt to explain the range and variety of themes we have presented in this paper.

Appendix—Sentence-Completion List

1   The most important thing for the future of psychiatry...
2   A psychiatrist should be careful...
3   Most patients think of the psychiatrist as...
4   Compared to what I thought a career in psychiatry would be like when I was in school, I have found out...
5   One thing you never get in psychiatry...
6   One thing that psychiatrists practicing in institutional settings seem to have in common...
7   One thing that psychiatrists in orthodox analytic practice seem to have in common...
8   Psychiatrists would perhaps be better off...
9   The most influential people in psychiatry...
10   Being a psychiatrist is like...
11   The trouble with most psychiatrists...
12   The nature of the psychiatric profession is such that...
13   My colleagues...
14   In order to get the most out of being a psychiatrist...
15   It is important to be the kind of psychiatrist...
16   What annoys me about psychiatry...
17   In psychiatry it is best to be thought of as...
18   When a psychiatrist seems extremely interested and concerned about the welfare of a particular patient...

For the purposes of this analysis, three of the 18 items (9, 17, 18) produced little or no codable data.

Table 1—Effectiveness of Treatment

Percentage* of Respondents in Each Category

	TOTAL	PRIVATE	ORGANIZATIONAL PRACTICE		
			Total	Military	State Hospital
	N = 152	N = 81	N = 71	N = 35	N = 36
Effectiveness of Treatment	59	53	65	69	61
Lack of standards and techniques	35	36	37	40	33
Ambiguity of results	31	28	34	37	31
Pretending to possess expertise	16	9	24	31	17

*All percentages are based on totals of respondents rather than number of responses. A respondent may be counted in more than one subtheme but is still only counted once in the major theme.

Table 2—Isolation

Percentage* of Respondents in Each Category

	TOTAL	PRIVATE	ORGANIZATIONAL PRACTICE		
			Total	Military	State Hospital
	N = 152	N = 81	N = 71	N = 35	N= 36
Isolation	63	63	63	66	61
Structured isolation	38	37	39	49	31
Isolated from colleagues	27	29	25	23	28
Communication difficulties	13	12	14	20	9

*All percentages are based on totals of respondents rather than number of responses. A respondent may be counted in more than one subtheme but is still only counted once in the major theme.

Table 3—Image Trouble and Status Problems

Percentage * of Respondents in Each Category

	TOTAL	PRIVATE	ORGANIZATIONAL PRACTICE		
			Total	Military	State Hospital
	N = 152	N = 81	N = 71	N = 35	N = 36
Image Trouble and Status Problems	74	68	80	94	67
Patient image trouble: Psychiatrist misperceived as too powerful	54	49	59	69	50
General image trouble: patient and public	18	17	20	34	5
Status problems in medicine	10	7	13	9	17
Psychiatrists create image trouble	15	6	25	43	8

* All percentages are based on totals of respondents rather than number of responses. A respondent may be counted in more than one subtheme but is still only counted once in the major theme.

Table 4—Personal Strains Created by the Work

Percentage* of Respondents in Each Category

	TOTAL	PRIVATE	ORGANIZATIONAL PRACTICE		
			Total	Military	State Hospital
	N = 152	N = 81	N = 71	N = 35	N = 36
Personal Strains Created by the Work	74	77	70	71	69
Work is too hard	47	46	46	43	50
Too much pressure	27	26	28	34	22
Not enough rewards	26	22	30	29	31
Too many temptations	16	22	11	9	14

* All percentages are based on totals of respondents rather than number of responses. A respondent may be counted in more than one subtheme but is still only counted once in the major theme.

Table 5—Negative Personal Characteristics

Percentage * of Respondents in Each Category

	TOTAL	PRIVATE	ORGANIZATIONAL PRACTICE		
			Total	Military	State Hospital
	N = 152	N = 81	N = 71	N = 35	N = 36
Negative Personal Characteristics	78	73	85	89	81
Overly superior, too much social distance maintained	66	59	75	71	78
Dependent and over-conforming	33	40	25	31	19
Mental illness	16	5	28	26	31

* All percentages are based on totals of respondents rather than number of responses. A respondent may be counted in more than one subtheme but is still only counted once in the major theme.

References

Armor, D., and Klerman, G. (1968), Psychiatric treatment orientations. *J. Health Soc. Behav.*, 9:243–254.

Caplan, G. (1964), *Principles of Preventive Psychiatry*. New York: Basic Books.

Daniels, A. K. (1972), Military psychiatry: The emergence of a subspecialty. In *Medical Men and Their Work*, ed. E. Freidson and J. Lorber, 145–162. New York: Atherton Press.

Frank, J. D. (1963), *Persuasion and Healing*. New York: Schocken Books.

Garfinkel, H. (1956), Some sociological concepts and methods for psychiatrists. *Psychiatr. Res. Rep.*, 6:181–195.

Hakeem, M. (1955), A critique of the psychiatric approach to crimend a correction. *Law Contemp. P. b.*, 23:650.

Kadushin, C. (1969), *Why People Go to Psychiatrists*. New York: Atherton Press.

Marmor, J. (1953), The feeling of superiority. *Am. J. Psychiatr.*, 110:370–376.

Miller, D., and Schwartz, M. (1966), County lunacy commission hearings: Some observations of commitments to a state mental hospital. *Soc. Prob.*, 14:26–35.

Riessman, F., et al. (eds.) (1966), *Mental Health in a Changing Community*. New York: Grune & Stratton.

Scheff, T. J. (1966), *Being Mentally Ill*. Chicago: Aldine.

Szasz, T. S. (1963), *Law, Liberty, and Psychiatry*. New York: Macmillan.

Chapter 7

George Ritzer

INDIGENOUS NON-PROFESSIONALS IN COMMUNITY MENTAL HEALTH: BOON OR BOONDOGGLE?

THE wide-ranging dissatisfaction of various minority groups in American society has spawned a series of brush fires, some of which, such as the ones at Attica prison, Kent State, Delano, the Marin County Courthouse, the 1968 Democratic convention, and Jackson State, have won national headlines. Other confrontations have generated far less notoriety but perhaps have similar (albeit less spectacular) consequences for American society. The conflict between minority-group clients and the professionals who offer them the services they need is merely one aspect of a far wider arena of conflict. Blacks, Chicanos, Puerto Ricans, women, students, and other minorities are in conflict with those in other service-delivery systems (police, politicians, professors, storeowners). While I have chosen to focus on clients versus professionals, many of the points discussed also apply to conflict between customers and those in other occupations.

The conflict between minority-group members and professionals is viewed as the "revolt of the client" by Haug and Sussman (1969). This includes the revolt of poverty clients against welfare caseworkers, black parents against ghetto school systems, university students versus their professors, and hospital patients in opposition to their physicians. There are a number of reasons for this widescale revolt of the client. Perhaps the most frequently cited explanation is that we do not have a sufficient number of professionals to provide the kind of service our society regards as its ideal. Yet it is also probably true that we have never had, or will we ever have, the number of professionals needed to match our ideals. Why then a revolt of the client at this point in history? The reasons, I think, must be traced to changes in society as well as in the relationship between clients and professionals.

Clearly the revolt of the client reflects the broader changes taking place in minority-group relations. With such cries as Women's Liberation, Black Power, and Red Power, Americans are rebelling against the authority of political leaders, school superintendents, prison wardens, policemen, and professionals. Whether it is due to changes within the total society or simply within minority groups, clients are now questioning the authority of professionals to make decisions that affect their lives.

However, we must also look at changes within the client–professional relationship. The professions have been traditionally differentiated from other occupations by their autonomy and the degree of control practitioners have over their clients. In fact, only the professions have clients—all other occupations have customers. Customers may question the authority of those who serve them, clients may not. While this view of the professional–client relationship is not isomorphic to reality, it is true that, in general, professionals have more control over their clients than those in other occupations have over their customers. Clients have always evaluated professionals (Freidson, 1960), and there is evidence to indicate that their evaluations are rather accurate (Kisch and Reeder, 1969). But whereas in the past it was individual clients who questioned professionals, today this confrontation is based in organized groups. In part, this is due to the increasing militancy of minority groups, but it is also due to the fact that the inadequacies of the professional have become far more obvious. This increased visibility can be traced to the mass media. Movies, television, and the news media have all made the public more aware of the ways professionals operate. Even though the media have romanticized the lawyer, physician, or school teacher, they have also provided greater publicity to professional failings, leading clients to question the professional's expertise as well as his claims to altruism (Haug and Sussman, 1969, p. 156).

Freidson (1971, p. 35) has recently noted that "The medical profession exercises a degree of control over the delivery of health services that precludes both effective and adequate health care for the majority of the client population." He adds that: "since the weaknesses I have outlined stem from professionalism itself, the medical profession cannot be expected to rectify them" (Freidson, 1971, p. 40). Similar statements could be made about every other profession. In recognition of these facts, clients are revolting.

Along with professionals and the professions,* the organizations in which professionals are employed are also under attack. Haug and Sussman (1969, p. 156) argue that these organizational delivery systems (hospitals, schools, mental health centers, welfare agencies) are assaulted for two very different reasons. On the one hand, they are viewed as "defective and insufficient" and criticized for not doing what they do very well. On the other hand, they are attacked because their delivery system "is too efficient and exceeds the appropriate bounds for power." This implies that their drive for bureaucratic efficiency ignores the individual needs of the client and that their power over the client has become too great.

The community mental health movement itself may be viewed as a response to the revolt of the client, of which the new careers movement is only one aspect. One of the major goals of the new careers movement has been the improvement of professional services to the poor. It arose to create "a *bridge* between the middleclass-oriented professional and the client from the lower socio-economic groups" (Reiff and Reissman, 1970). This bridging function was to be performed by the creation of a new role: the indigenous nonprofessional. The indigenous nonprofessional is recruited from the group being served and acts as an aide to and a link for the professional. Indigenous nonprofessionals, or new careerists, are also found in a variety of settings other than mental health.

Nonprofessionals have long been found in mental health,

*See Ritzer (1972) for a discussion of the difference between professions and professionals.

but the indigenous nonprofessional is very different from the paraprofessionals who preceded him. Hartog (1967) contends that the basic difference stems from the pool from which they are drawn. Paraprofessionals are not drawn from the groups being served, but are typically middle-class housewives and students interested in helping the deprived segments of society. In contrast, the indigenous nonprofessionals are drawn from a pool that Hartog labels "the unwanted." This group includes the impoverished, unemployed, retired, mentally and physically disabled, drug addicts, and school drop-outs. Thus they are drawn from the groups that are most likely to be served by community mental health centers.

Riessman, (undated, p. 1), as one of the founding fathers of the new careers movement, enunciated the following goals:

Provide millions of new jobs for the unemployed.
Create human service positions which cannot be automated out of existence.
Rehabilitate the poor through meaningful employment.
Provide more and "closer" service for the poor.
Reach the unreached.
Reduce the manpower shortage in education, health, and social work.
Free the professional for more creative and supervisory roles.

The new careers movement involves a number of essential elements:

1. It assumes that tasks performed by professionals can be broken down into smaller simpler tasks that can be handled by inexperienced people.
2. Those who are hired need not have any relevant training or experience, but are trained on the job.
3. The entry job of the indigenous nonprofessional is *not* a dead end. Attached to that entry position is a career ladder with "the ultimate option of becoming a professional" (Riessman, undated, p. 9).
4. The indigenous nonprofessional will free the professional

to perform more general functions such as supervision, planning, and training.

5. The indigenous nonprofessional, since he comes from the same group that he serves, will be able to perform traditional functions more effectively. Furthermore, he will be able to develop new functions since he is a peer and can act in a more subjective manner toward his clients.

6. Although it seeks to develop new functions and roles, the new careers movement is opposed to "reducing the quality of the service or deprecating the value of the professional" (Riessman, undated p., 10).

Indigenous nonprofessionals in the mental health field perform rather specific functions. First they are to provide psychiatric help for numerous persons otherwise unable to receive such assistance, supplementing the undermanned mental health professions in the community mental health setting. In addition, Hallowitz and Riessman (1967) list seven other roles:

Intervene in critical situations.
Engage comparatively pathological people in meaningful relationship.
Stimulate them to take action in their own behalf.
Mobilize community resources.
Serve as a bridge between the client-in-need and the professional service.
Interpret needs of the clients to professionals.
Serve as role models in the community.

Given these attractive and high-sounding goals, how have the indigenous nonprofessionals in mental health fared? There are some data on the success, but most are far from definitive. For example, in a review of studies on indigenous therapists Torrey (1969, p. 368) says, "They all conclude the same thing: that indigenous therapists are often effective in producing positive therapeutic changes." This claim is grounded in few hard data. Hughes *et al.* (1971) do present some hard data on the use of indigenous nonprofessionals in a community-based program for the treatment of narcotic addicts,

finding that the use of indigenous nonprofessionals (including an ex-addict who had kicked the habit four
weeks earlier) helped reduce the number of discharges against
medical advice from 60 percent of all those admitted to 10
percent. While these authors report that following the employment of indigenous nonprofessionals there was an increase
in the number remaining abstinent, the time span covered by
the data was very limited. Furthermore their results may have
been confounded by the introduction of other factors such as the
development of a halfway house for ex-addicts. Thus we cannot
accurately trace the increase in abstinence to the introduction of the indigenous nonprofessionals. Riessman and
Hallowitz (1967) report that two community mental health
centers in the Bronx, each employing a professional and
5 to 10 community mental health aides, were able to reach 6,620
new cases after only six months of operation. Here, however,
we have no report on the effectiveness with which all of these
new cases were handled.

Indigenous nonprofessionals in the mental health field *may*
help, but as yet we do not have enough long-run, large-scale
evaluative studies to confirm or deny this assumption. It would
seem however that the use of indigenous nonprofessionals in
mental health would be a boon to both needy clients and embattled professionals. The clients are being helped, at least in
part, by peers who presumably understand their needs. Furthermore, a new careerist is in a position to act as an "advocate"
for his constituency, making the helping agency more responsive
to its needs. Such a program would also seem to be a welcome
addition as far as professionals are concerned. Short on manpower, the professions are now aided by subordinates who
constitute no threat to their powerful position.

Yet the new careers movement has recently run into
problems with many professionals, clients, and even indigenous
nonprofessionals rejecting its basic principles. How can we
account for this apparent failure?

The new careers movement has never been intended to
revolutionize the delivery system despite the apparent need for
such basic change. The new careers movement was launched
to patch up a failing system, not to really change that system.

Basically, the new careers movement sought to *coopt* into the existing service delivery system some of the actual or potential enemies of that system. The basic goal was to defuse an explosive situation and any real gains in service were incidental. I do not contend that all those involved in the new careers movement were conscious of this objective, but it is certain that at least some of them were.

Others have attacked the cooptive aims of the community mental health and new careers movements. Haug and Sussman (1969, p. 158) contend: "The 'new careers' movement, although probably not developed as cooptation, may be discussed from this perspective." Miller *et al.*, (1970, p. 39) have attacked all poverty programs (including new careers and community mental health) for this very same reason:

> Since the declaration of the poverty war, the United States has moved toward policies that seek to include more people in the services and opportunities open to the affluent majority of the population. But acts of inclusion also exclude. Efforts to improve the conditions of the poor, when effective, generally result in improving the condition of those at the top of the bottom, leaving the bottommost untouched. Those left behind may be worse off than before. Their relative deprivation may grow, or their feeling about themselves may become negative. The selective mobility of some may mean the selective debasement of many others.

Statman (1970, p. 274) labels these programs part of a pacification effort:

> Regardless of the altruistic intent of the staff, federally funded community mental health programs aimed at the ghetto often serve solely to pacify the neighborhood—to mystify and mollify justifiable outrage and thereby prevent action for meaningful change. Our analysis suggests that by diverting neighborhood concern towards problems of "mental health" and away from efforts to confront the basic oppressive institutions in our society, such programs function to maintain the status quo rather than to advance the interests of the oppressed community....

Statman is really making two points. First, he is saying that community mental health programs, by coopting community agents, reduce the possibility of meaningful change. Second, he says that the focus on mental health makes it seem as if problems were individual, rather than institutional, problems. The goal is to do something about the "sick" individual rather than the pathological social conditions (e.g., racist institutions) that caused the individual's "sickness."

Even though it did not promise to revolutionize the service-delivery system, the new careers movement seemed to promise some changes in the system; yet from the beginning the program was subverted. The ways in which the new careers movement was subverted tell us a great deal about the chances of success of any reformist movement.

The jobs given to indigenous nonprofessionals were often meaningless. Despite some high-sounding words, the new indigenous nonprofessionals should have known what was in store for them. Note, for example, that Riessman said that indigenous nonprofessionals in education could take over such tasks as "tying children's shoelaces, taking attendance, etc." (Riessman, undated, p. 69). A good example of this in operation is the "family agent" who aids needy families by providing such "vital" functions as filling out forms for them or arranging for transportation to helping agencies (Crowne, 1969).

Although the indigenous nonprofessional must have been depressed by the nature of his work, he had still greater shocks in store for him. Lacking a meaningful job, he soon found he also did not have a career. Talking of new careerists in community mental health, Fields (1970, p. 58) says: "Without academic degrees, licensures or credentials, they have virtually no job mobility, whether vertically or horizontally." In fact, Riessman's provision of the ultimate option of becoming a professional can only be regarded as a cruel joke. As Haber (1968) has pointed out, this implied radical changes that professionals were not about to allow. Professionals have jealously guarded their right to license neophytes even after they have adequately completed the required training in professional schools. The new careers movement implied that one could become a professional without going through the training schools and without the blessings of the professional association. The new careerist could become a professional, or so he was told, by demonstrating superior performance on the job and by undertaking job-associated training and education. This clearly runs counter to the vested interests of the established professionals; it could mean the end of the training school, professional associations, and control of the profession by its elite members. The professionals were clearly not going to supervise their own demise. This is reflected in Haber's summary of evaluations of the new careers movement, where he concludes that the major problem was "resistance from professionals and administrative traditionalists" (Haber, 1968, p. 8).

One of the most astounding features of the new careers movement was the idea that the professionals would do a large part of the training of the indigenous nonprofessionals, which was supposed to enable the new careerist to ultimately become a professional. In other words, the established professional was supposed to contribute to his own devaluation. It is little wonder that another one of the major problems that has plagued the new careers movement has been an inadequate training program. But the failure of the training programs cannot be blamed totally on professionals since the money needed for such extensive efforts has not been forthcoming. Money that has been acquired has been for short-term purposes, not for such long-term goals as training. Furthermore, the business community has not become involved in the program as it was first hoped. Finally, relatively few colleges have provided needed courses for training efforts.

The training that has occurred has been typically oriented toward molding the indigenous nonprofessional into the model of middle-class respectability. Note the following description of an aide training program conducted by Howard University (Lynch *et al.*, 1966, p. 138):

The Howard University programs have been established on the following assumptions: It is assumed that the aides will need to revise and reconsider their customary standards and values in regard to employment, and they will have to comport themselves on the job. Many young people from disadvantaged backgrounds consider that to work hard is to be "square." They are unwilling to accept the fact that they have to dress appropriately, stick by the rules and routines, report punctually and regularly on the job, and, even, perhaps, change their customary manner of speech. They do not know how to understand the institutional structure, to use supervision or get help if things go wrong.

A similar description is advanced by Morrison (1970, p. 245) "The layman-turned-professional (i.e., case-aide community worker, indigenous nonprofessional) must shed some of his former 'positions' and begin to take on at least some of the trappings of professional expert if he is to 'know better' and help people." Thus, in many cases, community mental health training programs have deliberately sought to divest recruits of their indigenous background.

The new careers movement was also subverted by the selection of the participants. Ideally, all segments of the community served were to be represented among the indigenous nonprofessionals. However, there has been a disturbing tendency for those in charge of these programs to skim the "cream" off the top of the community. The cream, in this case, means those members of the community who best approximate the middle-class standards of those who do the selecting, as is clear in the following statement (Smith and Hobbs, 1966, p. 506, emphasis added):

> Specific tasks sometimes assigned to highly trained professionals (such as administrative duties, follow-up contacts, or tutoring, for a disturbed child) may be assigned to *carefully selected* adults with little or no technical training. Effective communication across barriers of education, social class, and race can be aided by the creation of new roles for *specially talented* member of deprived groups.

Such standards are hardly likely to ensure that a cross section of the community will be represented among the indigenous nonprofessionals.

Similar standards are implied by Hallowitz and Riessman (1967, p. 773) in their discussion of the selection procedures used in neighborhood service centers set up by Lincoln Hospital in 1965: "On the basis of this initial presentation, a number of applicants decided not to proceed with their application. Similarly, we were able to spot some who by their manner and behavior seemed inappropriate choices and were thus screened out." It is very likely that those who dropped out and were screened out were those who were most like the majority of the community and least like the middle-class standard. The principle that emerges is that if you must coopt members of the opposition, at least coopt those individuals who are going to cause you the least amount of trouble.

It is also apparent that those in power used the indigenous nonprofessional against his constituency rather than in its behalf. Note this description of the family agent discussed earlier: "The family agent is also expected to serve, in a subtle fashion, as a role model for the family. She (most of the agents are women) is supposed to be an agent of acculturation—in other words, an agent of change—and a means of helping the family become assimilated into the larger society" (Crowne, 1969, p. 182). There is much that is insidious in the preceding statement. It accepts the view that it is the individual who is to blame for his problems, not society. Thus it is the individual, not society who must change (become acculturated or assimilated). Furthermore, the indigenous nonprofessional is assigned the function of acculturation. Who is the indigenous nonprofessional helping here? The answer seems clear. By acting as a role model and helping another deprived family assimilate, she is helping to remove another thorn from the side of the establishment. There is a long tradition for such an approach in American society, which Ryan (1971) calls "blaming the victim."

Those who control the entry of people into the indigenous nonprofessionals have gone a step further. They employ some of the victims to "cure" others. Even those individuals who are inclined to work for their constituency face tremendous pressure to work in behalf of their employing agency. "If they (indigenous nonprofessionals) wish to ascend to administrative functions, the pressures to parrot existing behaviors are tremendous; thus as agents of the community they are often emasculated." (Fields, 1970, p. 58). Thus, by careful selection and by on-the-job pressure, those who control the various agencies are sure that the indigenous nonprofessional will do little or nothing to "rock the boat."

When professionals become involved in new careers programs they have made it clear that the new careerist will remain in secondary positions. The following statement is a good example of this position (Crowne, 1969, pp. 176-177):

> The greatest efforts at present are being directed toward the preparation of nonprofessional or ancillary workers. I do not want to denigrate this trust, but a word of warning seems in order: without supervisory *professionals* to train, direct, and assist mental health "support" personnel, there may be a dispersion and waste of talents and services that could be to the detriment of those seeking help.

It is clear that the established professionals never intended to dilute their position or to accept new careerists in anything other than menial and supportive positions. This is made even clearer by Willcox (1970, p. 349): "Community involvement does not mean community control. In the author's opinion, low-income people will not benefit from complete control of the New Careers program."

Numerous other reasons for the failure of the new careers movements could be examined at length:

1. The failure to give indigenous nonprofessionals a say in changes in the agency in question.

2. The propensity to give only dirty work to the indigenous nonprofessionals.

3. The overwork and underpay for many of the indigenous nonprofessionals.

4. The low morale of the indigenous nonprofessionals, which has resulted, among other things, in a growing unionization effort.

5. The difficulties in overcoming such problems in the training programs as the cost of paying people while they are in

training, overcoming the resistance of adults to returning to school, solving family problems resulting from combining work and training, and the difficulty in finding training techniques applicable to the kinds of adults found in these programs.

6. The techniques such as withholding information, making decisions of impact without consulting or informing the new careerist, failing to acknowledge the new careerists contribution and value, not treating them as colleagues, and failing to support changes within the agency.

Although most of these problems can be traced to external sources, some of them are based in the very nature of the role of the new careerist. According to Gartner (1970, p. 61) the indigenous nonprofessional must be "worker and consumer, force for change and member of the system, critic of professionalism and aspirant professional." It is plain that no individual could possibly balance all of these contradictory demands. Reviewing research on new careerists, Halpern (1969) concludes that Riessman may well have been wrong when he contended that the poor are helped best by those who are close to them in lifestyle. He cites studies that indicate that the nonprofessional may often experience role ambiguity, become authoritarian in defense of his helper role, or block upward communication. In his own study of a community mental health aide, Halpern found her in danger of becoming isolated: "She is vulnerable to accusations by her neighbors that she is a meddler, an 'Uncle Tom,' an opportunist, or a tyrant" (Halpern, 1969, p. 82). The community mental health aide's feelings of inadequacy and her growing recognition of her failings and those of her agency have all forced her to become very defensive about her position. Thus the program has been subverted by its own creation of unmanageable roles as well by a variety of external forces.

It seems evident to me that the new careers movement is an ill-conceived and unrealistic effort. The delivery of professional services to the poor will only be improved when we are willing to undertake a revolutionary change in that delivery system. In fact, many of the new careerists have now come around to this point of view. Haber (1968) has called for a truly radical new careers program. Such a program, according to Haber, would focus on attacking the centrality of the private economic system, the nature of the professions, the nature of work, and the nature of the bureaucracy. On the positive side it would be a struggle for community, the liberation of black people, and for popular control of government. I believe that a new careers movement dominated by this more radical set of goals has a far better chance of improving the services to the poor.

I agree with Haber's characterization of the established professions as enemies of efforts to improve community services; this is in stark contrast to the new careers advocates' view of the established professions as allies. Haber levels some heavy artillery at the professions. First, he feels that "few of the human service professions actually have a theory or a service technology which works" (Haber, 1968, p. 21). If applied to such occupations as teacher, social worker, and nurse, these assertions are quite correct. Whatever success is achieved in these occupations is achieved because an individual practitioner is authentic and honest and because he conveys respect and interest to those with whom he deals.

Haber's second critique is that "Much of professional education is useless, dull and vacuous, some is pernicious and a great deal has no relation to the problems of practice" (Haber, 1968, p. 21).Third, he contends that "professions, as now practiced, are elitest and authoritarian in their fundamental character, and hence they are both anti-democratic and supportive of the status-quo in their consequences" (Haber, 1968, p. 22). The professional usually regards his knowledge as his personal possession, he feels he has power over his client, he believes that the problems reside in individuals rather than in social systems, and his basic values often come from his conservative professional association. Haber recognizes that the new careers movement, if it worked, would only serve to shore up a system that is operating at the expense of the downtrodden.

By 1969 this type of thinking had taken hold of at least a segment of the new careers movement. The spring 1969 issue of the *New Careers Newsletter* carried the news of a basic change in the philosophy of the movement. It listed seven such changes:

1. New careerists no longer view themselves on the first step of a ladder toward becoming a professional, at least as long as the professions continue to exist as they are now constituted.

2. New careerists are already offering meaningful services of their own and need not be established professionals in order to provide such service.

3. For those who desire to become "community professionals" the route may not be nearly as long as was first thought.

4. "Large numbers" of new careerists may not, and/or may not want to, move to any ladder. They may simply want to stay where they are helping at the grass roots level in the community.

5. They have become highly critical of the established professions.

6. They are seeking to prevent cooptation.

7. They are seeking to change the old elitest relationship between board-staff-client.

This group of new careerists sums up their position in this way:

> "It (the new careers movement) is less concerned with individuals moving forward by themselves away from the group on a ladder toward professional or traditional careers. It is more concerned with new services, a new voice inside the system, new forms of participation, and a new responsive professional practice.... It does not want to patch up a system which is alien to the community, the poor, the consumer, the citizen."

Some new careerists, at least, have seen their initial errors and are moving in a more radical direction.

It is clear, however, that not all new careerists have changed. Rosen (1971) contends that two of the basic principles of the new careers movement are the provision of visible and accessible career ladders and the availability of formal education that can lead to professional credentials.

Some of those involved in the community mental health movement are coming to conclusions similar to those of radical

new careerists. Christmas *et al.* (1970) have attacked the
tokenism of most current community mental health centers and
outlined the need for truly radical change, based on their
experiences in the Harlem Rehabilitation Center. They criticize most community mental centers for using indigenous
nonprofessionals as links between community and professional,
as aides to overburdened professionals, or to perform the most
menial of tasks that the professionals are eager to avoid. They
eschew these goals and instead focus on what they consider the
more meaningful goals of developing "new professional, paraprofessional, and patient-client roles and new rehabilitative
services to meet the needs of the chronically mentally ill more
effectively, to broaden the mental health field, and to alter the
conditions that may themselves have been among the determinants of mental disorder" (Christmas *et al.*, 1970, p. 1480).
It is clear that most community mental health centers do not
have such revolutionary goals. In fact, Christmas *et al.* contend
that most current programs are token efforts aimed at creating
simply more temporary or dead-end jobs or, at best, some new
jobs. They urge a community mental health movement oriented
toward radical change, but they anticipate that (Christmas
et al., 1970, p. 1485)

> "it will require facing such issues as professional resistance,
> institutional vested interests, racist social policies and
> practices, community demands that exceed community
> cohesion, paraprofessional satisfaction with a larger slice of
> the status quo, and the limitations of knowledge of the
> mental health field."

I do not believe that my view of the initial failures of the new
careerist movement is idiosyncratic; in fact, it is coming to be
recognized by the new careerists themselves. The crisis throughout the New Careers Movement is apparent to all of those
involved. The *New Careers Newsletter*, which in 1969 heralded
the changes discussed previously, changed its title in 1970 to
The New Human Services Newsletter, with the explanation that the
New Careers Movement has not "entered upon the entire
agenda of human services issues" and the new title reflected

the broader concerns of the movement. Only two years later still another new title appeared on the masthead of the newsletter (*New Professional*) and still another new direction for the careers movement was in the winds. The rationale for this new shift was embodied in the following statement by the editors:

> "For years workers have been stigmatized by being called a variety of names from paraprofessionals to nonprofessionals and so on. New Professionals feel that their work is no less critical than that of professionals and in fact are primarily concerned with the delivery of quality services in their respective fields."

Along with this drive toward professionalization have come attacks on professional associations that discriminate against new professionals.

Like many occupations attempting to establish themselves, the new careerists have turned inward. Little is seen in the newsletter about helping the poor, but a good deal is written about solidifying the position of the new careerist in the establishment and as another enemy of the poor they were supposed to serve. All of the shifts imply a crisis in the new career movement, explicitly recognized by one of the founding fathers of the movement, Frank Riessman. In his description of the crisis Riessman (1972) lists the following things not accomplished by the movement:

> a leap in service productivity; a reorganization of human service practices and system; a piercing of the credential barrier so the paraprofessionals could become professionals; a marked change in professional associations and unions; nor did it develop in the paraprofessionals an attitude of being major social change agents, activists, etc.

In terms of the weaknesses of the movement Riessman (1972) includes "the continuing distance between paraprofessionals and the community, the limited activist role of paraprofessionals, and the dilution of the new careers concept into a shredding out of tasks via one form of job task analysis rather than reorganization of the whole field of professional practice."

The basic reason for this "crisis" lies in the fact that the new career movement never was aimed at a "reorganization of the whole field of professional practice." Instead it was designed as a response to the "revolt of the client" through the palliative of coopting some of the clients to act as links between the embattled professionals and the angry clients. The whole idea of a link was inadequate from its initial conception. Inadequate from the beginning, the new careers movement was made even more pathetic by the ways in which it was subverted when put into practice. Indigenous nonprofessionals were doomed to lives as "marginal men" acceptable neither to professionals nor to clients. Despite the fact that they were rejected by professionals, they are drawn to the apparent status and rewards of professionalism, hence the current desire to be labeled new professionals and accepted by professional associations. As they move in this direction, they have become part of the problem rather than part of the solution, at least from the client's perspective.

The new careers movement in community mental health has had an effect on the revolt of the client, but not in the way its founder expected. The founding fathers had hoped that the movement would satisfy the needs of the revolting clients. Instead it has only succeeded in adding a new target for clients in revolt: the indigenous nonprofessional.

The simple fact is that our professional delivery system needs a total overhaul. Along these lines we might emulate the changes that have taken place in public health care in Cuba. According to several observers: "The most unique feature of the Cuban health system, and perhaps the one most responsible for its success and the high regard in which it is held by the people, is the extent to which citizens participate in the planning and modification of health policy" (Roy *et al.*, 1971, p. 45). This is what is required—the participation of the citizenry in the planning and modification of all of those agencies which provide services to the poor (and every other segment of American society). This goes for community mental health centers, welfare agencies, hospitals, and schools. As Roy *et al.* (1971, p. 46) points out, this "entails a radical, even a revolutionary revision of the prevailing thought and practice in the United States." Are we ready for such a revolution that transfers power from the elites to the community? Episodes such as the one in Ocean Hill–Brownsville indicate that we are not. The new careers and community mental health movements, even in their new radical form, are only small steps in that direction.

References

Christmas, J., Wallace, H., and Edwards, J. (1970), New careers and new mental health services : Fantasy or future? *Am. J. Psychiatr.*, 126:1480–1486.

Crowne, L. J. (1969), Approaches to the mental health manpower problem: A review of the literature. *Ment. Hyg.*, 53:176–187.

Fields, R. M. (1970), The politics of community mental health. *Soc. Pol.*, 1(September/October): 57–59.

Freidson, E. (1960), Client control and medical practice. *Am. J. Sociol.*, 65:374-382.

————— (1971), Professionalism: The doctor's dilemma. *Soc. Pol.*, 1 (January/February):35–40.

Gartner, A. (1970), Organizing paraprofessionals, *Soc. Pol.*,1 (September/October): 60–61.

Haber, A. (1968), Issues beyond consensus. Working paper presented to the National Council for New Careers Organizing Conference, Detroit.

Hallowitz, E., and Riessman, F. (1967), The role of the indigenous nonprofessional in a community mental health neighborhood service center program. *Am.J. Orthopsychiatr.*, 37:766–778.

Halpern, W. I. (1969), The community mental health aide. *Ment. Hyg.*, 53:78–83.

Hartog, J. (1967), A classification of mental health non-professionals. *Ment. Hyg.*, 51:517–523.

Haug, M. R., and Sussman, M. B. (1969), Professional autonomy and the revolt of the client. *Soc. Prob.*, 17:153–161.

Hughes, P., *et al.* (1971), Developing inpatient services for community-based treatment of narcotic addiction. *Arch. Gen. Psychiatr.*, 25:278–283.

Kisch, A., and Reeder, L. (1969), Client evaluation and physician performance. *J. Health Soc. Behav.*, 10:51–59.

Lynch, M., Gardner, E., and Felzer, S. (1966), Training for new careers. *Commun. Ment. Health J.*, 6 (February): 3–12.

Miller, S. M., Roby, P., and Steenwijk, A. (1970), Creaming the poor. *Transaction*, 7 (June):38–45.

Morrison, A. P. (1970), Consultation and group process with indigenous neighborhood workers. *Commun. Ment. Health J.*, 6 (February).

Caree Newsletter (1969), 3 (spring).

Reiff, R., and Riessman, F. (1970), The indigenous nonprofessional: A strategy of change in community action and community mental health programs. *Commun. Ment. Health J. Monog.*, 1:3–31.

Riessman, F. (no date), *New Careers: A Basic Strategy against Poverty*. New York: A. Phillip Randolph Educational Fund.

——— (1972), The crises in new careers. *New Hum. Serv. Newsl.* 2 (Spring) : 2.

———, and Hallowitz, E. (1967), The neighbourhood service center: An innovation in prevention psychiatry. *Am. J. Psychiatr.*, 123.

Ritzer, G. (1973), Professionalism and the individual. In *The Professions and Their Prospects*, ed. Eliot Freidson. Beverly Hills: Sage Publications.

Roy, J., *et al.* (1971), Public health care in Cuba. *Soc. Pol.*, 1 (January/February): 41–46.

Rosen, S. (1971), Upgrading and new careers in health. *Soc. Pol.*, 1 (January/February):15–24.

Ryan, W. (1971), *Blaming the Victim*. New York: Pantheon.

Smith, M. B., and Hobbs, N. (1966), The community and the community mental health centre. *Am. Psychol.*, 21:499–509.

Statman, J. (1970), Community mental health: The evolution of a concept in social policy. *Commun. Ment. Health., J.*, 3 (spring): 5–12.

Torrey, E. F. (1969), The case of the indigenous therapist. *Arch. Gen. Psychiatr.*, 20: 365–373.

Willcox, A. F. (1970), The new professionals: Practical aspects of the use of new careerists in public health agencies. *Ment. Hyg.*, 54:347–356.

Chapter 8

Gary L. Albrecht

THE INDIGENOUS
MENTAL HEALTH WORKER:
THE CURE-ALL FOR WHAT
AILMENT?

IN Chapter 7 George Ritzer exposes a raw nerve of modern American society. In an era when the services sector of the economy is growing at an unpredecented rate, Ritzer asserts that there is a fundamental conflict between those who control resources and those who consume the services. The evidence clearly supports Ritzer's contention.

This "revolt of the client" (Haug and Sussman, 1969) has stunned almost every managerial and professional group. The consumer has felt so disinfranchised and powerless that public delight is expressed when an individual can "rip off" the establishment. The anonymous D. B. Cooper suddenly appeared on T-shirts around the country and became an overnight folk hero after he single handedly "ripped off" a major airline in spectacular fashion. Intense pride is taken in those individuals and groups who successfully stand up to the establishment and demand their rights. Revolt against systems of medical-care-delivery is now assuming increasing prominence.

Given these facts, Ritzer examines the case of the indigenous nonprofessional community mental health worker as a response by the establishment to this revolt of the client. He contends that the medical profession does not intend to alter professional–client relationships. Instead, according to Ritzer, the indigenous mental health worker movement had become a boondoggle.

The indigenous workers have been coopted from their own communities. Alleged changes are introduced into the medical delivery system that do little to alter the traditional professional power structure. False promises of career training and mobility are held out and never fulfilled. In addition, the indigenous worker frequently finds himself caught in role conflict between the community and the establishment. Whose side is he on? Although some of the original ideas of this movement were worth exploring and certainly well intentioned, the results have been less than successful.

I would agree with Ritzer that there is a revolt of the client, that the indigenous community mental health workers have been coopted, that there is excessive stress and role conflict in this occupation, and that the movement has been less than successful. I disagree however with Ritzer's ideological approach to the problem. The advocates of the indigenous community mental health worker movement espouse the ideology of the establishment. Ritzer has responded with the ideology of the advocates of radical change and revolution. But what are the facts? The solutions to problems must ultimately be judged in terms of empirical data, not solely in terms of some ideology.

The International Health Care Crisis

At first, the indigenous community mental health worker seems an appropriate response to the international health-care-delivery problem. In a somewhat Pollyannaish fashion the indigenous nonprofessional has been championed as a major source of change in health-care-delivery systems (Reiff and Riessman, 1965; Finestone and Sobey, 1969; Grosser et al., 1969; Crowne, 1969; Halpern, 1969; Sobey, 1970; Riessman, 1971a). Can the better utilization of the indigenous-health-worker role drastically alter and improve health services? There are many critics who say no (Davis, 1971; Birenbaum, 1971).

The problem of economical and effective health-care-delivery is found in every country of the world. No nation has solved these delivery problems to the satisfaction of its citizens or the professional community. The importance of the social organization of medical-care-delivery was first recognized by physicians through extensive field experience in both developing and industrialized countries. The physician in the developing nation is usually faced with massive health problems and has very meager resources at his command. How do a few trained physicians deal with every possible variety of health problem in an uneducated population that is often massive and rapidly expanding in size? The overwhelming nature of these circumstances forced physicians and administrators in these countries to face the question of how a few men could best utilize limited resources for the medical needs of these large populations. The tentative answers to this question focused upon public health measures, prevention, education, full utilization of existing community structures, and maximum use of the physician's skills. Critical evaluation of medical-care systems eventually spread to industrialized countries. The careful examination of national priorities in health-care-delivery has raised many salient questions and a great deal of anxiety, but has suggested few solutions.

Querido (1963), King (1966) and Bryant (1969) began to ask the right questions. How much is a country willing to spend on medical care? Who shall receive this medical care? What are the criteria of successful or good health care? Must all of the people of a community or nation be reached? If there are insufficient resources for all of the individuals in a community, who shall be served and who shall be excluded? Should one person receive the benefits of kidney dialysis or open heart surgery while thousands of others suffer malnutrition or go without cholera vaccine? Who should have the power to make these decisions? Given these issues, Bryant (1969, p. ix) says that it is as difficult to deliver health care in Malawi, one of the poorest nations in the world, as it is in the United States, one of the richest nations in the world.

Senator Edward Kennedy's hearings on the health care crisis in America alerted the American public to the fact that health care is the "fastest growing failing business in the Nation, a $ 70 billion industry that fails to meet the needs of our people"

(Committee on Labor and Public Welfare, U.S. Senate, 1971). If personal experience were not a vivid reminder, Kennedy's subcommittee pointed out that medical costs are out of control, that there is an acute shortage of medical personnel, that the delivery system provides many obstacles for the consumer and serves special-interest groups, and that quality of care is not uniform. In testimony before this subcommittee, Rashi Fein stated that total health expenditures were 5.3 percent of the gross national product in 1960 and had risen sharply to 7.0 percent in 1970. For 1980 the estimates range from 8 to 9.8 percent of the gross national product of the country to be expended on medical care (Committee on Labor and Public Welfare, U.S. Senate, 1971, pp. 136–137). The sobering fact is that the United States will soon be spending 1 of every 10 dollars in the GNP on medical care. Since Americans have the highest standard of living of any people in the world, these percentages add up to a great deal of money.

Furthermore, twenty billion dollars have been spent on biomedical research in the United States since the late 1940s. What kind of health care is being delivered as a result of this extraordinary outlay of research money? The answers to this question are embarrassing (Bevan, 1971). Americans are not the healthiest people in the world. Twenty years ago the United States ranked sixth in the world in life expectancy for females, seventh in infant mortality, and tenth in life expectancy for males. In 1971 Americans ranked eighth in life expectancy for females, thirteenth in infant mortality, and twenty-seventh in life expectancy for males. In terms of these indicators, American health status is falling behind rather than catching up with other countries of the world (Committee on Labor and Public Welfare, U.S. Senate, 1971). It is becoming increasingly apparent that sheer expenditure of vast sums of money does not guarantee improved health care.

Within the United States there are obvious geographical, socioeconomic, and racial differences in the availability of health resources (Bevan, 1971). However, we could argue that health care in the United States will improve because people are migrating toward the city and the adjusted median family income is continually rising. Thus, families will have more money for health care and will be located in an urban area where it is available. Past experience and future predictions do not support this reasoning. The distribution of medical care in urban areas is by no means equitable or satisfactory (Strauss, 1970; Ehrenreich and Ehrenreich, 1970). Furthermore, Rainwater (1972) clearly points out that although the median familly income will continue to rise, there is no indication that this income will be distributed more equitably in the future than it is now. The poorest 20 percent of the population will still be receiving less than 5 percent of the total personal income of the country. So while the upper and middle classes struggle with the problems of more money to spend and more leisure time (Linder, 1970), the lower social classes will still be concerned with survival and meeting daily needs. As long as the delivery system remains unchanged and access to it is limited, there seems no reason to believe that all citizens eventually will receive adequate health care.

A typically American solution to the current health care delivery crisis would be to pour more money into the present system. Money does not, however, seem to be the major part of the solution; the use and appropriation of money seems in fact to be an integral part of the problem. The American medical establishment is making a great deal of money from the present system. They are comfortable, enjoy high prestige, and oftentimes spectacular income (Bogue, 1969, pp. 428–462). In the last 10 years physician fees have risen twice as rapidly and hospital charges four times as fast as other items in the consumer price index (Ehrenreich and Ehrenreich, 1970, pp. 133–146). Why should they change the system that is yielding such rewards? Hospitals are benefiting, researchers are benefiting, and many service industries are benefiting. The individual consumer appears to be the sole loser. Bevan (1971) suggests that the current health care delivery system suffers because insurance plans are spotty and the individual must often pay heavily for medical care. In this era of third-party payments, however, there is little incentive for the health care delivery system to be efficient.

If there were only a 5 percent improvement in the utilization of health resources in the United States a saving of $2.5 billion would be realized (Bevan, 1971). However the complacency with the *status quo* is nowhere more evident than in the assumptions made by the Department of Health, Education, and Welfare in planning future health expenditures (Committee on Labor and Public Welfare, U. S. Senate, 1971, p. 140).

1. The current public medical care programs will continue with no major change in scope and type of benefits or in persons served.

2. Financing of health care services through public and private sources will remain at approximately the same relative proportions as in 1968.

3. No major changes in the organization and delivery of health care services will take place by 1980.

4. Medical care outside the hospital will continue to be provided primarily by solo practitioners.

The Department proceeds to argue that health care in America is a business like any other business, with the major goal of making money. If the system is making money and amply rewarding the workers in the system, why introduce any major changes in goals or in structure? Roemer (1971a, p. 31) concurs with this appraisal: "The basic fault in American health service is the discrepancy between our assertion of health care as a basic human right and our practice of treating it as a market-place commodity." The delivery of medical care in the United States involves buying and selling on an individual level. This service is organized in a very different fashion than other essential services, such as police and fire protection, education, and sanitation, which are organized to provide easily accessible services to all individuals. Roemer argues that health services should follow these patterns of organization.

As criticism of this entrepreneurial approach to the delivery of an essential service has mounted, the government and medical institutions and professions have begun to search for ways to blunt it. Both in psychiatric and medical practice the indigenous health worker has been a very facile answer in responding to pressures for change in the system. Patients could be treated within their own communities by individuals who understood them. Professionals could now reach more patients, cost per treatment would decline, the need for hospital beds would decline, and individuals in the community would have more immediate access to treatment. Thus the indigenous mental health worker movement seemed designed to alleviate the criticism of the health care delivery system (Stretch, 1969). Furthermore, at a time when racial tensions were rising, it allowed the government to hire and train minority-group people to work in their own neighborhoods, reducing unemployment as a side effect.

While the movement provided a semblance of change, it had little or no effect on the entrepreneurial nature of health service. When minority groups and communities were calling for a voice in politics, the movement gave residents of communities a chance to speak but gave them little real power. The government, medical institutions, and professionals still had complete control of the delivery system. Ritzer concludes that the movement was a boondoggle. He bases his argument upon scanty evidence, however. He does not carefully examine the reasons for the instigation of the movement or its manifest and latent goals but instead argues that the movement was doomed to failure from the start. He then proceeds to argue from an ideological position that the movement did not aid the individual worker or the community but instead served as a convenient mechanism of cooptation.

Conceptual Basis of the
Indigenous Worker Movement

The indigenous worker movement was established to improve health-care-delivery services, and there is evidence to indicate that this is a viable goal. For example, early ethnographers left little doubt that mental illness was successfully treated in many parts of the world by indigenous therapists. As colonies became settled, the residents were exposed to Western medical practices. The result was often a curious mix of beliefs, magic and science. At first, the role of the local priest or medicine man was belittled. However, Kiev (1964, 1972) has reported a wide variety of instances in which indigenous therapists have effectively treated psychiatric disorders. Shakman (1969) found that indigenous therapists in the Philippines were successful in treating pain, anxiety, infertility, pruritus, and headaches, utilizing a variety of different treatments. Torrey (1969) summarizes a large body of cross-cultural research that all seems to indicate that indigenous spiritualists, mediums, shamans, curanderos, and native healers are effective psychotherapists. Reviewing studies conducted in the United States, he also concludes that parents, former addicts, housewives, lay counselors, case aides, medical technicians, and students can effect improvement in psychiatric problems (Torrey, 1969).

In Africa (Alland, 1964), Trinidad (Simpson, 1962), and in the Puerto Rican community of New York City (Lubchansky *et al.*, 1970) a mix between traditional healers and modern medicine is found. The community often has more trust in the indigenous healers, but there is awareness that modern medicine can also produce significant positive results. In a study in a southern black community, Hall and Bourne (1972) conclude that community residents depend upon both the large city charity hospital and the indigenous therapists in the community. They found four distinct types of indigenous therapists: the root doctor who used herbs as his therapy; the faith healers who depend upon the "spirit" for their results, the magic vendors who used herbs and magical devices, and the neighborhood prophets who relied on dreams and direction from "the Lord" for their advice. Many of the older community residents turn to the indigenous therapists as a supplement to or in place of treatment that they could get at the city hospital.

Evidence from numerous studies strongly supports the contention that indigenous mental health workers can be effective therapists. Why then do Ritzer and other observers of the indigenous community mental health workers movement denounce it as a failure (Freidson, 1971; Haug and Sussman, 1969; Miller *et al.*, 1970)? The answer lies in the goals of the movement.

Confusion over Goals

Although the major goal of the indigenous mental health movement was to assist in health-care-delivery, everyone expected much more. Introduction of indigenous workers was supposed to dramatically change the entire health-care-delivery system. The movement was supposed to solve many of the problems of health-care-delivery in the United States, quiet restive minorities, and enable unskilled workers to pull themselves up by their own bootstraps (Wolfe, 1957). If the movement was to be judged by these criteria, it was doomed to failure from the very beginning.

In many respects, the indigenous mental health worker movement is but a "Great White Hope." The movement is advertised as an attack on an extensive set of complex problems (Hallowitz and Riessman, 1967; Morrill, 1968; Riessman, 1971b; Johnson, 1971; Bullough and Bullough, 1971). The white, middle-class establishment holds a vested interest in the success of the indigenous mental health worker movement because it seemingly offers solutions to many problems without essentially changing the medical delivery and reward system. Medical professionals and organizations may continue to control, as well as to be amply reimbursed. Although indigenous mental health workers have been admitted into the medical delivery system, their status, power, occupational mobility, and salaries have been carefully controlled. A look at the immediate future indicates that there will be no significant change in the control of the American medical system by white males (Cogan, 1968; Carnegie Commission on Higher Education, 1970). Since the medical profession has structured the nursing occupation so that it is a dead-end job with little opportunity for upward mobility (Bullough and Bullough, 1971), there seems no reason to believe that indigenous mental-health workers will be given great opportunities for occupational mobility (Fields, 1970). Thus, the indigenous workers are experiencing increasing stress because they do not have an opportunity for job advancement, their salary range is very limited, and there are often definite misunderstandings about job expectations (Boyette *et al.*, 1971). Certainly they are expected to improve health-care delivery. However, they are also expected to increase their skills and become occupationally mobile. Yet the structure of the system does not permit this (Carnegie Commission on Higher Education, 1970; Holden, 1971a). The indigenous worker expects to be welcomed as part of a health care team but is called a "subprofessional, para-professional, aide or assistant" (Boyette *et al.*, 1971). This less-than-full acceptance is emphasized by the fact that the professionals on the health teams communicate fully among themselves but inadequately to the members of the team who do not hold professional status (Torrens, 1971). The indigenous workers frequently come from the communities in which they are to work but often are not asked for suggestions about deal-ing with the community (D'Onofrio, 1970); this contrasts with their expectations for decision making about community health and welfare (Wise *et al.*, 1968; Silver, 1969). The com-munity and the indigenous workers anticipated basic structural changes in the medical system, only to discover that the medical institutions and professions were resistant to these changes (Holden, 1971b). The new professional working in the field is instructed to perform only a specific task when he finds entire sets of problems. (D'Onofrio, 1970). He is confused as to whether he should limit his efforts to a part of a person or family or attack the entire problem. The indigenous mental health worker is viewed by the establishment as a representative of his community and by the community as a member of the establishment. This classic problem of being caught in an overlapping role produces dissatisfaction both on the part of management and the community and alienates the individual as well (Aiken and Hage, 1966).

There is a serious question as to whether the middle and upper classes genuinely desire to eliminate poverty and its associated problems. The provision of excellent medical care to the poor, which constitutes an indirect attack on poverty, might not be in the best interests of the affluent. Rainwater (1972) asserts that the poor will be with us for the years to come; they are simply "functional." Gans (1971) argues that the "good life" and security of the affluent is dependent upon the existance of poverty. The poor provide a labor pool for the dangerous, menial, and demeaning jobs necessary in an industrial society. The poor consume half-used goods no longer desired by the affluent. The poor provide the *raison d'etre* of most private and governmental social agencies. They serve to define the norms for society (Erikson, 1966; Matza, 1969). Their deviancy provides the affluent with pride and elevates the value of middle-class culture. Gans concludes that the poor bear the financial and human costs upon which an industrialized society is built and maintained. For these reasons, equity in health-care-delivery may not make a great deal of sense for the affluent.

Given the many functions of poverty, the confusion of goals, and the ambiguous role definitions of the indigenous worker, it is little wonder that the movement has received mixed reviews. What criteria of success can be used to elevate the movement? As we have seen, this depends in large part upon an individual's reference group, place in society, and ideology. What is success for one group spells failure to another. Keeping in mind these diverse and even conflicting goals for the movement, let us examine what objective data there are on the achievements of indigenous mental health workers.

Unfortunately the majority of literature is based on what ought to be, on conjecture, and on limited clinical experience. Usually the virtues of such an approach are extolled (Heyssel, 1972; Sanazaro, 1972; Simpson, 1969). For example, systematic evaluation of training efforts are almost unknown. Lynch *et al.*, (1968) praise the experience of training indigenous therapists in the community where they are going to work. They argue that the therapists thus acquire a deeper knowledge of their community under professional supervision. Callan (1970) suggests that supervision be a continuing educational experience that helps aides become more knowledgeable and effective in their jobs. The interactional approach to training is favored by Carlaw (1970), since it attempts to avoid the authoritarian relationship of trainer to trainee. Hoff (1970) emphasizes that careful training is imperative for effective performance but does not set forth carefully articulated goals for a training program. The importance of making use of blacks who are knowledgeable of both mental health and the target community in mental health professional training programs is pointed out by Lawrence (1972). The military, which has used paraprofessionals for many years, does not have all of the political and personnel problems found in the community mental health center. Military paraprofessionals know what is expected of them, they know that they will only have to perform that job for a definite length of time, that they are accepted by their clients, and that their efforts will be appreciated. In civilian life these goals, roles, functions and rewards are not so clear and compatible (Heath and Pelz, 1970). Ritzer's assertion, however, that there is very little hard evidence on the effectiveness of indigenous workers is not totally true. Indigenous therapists can and do give effective therapy. Aside from the cross-cultural literature, there are representative studies done in the United States. Rice and Bernstein (1971) report that community mental health workers were accepted by 95.5 percent of the families with children in school in an Appalachian community. After health-status evaluations, the workers informed the families and the community of their medical problems, and a coordinated program to meet these needs was established. In a controlled experiment where both medical and nonmedical therapists treated patients with psychoneurosis, personality disorders, and adolescent adjustment reactions, no significant differences were found in patient outcome (Cline and Rouzer, 1971); nonphysician therapists were just as effective (or ineffective) as trained psychiatrists. A study of 346 cases in Vermont, which were handled by indigenous nurses who had received a six-month training in crisis intervention, demonstrated 80 percent of the nurses were successful in crisis intervention (Marshall and Finan, 1971). In a study of community health aides, 275 mothers were randomly assigned to the aides, public health nurses, and physicians for instructions about home care of an upper respiratory infection. Regardless of who administered the treatment, there was no significant difference in whether mothers complied with the instructions (Cauffman *et al.*, 1970).

Some critics have argued that the services given through community mental health clinics and neighborhood health centers are more expensive than care given through traditional channels. Sparer and Johnson (1971), however, present data that show that neighborhood health centers provide clinical service at costs comparable to other providers. Adamson (1971) reports that the use of physicians' associates and assistants has significantly increased the productivity of the physician. The physician with this type of help can see more patients per hour and provide better care. This growing number of empirical studies indicates that indigenous workers are effective, cost no more than traditional treatment methods, and increase the physicians' productivity. Better methods of measurement are currently being developed. Chinsky and Rappaport (1971) present useful instrument for evaluating the behavior of nonprofessional mental health workers, and Roemer (1971b) offers sound advice for evaluating the effectiveness of health service programs.

In light of this evidence I disagree with Ritzer that there is little firm evidence on the effectiveness of indigenous nonprofessionals. However, he is probably correct when he asserts that the nonprofessionals are not as successful as their advocates had hoped. If the major goal of the indigenous nonprofessional is solely to render effective therapy and service, then the movement seems able to meet this goal. Yet many hoped the movement would solve a host of more complex problems; there it has been largely unsuccessful. The medical establishment is still in control of health services, health professionals continue to be amply and often over rewarded for their work, the poor remain poor, and access to medical school and administrative positions has not been opened to indigenous workers. The indigenous worker has confused role expectations, he is often disliked both by the establishment and his own community, he lacks occupational mobility, his salary is limited, and he is not fully accepted on the health care team by the professionals. On the other hand, mental health centers have served as a political background in many locales, and the community has used them to assert power and win concessions from public agencies and the government; in several instances the poor have rebelled against their being used in research by universities that have entered their communities, and in part the centers have continued to pressure the medical profession into reexamining the priorities of service, research, and training. In a sense, the indigenous mental health nonprofessionals have indeed been coopted, but the movement has achieved some of its goals. Ritzer does not examine the full complexity of these issues, since he concentrates his discussion on the goals of the individual indigenous mental health workers. Certainly one of the major unplanned consequences of the indigenous community mental health worker movement is community political activity and exercise of power that revolves around mental health centers and their programs in local neighborhoods. In failing to recognize the multiple goals and consequences embodied in the movement, Ritzer tends to provide a one-sided and simplistic view of the problem.

Ritzer makes many sound points, but his argument suffers because it is based more on ideological position than on empirical data. Ritzer cites the need for revolutionary change in the delivery of services. Why is revolutionary change needed? What are the goals? From examining the available information, I agree that the indigenous community mental health worker movement has not been an unqualified success and that the general health-care-delivery system as it now exists is both expensive and inefficient. I do, however, take strong exception to Ritzer's arguing from an ideological position without basing his argument on the empirical data. Espousal of a radical position in itself is no better than identification with the *status quo*: both positions are based on ideology. The success of an institution or movement should be based on whether or not it achieves its goals. Science and empirical research can answer that question. Science cannot decide whether the goals are good. There are sound data to document that the indigenous mental health worker movement and the health-care-delivery system have not met their goals. But whether all Americans should have the same quality health care and economic independence is an ideological issue. Given some public consensus on goals, I would rather argue from data than from the ideological position that radical revolution is good. What are the goals of the radical revolution? If the goals of the community can best be served by radical revolution, then radical revolution is the answer. If not, then other solutions might be in order. The issues present an empirical question that must be judged in light of data. Radical organizational and programatic change might well be the solution to an improved health-care-delivery system. But will such a program meet the needs of the nation, the middle and upper classes, the poor, the majority groups, the minority groups, the local community, the city and county, the individual indigenous mental health worker and the professional? I think not. Many of these goals and needs are incompatible. Whose goals should then be met? This problem should be confronted in the political arena, not in the scientific community.

The literature on indigenous mental health workers is replete with suggested improvements in the health-care-delivery system that are based on values. Scott (1969) points out that medical institutions and professionals encourage the client to become dependent upon them. This runs counter to the value of individual independency as the goal of treatment. Reynolds and Bice (1971) show that medical interns have much higher evaluations of the medical staff than they do of patients. These data suggest that patients are not treated as equals. On the positive side, Bohr and Kaplan (1971) indicate that employee protest in medical institutions can positively alter the nature and quality of health-care-delivery. Davis (1971) and Holder and Dixon (1971) conclude that decentralization of services and community participation in decision making are necessary ingredients in successful neighborhood health delivery. This approach restores power to the individuals and the community (Moore, 1971) and makes the health clinic a political action unit (Berlin, 1971; Torrens, 1971). Finally if there is equality for all, the consumer should have some say about the services and product that he is consuming (Ishiyama, 1970; Sellers, 1970; Bohr and Kaplan, 1971; Moore, 1971).

These conclusions support and reflect values about health care that most Americans accept. Research can empirically test whether programs, institutions, and individuals attain these goals, but it cannot set these goals or necessarily select which ideological position is best. The public good and decisions based on the values of the society are not always rewarding to every individual and group. It is in this light that we must continue to examine the community mental health movement and its efforts to bring about social change.

References

Adamson, T. E. (1971), Critical issues in the use of physician associates and assistants. *Am. J. Public Health*, 61:1765–1779.

Aiken, M., and Hage, J. (1966), Organizational alienation: A comparative analysis. *Am. Sociol. Rev.*, 31:497–507.

Alland, A., Jr. (1964), Native therapists and Western medical practitioners among the Abron of the Ivory Coast. *Trans. N. Y. Acad. Sci.*, 26:719–725.

Berlin, I. N. (1971), Professionals participation in community activities: Is it part of the job? *Am. J. Orthopsychiatr.*, 41:475–505.

Bevan, W. (1971), The topsy-turvy world of health-care-delivery. *Science*, 173:985.

Birenbaum, W. (1971), The more we change, the worse we get. *Soc. Pol.*, 2 (May–June):10–13.

Bogue, D. J. (1969), *Principles of Demography*. New York: Wiley.

Bohr, R. H., and Kaplan, H. M. (1971), Employee protest and social change in health care organization. *Am. J. Public Health*, 61:2229–2235.

Boyette, R., Blount, W. and Petaway, K. (1971), The plight of the new careerist. *Am. J. Orthopsychiatr.*, 41:237–238.

Bullough, B., and Bullough, V. (1971), A career ladder in nursing: Problems and prospects. *Am. J. Nurs.*, 71:1938–1943.

Bryant, J. (1969), *Health and the Developing World*. Ithaca, N.Y. : Cornell University Press.

Callan, L. B. (1970), Supervision, the key to success with aides. *Public Health Rep.*, 85:780–787.

Carlaw, R. W. (1970), The development of interaction as an approach to training. *Public Health Rep.*, 85:754–759.

Carnegie Commission on Higher Education, (1970), *Higher Education and the Nation's Health—Policies for Medical and Dental Education*. New York: McGraw-Hill.

Cauffman, J. G., *et al.* (1970), Community health aides: How effective are they. *J. Public Health*, 60:1904–1909.

Chinsky, J. M., and Rappaport, J. (1971), Evaluation of a technique for the behavioral assessment of nonprofessional mental health workers. *J. Clin. Psychol.*, 27: 400–402.

Cline, D. W., and Rouzer, D. L. (1971), The nonphysician as primary therapist in hospital psychiatry. *Am. J. Psychiatr.*, 128:407–411.

Cogan, L. (1968), *Negroes in Medicine. Report of a Macy Conference.* Baltimore: Johns Hopkins University Press.

Committee on Labor and Public Welfare, U. N. Senate, (1971), *Health Care Crisis in America*, 1971. Washington, D.C.: U. S. Government Printing Office.

Crowne, L. (1969), Approaches to the mental health manpower problem. *Ment. Hyg.*, 53:176–187.

Davis, J. W. (1971), Decentralization, citizen participation care. *Am. Behav. Sci.*, 15:94–107.

D'Onofrio, C. (1970), Aides—Pain or panacea? *Public Health Rep.*, 85: 788–801.

Ehrenreich, B., and Ehrenreich, J. (1970), *The American Health Empire*, New York: Random House.

Erikson, K. T. (1966), *The Wayward Puritans.* New York: Wiley.

Fields, R. (1970), The politics of community mental health. *Soc. Pol.*, 1 (September–October):57–59.

Finestone, S., and Sobey, F. (1969), *Non-Professional Personnel in Mental Health Programs: A Survey.* Washington, D.C.: The National Clearinghouse for Mental Health Information.

Freidson, E. (1971), Professionalism: The doctor's dilemma. *Soc. Pol.*, 1 (January–February):35–40.

Gans, H. J. (1971), The uses of poverty: The poor pay all. *Soc. Pol.*, 2(July–August): 20–24.

Grosser, C., Henry, W. E. and Kelly, J. G. (1969), *Nonprofessionals in the Human Services.* San Francisco: Jossey-Bass.

Hall, A. L., and Bourne, P. G. (1972), Indigenous therapists in a black urban community in the South. Unpublished manuscript.

Hallowitz, E., and Riessman, F. (1967), The role of the indigenous nonprofessional in a community mental health neighborhood service center progam. *Am. J. Orthopsychiatr.*, 37:766–778.

Halpern, W. (1969), The community mental health aide. *Ment. Hyg.*, 53:78–83.

Haug, M. R., and Sussman, M. B. (1969), Professional autonomy and the revolt of the clients. *Soc. Prob.*, 17:153–161.

Heath, A., and Pelz, D. R. (1970), Perception of functions of health aides by aides themselves and by others. *Public Health Rep.*, 85:767–772.

Heyssel, R. M. (1972), The health services delivery system. *Bull. N. Y. Acad. Sci.*, 48:166–172.

Hoff, W. (1970), The importance of training for effective performance. *Public Health Rep.*, 85:760–765.

Holden, C. (1971a), Community mental health centers: Growing movement seeks identity. *Science*, 174:1110–1113.

——— (1971b), Community mental health centers: Storefront therapy and more. *Science*, 174:1219–1221.

Holder, H. D., and Dixon, R. T. (1971), Delivery of mental health services in the city of the future. *Am. Behav. Sci.*, 14:893–908.

Ishiyama, I. (1970), The mental hospital patient—Consumer as a determinant of service. *Ment. Hyg.*, 54:221–229.

Johnson, C. T. (1971), Paraprofessionals bridging the gap. *Am. J. Orthopsychiatr.*, 41:234–235.

Kiev, A. (1964), *Magic, Faith and Healing.* New York: Free Press.

—— (1972), *Transcultural Psychiatry.* New York: Free Press.

King, M. (ed). (1966), *Medical Care in Developing Countries.* Nairobi: Oxford University Press.

Lawrence, L. E. (1972), On the role of the black mental health professional. *Am. J. Public Health*, 62:57–59.

Linder, S. (1970), *The Harried Leisure Class.* New York: Columbia University Press.

Lubchansky, I., Egri, G., and Stokes, J. (1970), Puerto Rican spiritualists view mental illness: The faith healer as a paraprofessional. *Am. J. Psychiatr.*, 127:312–321.

Lynch, M., Gardner, E. A., and Felzer, S. B. (1968), The role of indigenous personnel as clinical therapists. *Arch. Gen. Psychiatr.*, 19:428–434.

Marshall, C. D., and Finan, J. L. (1971), The indigenous nurse as crisis counselor. *Bull. Suicidol.*, 8:45–47.

Matza, D. (1969), *Becoming Deviant.* Englewood Cliffs, N. J.: Prentice-Hall.

Miller, S. M., Roby, P., and Steenwijk, A. (1970), *Creaming the poor. Transaction*, 7:38–45.

Moore, M. L. (1971), The role of hostility and militancy in indigenous community health advising groups. *Am. J. Public Health*, 61:922–930.

Morrill, R. G. (1968), Group identity, marginality, and the nonprofessional. *Arch. Gen. Psychiatr.*, 19:404–412.

Querido, A. (1963), *The Efficiency of Medical Care*, Leiden: H. E. Stenfert Kroese.

Rainwater, L. (1972), Post-1984 America. *Society*, 9:18–27.

Reiff, R., and Riessman, F. (1965), The indigenous nonprofessional: A strategy of change in community action and community mental health programs. *Commun. Ment. Health J. Monog.*, 1:3–32.

Reynolds, R. E., and Bice, T. W. (1971), Attitudes of medical interns toward patients and health professionals. *J. Health Soc. Behav.*, 12:307–311.

Rice, T. J., and Bernstein, S. B. (1971), The process of community interventions in an isolated Appalachian mountain hollow. *Med. Care*, 9:365–371.

Riessman, F. (1971a), When it Comes to the poor—Suddenly, doctors aren't the answer. *Soc. Pol.*, 2 (September–October):3–4.

—— (1971b), The vocationalization of higher education: Duping the poor. *Soc. Pol.*, 2 (May–June):3–4.

Roemer, M. I. (1971a), Nationalized medicine for America. *Transaction*, 8 (September): 31–36.

—— (1971b), Evaluation of health service programs and levels of measurement. *Health Serv. Ment. Health Admin.*, 86:839–848.

Sanazaro, P. J. (1972), Health services research and development. *Bull. N. Y. Acad. Sci.*, 48:157–165.

Scott, R. A. (1969), *The Making of Blind Men.* New York: Russell Sage Foundation.

Sellers, R. V. (1970), The black health worker and the black health consumer— New roles for both. *Am. J. Public Health*, 60:2154–2170.

Shakman, R. (1969), Indigenous healing of mental illness in the Philippines. *Int. J. Psychiatr.*, 15:279–287.

Silver, G. A. (1969), What has been learned about the delivery of health services to the Ghetto. In *Medicine in the Ghetto*, ed. J. C. Norman, New York: Appleton-Century-Crofts.

Simpson, G. A. (1969), Family health worker on the community level. *Ann. N. Y. Acad. Sci.*, 166:916–926.

Simpson, G. E. (1962), Folk medicine in Trinidad. *J. Am. Folkl.*, 75:326–340.

Sobey, F. (1970), *The Nonprofessional Revolution in Mental Health*. New York: Columbia University Press.

Sparer, G., and Johnson, J. (1971), Evaluation of OEO neighborhood health centers. *Am. J. Public Health*, 61:931–942.

Strauss, A. (ed). (1970), *Where Medicine Fails*. Chicago: Aldine.

Stretch, J. J. (1969), Community mental health as a pacification program: A radical critique. *Commun. Ment. Health J.*, 3:5–12.

Torrens, P. R. (1971), Administrative problems of neighborhood health centers. *Med. Care*, 9:487–497.

Torrey, E. F. (1969), The case for the indigenous therapist. *Arch. Gen. Psychiatr.*, 20:365–373.

Wise, H. B., Levin, L. S., and Kurahara, R. T. (1968), Community development and health education: I. Community organization as a health tactic. *Milbank Mem. Fund. Q.* July.

Wolfe, D. M. (1957), *The Image of Man in America*. New York: McGraw-Hill.

Index